WITHDRAWN

An Introduction to the Study of Sexuality

Roger Horrocks

Consultant Editor: Jo Campling

First published 1997 by
MACMILLAN PRESS LTD
Houndmills, Basingstoke, Hampshire RG21 6XS
and London
Companies and representatives
throughout the world

ISBN 0–333–65138–3 hardcover
ISBN 0–333–65139–1 paperback

A catalogue record for this book is available
from the British Library.

This book is printed on paper suitable for recycling and
made from fully managed and sustained forest sources.

10   9   8   7   6   5   4   3   2   1
06 05 04 03 02 01 00 99 98 97

Printed and bound in Great Britain by
Antony Rowe Ltd, Chippenham, Wiltshire

Published in the United States of America by
ST. MARTIN'S PRESS, INC.,
Scholarly and Reference Division
175 Fifth Avenue, New York, N.Y. 10010

ISBN 0–312–17281–8 cloth
ISBN 0–312–17282–6 paperback

For Rachel

Sex contains all, bodies, souls,
Meanings, proofs, purities, delicacies, results,
promulgations.

Walt Whitman, *Leaves of Grass*

Contents

Acknowledgements

Many thanks go to Jo Campling, who has been most helpful, and also to Annabelle Buckley at Macmillan. I very much appreciate the comments of the anonymous reader, which were most useful.

The library of University College London has been a lode-mine of material in researching this book, and I thank the staff for their help.

I am very grateful to my own clients, whose life-stories have taught me more than any textbook could.

Several people have listened to me tirelessly as I went through the inevitable ups and downs involved in writing this book – I am particularly grateful to Sybilla Madigan and Victoria Zinovieff.

Thanks and love to Rachel Floater for being there.

ROGER HORROCKS

1 Introduction

What is sexuality? How can it be studied? This book sets out to answer these questions within the limited space available. Rather than investigate sexuality in depth from one point of view – for example, psychologically, historically or sociologically – I have chosen to take a bird's-eye view of a number of approaches. This has the disadvantage of treating each area rather superficially, but it has the advantage of permitting comparisons and links to be made between a variety of standpoints.

Sexuality is not a simple or uniform phenomenon: it embraces many aspects of human existence, such as the economic, social, political, psychological, emotional, spiritual, physical, genetic, and so on. It therefore seems difficult to develop a one-dimensional or monistic theory of it. It also seems impossible to give a comprehensive account of it: we have to be highly selective about the sub-topics within sexuality that we study.

On what basis can one make such a selection? Three criteria have guided my choice of topics. First, certain topics have great contemporary significance in the study of sexuality, for example, the various debates and controversies in feminism and gay studies. Perhaps the most important issue here is the relation between gender and sexuality. Second, one cannot help gravitating to topics that are personally interesting and provocative: thus I have allotted three chapters to the psychoanalytic treatment of sexuality, since I am professionally involved in this, and keenly interested in it. Third, I have also tried to cast my net widely, and attempted to include a variety of approaches and models of sexuality. This encourages comparison between different approaches, and prevents too blinkered an approach. In particular, I have tried to give some account of both socio-political and psychological approaches to sexuality: these seem so different, and even at odds with each other, yet both are vital. I have also included a chapter on the relationship between sexuality and spirituality, since it strikes me that this is often ignored in studies of sexuality.

This book is definitely not intended to be a guide to sexual techniques, nor as a spur to sexual excitement, but rather focuses on the different ways in which human sexuality has been described in the West. Thus, I am concerned with some of the meanings that have been

1

ascribed to sexual desire and sexual experience, and some of the theoretical models within which sex and sexuality have been described and explained.

ORGANIZATION OF THE BOOK

The book falls broadly into two parts. In Chapters 2–7 I have tried to set out some of the important paradigms within which sex and sexuality have been approached in Western culture. I have focused on Christianity, psychoanalysis (looking at Freud and Lacan), social constructionism and the relation between sexuality and spirituality.

In Chapters 8–10 I have examined a number of topics that are important in the contemporary study of sexuality, including the contributions of feminism and gay studies, and the confused and complicated area of male sexuality.

In the main, this book provides a discussion of various theoretical issues that have arisen in the study of sex and sexuality, but I have also attempted to provide some practical examination of various texts, and I have contributed some vignettes from my own work as a psychotherapist.

2 Christianity and Sex

Any discussion of sexuality that ignores the Christian view is incomplete, not simply because historically Christianity has dominated Western thinking for a very long time, but also because it is still with us, even if in an unconscious or degenerate form. The equation of sex with 'sin', the use made of sexual scandals in the tabloid press, and the enormous guilt shown by individuals as they begin to unravel their complex attitudes towards sex – these are just some of the indications that our attitudes are still heavily influenced by the ancient Christian view.

In addition, politicians of both right and left still pay homage to 'traditional values' and 'family values' and some kind of nominal Christianity. They are still able to appeal to some common stock – incoherent as it may be – of myths and beliefs about sex and sexuality. Certainly in America, the Christian standpoint is enormously important in political life, usually associated with a right-wing position that is anti-abortion and 'pro-family'. Here we get an indication that sexuality has been, and is, of great importance politically, particularly as it connects with family structure and the perceived stability of the state.

In addition, Christian attitudes towards sex have not just been the subject for debate by intellectual clerics, but have penetrated popular thinking. This is important, for while academic scholars may often ignore Christian thinking, it may still be found alive and well in the market-place, or for that matter, in the bedroom. In my work as a therapist, it is clear that many people are still haunted by feelings of guilt and sin, which are partly identifiable as 'Christian'.

It is a daunting task to retrace the history of Christian attitudes to sex. In the first place, one cannot speak of a homogeneous 'Christianity', since we are speaking of a movement that has straddled the Roman Empire, the medieval world, the Renaissance and Reformation, the Enlightenment, and the turbulence of the nineteenth and twentieth centuries, which have seen Christianity suffer enormous blows to its prestige. Obviously, I cannot attempt to encompass this enormous time span: I shall select several 'moments' in the development of Christian thought about sex, moments which seem to illustrate some key themes and attitudes.

CHRISTIANITY AND POLITICAL POWER

From one point of view, Christianity can be seen as an individual form of spiritual self-analysis, but this is clearly inadequate as a historical description, since the Christian churches have been powerful social and political institutions, within which the individual is subject to a high degree of control, not to say coercion.

The various churches have been – and still are – nakedly political bodies, operating both internationally and nationally as powerful and prestigious forces. They have waged wars, controlled governments, incited rebellion against some rulers and demanded loyalty to others, and they have continually intervened in economic, social and political conflicts. Examples of the political weight exerted by Christian bodies are legion – one can cite the role of the Catholic Church in the Spanish Civil War, exhorting opposition to the 'red horde'; or the Henrician reforms in England in the sixteenth century, which swept aside many of the powers of the Vatican and led to the foundation of the Church of England; or the role of the Catholic Church in modern Ireland, still very much a power in the land.

This is the extraordinary fact about Christianity – it has operated both at the political macro-level of government, diplomacy and war, and also at the individual level, in terms of morality and conscience. In this sense, it is one of the most efficient and thoroughgoing multi-level political institutions that has existed in Western society.

The first great manifestation of this occurred when Christianity became linked with the Roman Empire in the fourth century AD, and thereby tied in with a political Establishment. Whereas in earlier periods Christians had been persecuted by Rome, in 313 the emperor was converted to Christianity, and an edict of 380 made it the official state religion, and non-compliance was punished by the emperor.[1] The third and fourth centuries also saw many Roman aristocrats become converts, so that from being the faith of slaves and other marginalized people, Christianity began to occupy the centre of power.[2]

This coming together of church and state is one of the historical developments in Christianity that twentieth century liberation theologians have objected to most intensely: 'succeeding generations began to give way to the temptation of viewing Christianity as a political religion that was useful to the Roman Empire'.[3]

Similar links between church and state, or between church and important political bodies, have continued down to the present day.

One can cite, for example, the English Civil War, which was partly fought in religious terms over the issue of a state church versus the religious sects, such as the Baptists, who elected their own ministers.[4] Even today in Britain, the bishops of the Church of England sit in the House of Lords, the head of the Church is the ruling monarch, and bishops are partly selected by the prime minister.

These political considerations are important when we consider Christian views on sexual relations, for these are not simply other-worldly or 'spiritual', nor are they absolute and unchanging; they inhabit shifting socio-political contexts and take shape within such contexts. A very clear example can be found in relation to the Christian attitude to marriage, for in the first centuries of Christianity, the Church was not overly concerned with marriage, and only began to treat it seriously in the medieval period. This can be seen partly as an attempt to exert political power over people's lives, and not simply as a pastoral or moral issue. The ban on clerical marriage was also late in the development of the Church's teaching on celibacy and marriage, and was seen by critics as an exertion of papal power: 'the real papal agenda was not moral reform, but rather the assertion of power, that by forcing men to give up their wives, the movement sought to gain greater control over men's lives'.[5]

CHRISTIAN DUALISM

It is generally accepted that ancient Judaic thought did not see sex as an evil, and did not split body and soul to the extent that Christianity eventually did. Of course Judaism exacted severe penalties for adulterous sex, and took a heavily patriarchal view of female sexuality, but sex within marriage was considered good, or even delightful. Furthermore, it seems to have been accepted that women had the right to sexual satisfaction within marriage, and Jewish texts even condoned oral sex between man and wife.[6]

Thus if we accept that in many ways Christianity was originally a 'messianic Jewish sect', that is, has Judaism as a direct progenitor,[7] none the less there appears to be a clear disjunction between the respective treatments of the body and sex. Christianity became in many ways an anti-materialist religion, propounding the body/soul split with a remarkable vehemence and hatred for the body. The body became an encumbrance that had to be endured and renounced in one's spiritual development.

Part of this break from Jewish thinking can be ascribed to the influence of Greek thought on Christianity, which was considerable. For example, neo-Platonic philosophy was heavily indebted to the notion of an immaterial world, perfect in comparison with the earthly imperfect one. Such ideas were very influential on Christianity: for example, the idea arose that Christ's fleshly identity was apparent not real, since 'historical existence [is] the sphere of corruption and un-reality, participation in which would be derogatory to the divine'.[8]

Christianity was also heavily influenced by Gnosticism, which tended to view the material world as inferior to the spiritual world; in its extreme versions, it saw matter as evil or as an imprisonment for the human soul. Although Christianity conducted fierce polemics against Gnosticism, Gnostic ideas undoubtedly permeated some streams of Christian thought, and the Gospel of John was interpreted in a Gnostic manner by some groups.[9]

Thus, Christianity was not alone in its suspicious attitude towards bodily pleasures. Other religious movements such as Gnosticism, Zoroastrianism, and Manichaeism took an ascetic standpoint towards sex, and perpetrated a split between body and soul. In a sense, a massive tide of 'other-wordliness' or asceticism swept through the Mediterranean. One might see this as an escape from political turmoil, from material oppression and poverty, just as Christ's other-worldli-ness could be seen as an escape from Jewish oppression and the political and military struggles that had developed against the Roman state.

More generally, it is arguable that a huge split between reason and emotion was going on in human consciousness, a split which can be seen as part of the emergence of the modern world. The emergence of rational thought within religion has been described by E.C. Whitmont as a shift from magical and mythological consciousness towards mentation, which is the patriarchal form of ego consciousness. This form of thinking splits psyche from physics, and ultimately anticipates and leads towards Cartesian dualism.[10]

Within such a dualism, sexual pleasure is always regarded with suspicion, since it seems to represent the extreme of corporeal plea-sure, an animal-like sensuality that reason shrinks from. But Christianity is a highly paradoxical religion: it also retained many elements of mythological thinking – the revelation of the numinous through highly revered symbols which defy intellectual analysis.

Christian dualism has far-reaching implications: arguably it articu-lates a major shift in human consciousness – the creation of the rational subject, who is forever torn from the object, and yearns for reunion with it. Moreover, this focus on rationality and subjectivity was to intensify in Christianity during the Renaissance and the Reformation, when the sensual imagery of Catholicism was demolished.

THE NEW AGE

It is also likely that Christian other-worldliness developed as a reaction to other, less ascetic pagan religions or cultures, which were perceived as a threat: 'the paganism of the Byzantine world...had become a syncretistic religion with very disturbing elements of ecstatic frenzy and sexual promiscuity, and one of the most prominent figures was the Mother Goddess'.[11] In *The City of God*, Augustine, the former Manichean, is full of contempt for the former sexual rituals and orgies of pagan Rome: 'The Great Mother surpassed all the gods, her sons, not by reason of the greatness of her divine power, but in the enormity of her wickedness.'[12]

But there are less lurid reasons why early Christians rejected the sexual mores of pagan society: the Christian who became celibate was not simply renouncing sex, but a defined place in society, that is, a *socialized and politicized form of sexual relations*. The early Christians saw themselves as opposed to the orthodox world of family, children and responsibilities:

> In classical Greek and Roman society, a young man or woman who hesitated or refused to marry the person chosen by his or her family would be considered insubordinate or possibly insane.... Young men were expected to marry between the ages of seventeen and twenty-five and then to place themselves at the service of their communities, according to their family tradition and circumstances.[13]

In this sense, the early Christian rejection of sexual relations was seen as a detachment from social obligations and the claiming of a new kind of human freedom. This was entirely in accord with the radical message that had been preached by Jesus:

> I came to cast fire upon the earth; and would that it were already kindled!...Do you think that I have come to give peace on earth? No, I tell you, but rather division; for henceforth in one house there will be five divided, three against two and two against three; so they

will be divided, father against son and son against father, mother against daughter and daughter against her mother.[14]

There is little doubt that this radical social gospel, whose message has been diluted and blunted in the intervening two millennia, was taken seriously by Christians in the first centuries after Christ's death. Christianity was set to turn the world upside down, and part of this involved the rejection of family ties, prescribed sexual relations and the acquisition of wealth: 'the coming new age demands new – and total – allegiance, no longer to family and nation, but to the coming kingdom'.[15]

Thus Christian asceticism was part of a radical social movement, which rejected the social expectations both of the Jewish and the pagan worlds. And this movement initially appealed to the rejects of Roman society: slaves, women, those who were not Roman citizens.[16] Some accounts describe how women who rejected marriage were able to become powerful figures in the local church and community; in this sense, the rejection of sex and the valorization of virginity gave freedom to some women, for it liberated them from the shackles of marriage and procreation:

> The enthusiasm with which they took to the ascetic life, their repugnance for sexual relations within a marriage which had been forced on them, and the chance to be recognized in a way of life in which they could be men's equals made the women of the Empire one of the principal forces in the transformation of the ancient world.[17]

This is the crucial point about the ascetic or anti-sex movement of early Christianity: sexual relations were being viewed in their social and political dimensions. Those who turned against the world of Roman society, and its structures of family and kinship, in anticipation of a new world order, were turning against the prevalent political structuring of sexual relations, and not against 'sex' in abstract. This theme will recur again and again throughout this book: sex is apprehended and practised by people within a socio-political context.

AUGUSTINE: THE CITY OF GOD AND THE CITY ON EARTH

The theologian Elaine Pagels has argued in her books *Adam, Eve and the Serpent* and *The Gnostic Gospels* that the religious currents that have existed within Christianity are not simply spiritual schools, but also express political viewpoints. In this sense, the coming together of Christianity with the Roman Empire was a momentous change, which affected all aspects of the faith. From having been a group of outcasts, actively persecuted by the state, seen as dangerous radicals who denied the power of the Emperor, Christianity became the official state religion, and punishment was exacted on those who refused to convert.

These changes have great implications for the treatment of sexual relations, for if in the early Church celibacy was seen as a rejection of the status quo and an anticipation of the new age to come, in the post-imperial era this changed. Christians were no longer at loggerheads with the state; the radicalism of Christ's message – 'You cannot serve God and mammon'[18] – began to be diluted. Eventually, of course, the Church was to become itself a mighty political power, fabulously wealthy, its bishops, cardinals and popes often political potentates.

In fact, the christianization of Rome had a contradictory effect on sexual ethics, for as Christians became more powerful in the secular sense, for some this amounted to a diluted semi-pagan Christianity, and made them yearn for the old anti-state faith of the underdog. Thus asceticism retained its appeal for those who looked for a spiritual authenticity that rejected the world of Mammon. This can be seen in the growth of monasticism, which also featured a turning away from material concerns, including sex, and the creation of a microcosm of the 'City of God' on earth. The 'Desert Fathers' were Egyptian monks who went out into the desert, in order to escape, not just from sexual relations, but all forms of dependence on the secular world.[19]

Part of the tension in the christianization of Rome concerns the postponement of the Parousia – the second coming of Christ. This had been a tension in Christian belief and practice since the first century, for the very earliest Christians were convinced that the new age was very close, and therefore many practical problems in the real world could be ignored. But the delay in the arrival of the kingdom had forced Christians to pay attention to the present, and in particular the organization of churches and local communities.[20]

This tension was given added piquancy by the conversion of Rome: relief at the Roman acceptance of Christianity was tempered by the awareness that the new age so eagerly anticipated by the early Christians – 'this generation will not pass away before all these things take place'[21] – was being put off apparently indefinitely. Meanwhile Christians had to coexist with the secular Roman state. What kind of theology could deal with this? Granted that Christians still yearned for the 'world to come', which would change everything, yet they had to live in the present world.

The key theologian who worked on these issues was Augustine, whose massive writings cover a vast range of topics. Augustine developed a sophisticated theology concerning the relations between religion and state, arguing that Christians were not capable of self-government – thus contradicting the fervent hopes of the early Christians – and that a certain degree of corruption in church and state was inevitable, given the inherent sinfulness of human beings: 'Augustine draws so drastic a picture of the effects of Adam's sin that he embraces human government, even when tyrannical, as the indispensable defence against the forces sin has unleashed in human nature.'[22]

Within this schema, the theology concerning sex became both more pessimistic and more pragmatic. The optimism of the early Christians, and other groups such as the Gnostics – both that 'the kingdom' was very close, and that it was possible now to reject social ties, including sexual ones, and carve out one's own moral freedom – gave way to a theological pessimism about human freedom, which was seen as severely limited and inherently tainted by sin.

But this in fact gave the Church an essential importance. If the Christian radicals had not seen the need for an elaborate ecclesial structure, since the coming of the kingdom was at hand, now it could be argued that only the Church stood between the human being and damnation. The Gnostics and other groups were condemned partly because they suggested that human beings could govern themselves, and could find their own salvation within themselves.

Augustine went through various changes of opinion concerning sex, but in *The City of God* he argues in quite a subtle fashion that sex was created by God, and is therefore not in itself sinful, but is corrupted by the fundamental disruption of human will caused by the original disobedience of Adam and Eve:

> The corruption of the body, which weighs down the soul, is not the cause of the first sin, but its punishment. And it was not the corruptible flesh that made the soul sinful; it was the sinful soul that made the flesh corruptible.[23]

The problem with sexual desire is that it does not obey the will, and human will is now at odds with the divine will:

Is there any reason why we should not believe that before the sin of disobedience and its punishment of corruptibility, the members of a man's body could have been the servant of man's will without any lust, for the procreation of children? It was because man forsook God by pleasing himself that he was handed over to himself, and because he did not obey God, he could not obey himself. Hence came the more obvious misery where man does not live as he wishes to live.[24]

What is fascinating about this analysis of desire is that Augustine posits an internal conflict in the human being: his will is contradicted by his own lusts – 'he could not obey himself'. Augustine spends some time pointing out how many bodily organs do obey the individual's will, but not the sexual organs. They are excited by lust, and even that is not predictable.[25]

We could argue that Augustine is grappling with the conflict between conscious and unconscious desire, a conflict which Christianity was to equate with the basic struggle between good and evil. Thus having an erection in itself is not evil, but 'the genital organs have become as it were *the private property of lust*, which has brought them so completely under its sway that they have no power of movement if this passion fails' [added emphasis].[26] It is the unconscious motivation for lust that Augustine objects to: it is neither rational, predictable nor controllable.

The separation from God embodied in Adam's first disobedience had resulted in an internal fracturing in the human being, who no longer existed as a unity, but was at war with his or her own self. True, human beings could learn to control their own desires, but Augustine points out that this only results in a neurotic mentality: 'this control entails coercion and struggle, and the situation does not represent a state of health in accordance with nature, but an enfeebled condition arising from guilt'.[27] Human beings are in a no-win situation: they either give in to lust, and become even more separated from God, or they struggle against it, forever at war with themselves.

One could object at this point that Augustine is carrying out a massive rationalization, and is concealing some deeper distaste for sex. For his argument concerning the autonomy of sexual desire applies to many bodily functions: does my heart beat because I will it? Does the peristalsis in my digestive tract obey my will? Do my pupils dilate at will? Clearly many bodily functions are not subject to the will, but are not considered sinful. But heartbeats and peristalsis are not the source of great pleasure for human beings, and Augustine gives every indication of having had personal experience of sexual pleasure:

> So intense is the pleasure that when it reaches its climax there is an almost total extinction of mental alertness; the intellectual sentries, as it were, are overwhelmed.[28]

Within the highly rational theology that Christianity was developing, heavily influenced by Greek philosophy, it is this 'extinction of the mind' that is found to be so awful, and so contrary to human will and divine will. The bifurcation of body and soul, desire and reason, has produced a theology and a psychology based on a titanic and internecine struggle within the personality. In a sense, Augustine claims, we are lost in this struggle, we can never win, unless God intervenes. But in addition, until God finally brings about the end of time and the dawn of the new age, we need church and state as props to get us along.

This theology of reason and will versus desire was to dominate Christianity for a long period. It is not simply a theory of desire, but also a theory of ecclesiology, and a theory of politics. Since human beings are so depraved, they cannot claim to have any salvation: 'So long, therefore, as there is in us this weakness, this disease, this lethargy, how shall we dare claim that we are saved?'[29] Augustine rails at those schools of philosophy, such as Stoicism, that claimed that life could be accepted as it was. How could this be, he retorts, when many such pagan schools advocated suicide if life becomes too difficult? No, Augustine insists on the misery of this present life: 'we are beset by evils, and we have to endure them steadfastly until we reach those goods where there will be everything to supply with delight beyond the telling'.[30]

Theologically, this means that human beings are lost without divine grace; spiritually, they are therefore dependent on the Church to help them; politically, they are reliant on Christian emperors:

> We Christians call rulers happy if they rule with justice... if they are slow to punish, but ready to pardon; if they take vengeance on wrong because of the necessity to direct and protect the state, and not to satisfy their personal animosity... if, when they are obliged to take severe decisions, as must often happen, they compensate this with the gentleness of their mercy and the generosity of their benefits.[31]

Robert Markus uses the term 'Christian mediocrity' to describe the subject of Augustine's mature thinking.[32] Augustine did not see the Church as a pure spotless élite, as some Christians had done; he did not see the secular state, even when directed by Christian emperors, as inherently wise or good; Christians themselves were full of sin, and could only look forward to salvation at the end of time. This was simultaneously an attack on the perfectionism which had permeated many radical Christian teachers and groups – claiming that eschatological purity could be established now on earth – and also a justification of the present impurity of individuals, church and state.

I am not suggesting that there was a conscious cynical conspiracy to find a rationale for the growth of the Church; rather that theological theorization is inevitably ideological, and part of the Augustinian ideology was that the individual human was lost without mother Church. If the second coming was postponed, then the Church was vital as its midwife, and also as a help for human beings struggling with their own sinfulness. Of course, this was wonderfully convenient, and as fine a piece of self-advertisement as one will find in human history!

It also had implications for the role of the state, for if the individual was basically lost to sin, then not only was a powerful Church necessary to fight 'the world, the flesh and the devil', but a powerful state might also be necessary to bolster the Church. It is significant that Augustine himself, in his controversy with certain Christian groups, did not shrink from using the power of the Roman state against them, even including military force.[33]

Augustine has constructed a dazzling double bind: human beings are depraved and cannot save themselves, but are dependent on God's grace. But, while we wait for the end of the old age, with its temptations and its vices, we must seek advice and leadership from church and state.

One can only be impressed at the masterly synthesis that Augustine achieved in his theology, and that was to dominate the Catholic Church well into the Middle Ages. Augustine had brought together the theology of sin, a theory of government, and a theology of the Church, as well as an understanding of the linear direction of history as opposed to the ancient cyclical view.

It has always been tempting to demonize Augustine and portray him as the sex-hating theologian who set the Church on its path of misogyny. However, such an approach tends to isolate Augustine from his social and historical context. His theology was a perfect fit for a patriarchal church, which was losing its radical roots and adapting itself to the secular world.[34]

It is clear from the above cursory account that the Augustinian theory of sex was not simply a moral and theological one, but also a socio-political one. In the first place, marriage is the right place for sex, for marriage was created by God for procreation.[35] Thus sex is firmly placed within a tightly restricted social context. But secondly, sex is so dangerous, and so emblematic of human beings' tendency to follow their own pleasures, and not their own rational will (and therefore God's will) that they cannot be left to themselves. The whole panoply of church and state are required, or human beings, left to their own devices, will inevitably fall into perdition.

Augustine is using one of the classic conservative arguments: human beings are so depraved that coercion is required to keep their depravity in check. Certainly the Catholic Church was to use Augustinian theology as a defence of its own deployment of coercive force against those whom it saw as a danger, for example, the medieval Cathars and the Knights Templar.[36]

THE VIRGIN MOTHER

The Christian God is a rational patriarchal God, who created an ordered universe, disrupted only by human disobedience. Thus in Christianity, patriarchal rationality found a new synthesis, a new self-consciousness that simultaneously permitted brilliant feats of philosophical reasoning, and also excoriated women, sex and indeed any kind of sensual existence.

Women were targeted as emblems of the sensual – bleeding in menstruation, conceiving babies in their wombs, giving birth to them and breast-feeding them – and gradually the increasing rationality of Christianity found these sensual aspects unbearable and drove them underground. This can be seen above all in the growing accretion of theology concerning the Virgin Mary, about whom the most arcane and casuistical ideas were proposed. For example, medieval theologians argued about whether Mary, undoubtedly free from the stain of sexual intercourse, also remained a virgin during and after childbirth. That is, not only was her body refused any sexual contact during the conception of Jesus, but her body was to remain 'intact' – the hymen undisturbed – during childbirth.[37]

The 'filth of the flesh' must not contaminate the mother of God – but this purification of Mary simultaneously downgrades and humiliates real women, who do experience sexual intercourse and childbirth. Eventually even the images of Mary breast-feeding Jesus were censored, as she became more and more exalted and non-human.[38]

One can suggest also that this concentration on the body of Mary expressed a fascination with female sexuality, masked by prurience and distaste. In a sense, Mary is subject to an ongoing gynaecological examination by medieval theologians, who compulsively examine that which they abhor, much as present day anti-pornography activists cite massive amounts of porn.

It is arguable that the prominence of Mary in Catholicism and in the Eastern Church does show the contradictory presence of the feminine within the concept of the divine. Many scholars have shown that the image of the virgin mother is an ancient pre-Christian one, and is not necessarily anti-sex or anti-women. For example, virginity can refer to a self-sufficiency in the goddess or in a woman, who does not require fertilization from an external male source.[39] One can also mention here the Gnostic texts, which accorded much importance to the feminine, and spoke of 'God the Mother' as well as 'God the Father'.[40]

But in the Christian scheme, the ancient symbol of the virgin goddess became an anti-sexual and misogynist image:

> the literalization of the virginity of Mary, like the literalization of Eve's role as the wicked temptress of Genesis, broke the heart of Christianity.[41]

Ean Begg's reference to Eve is important, for Christian theologians repeatedly used the myth of Adam and Eve to show that it was a woman who had originally disobeyed God and seduced the male into disobedience. Thus Eve and Mary formed a polarity within the feminine: 'in place of the virgin Eve, mediatrix of death, a virgin has been filled with God's grace, to be the minister of life'.[42]

And of course, Eve's disobedience was linked with the shame felt by Adam and Eve at their nakedness, and the curse placed by God upon women because of Eve's frailty: 'I will greatly multiply your pains in childbearing; in pain you shall bring forth children, yet your desire shall be for your husband, and he shall rule over you.'[43] This Genesis text neatly brings together sexual desire, childbirth, and male domination as punishments given to women for their frail and seductive nature, and Christian theologians never tired of using it to justify their misogyny and distaste for sex and reproduction.

The Eve/Mary split can be seen as the prototype of the whore/Madonna split which continues to exist as a patriarchal view of women. Another biblical reflection of it can be found in Mary Magdalen, a reformed prostitute, who now repents of the pleasures of the flesh.

The evolution of the myth of the Virgin Mary took a further twist in the Reformation, which took the bowdlerization of women and 'the feminine' a stage further. Mary was completely excised, all images were smashed, all types of sensual symbolism – music, incense, decorations, statues – were abolished. If medieval Christianity had blended rationality with a magical, pagan appreciation of 'signs and wonders', Reformation Christianity expelled the magic and adhered to the patriarchal Word alone. Here was a religion entirely suited to the coming age of science, industry and commerce. All superstitious accretions were cut away, so that Christianity became both rational and efficient.

Thus in Christianity, reason became Lord, and sensual existence was cast out into the outer darkness.

CONTROL, POWER AND TERROR

The Christian attitude of suspicion, even hatred, towards the body, and particularly sexual desire, is very long-lasting. It has survived for two thousand years, and although churches in the twentieth century have adapted considerably to secular thinking about sex, there is still a sense of restrictiveness and distaste in their teaching about it. Thus the contemporary Catholic catechism has a section entitled 'Self-control', which is defined as one of the 'cardinal virtues'. In relation to sex, self-control is described as 'chastity', which means:

> being warm and affectionate but not flirtatious with others; by ensuring that embraces and other bodily gestures are genuinely signs of friendship; and having genital sex only with the one to whom we are exclusively committed in marriage.[44]

Furthermore, we fail in the exercise of chastity by practising sex 'without friendship', or with no view to procreation; by masturbating; by sex 'simply for individual gratification'; by promiscuity, fornication, perverse or homosexual intercourse; and by 'self-indulgent sexual fantasies'.[45]

That is a pretty comprehensive list! If one were seriously to follow it, one would surely end tying oneself up in knots, trying to ascertain if a gesture or a look or an embrace contained any vestige of flirtatiousness or individual gratification. The strictures about sexual fantasies strike me as quite bizarre: all fantasies are 'self-indulgent'; furthermore, how is one to prohibit them? Are fantasies subject to the will?

But what is truly extraordinary about this teaching is how ancient it is. How has it been possible for such an anti-sexual ethic to become a permanent part of a religious system, and indeed of a cultural system? I would like to draw together some of the ideas that have been discussed in this chapter, and also suggest some alternative ones.

In the first place, as a patriarchal system of ideas and power, Christianity has been concerned to control women's bodies, and women's sexuality. Thus the linkage of sex with procreation has been a constant theme in Catholic teaching; the pursuit of sex purely for pleasure has been condemned as a mortal sin, and the use of contraception and abortion condemned out of hand. The function of female sexuality is to produce children, and any pleasure obtained is a by-product.

This has also involved a projection onto women of lasciviousness and sinfulness. In the paradigmatic story of paradise, Eve brings about the downfall of humanity through her temptation of Adam, and this story has been used continually to point out that men must beware of women's sensual powers of bewitchment. The witch trials made this misogyny more explicit and lurid, but it has always existed as a basic undercurrent.

Second, one can suggest that Christian teachings on sex served to control human bodies in general. Here one can refer to what Michel Foucault calls 'bio-power', that is, the exertion of power over bodies.[46] Here, the alliance between Christian church and the political state is important, since the 'Christian state' was able to use religious teaching to control its citizens.

Third, in its stress on marital and reproductive sex, and the condemnation of sexual pleasure outside these bounds, Christian teaching has helped to buttress the conservative forces in society. The concepts of 'deviation' and 'perversion' in sexual matters have been judged as moral, and not simply statistical, abnormalities.

But I think it would be a superficial judgement simply to argue that Christianity has exerted a form of control over people's sexuality. That is a rather paranoid view of history: the 'rulers' exert power over the 'ruled' via a number of strategies, of which the doctrine of original sin is central. This view is rather too 'top-down': messages are transmitted from the top down to a set of passive dupes. This leaves out of account the meaning of Christianity for 'the ruled', who also play their part in the whole system of sexual signification.

In the first place, it is arguable that sex has caused intense fear amongst people in many cultures. One might argue that it is the churches that have instigated that fear, but surely there is a more primitive fear: sex connects with death and mortality. Sex does cause the procreation of children, yet to have a child reminds the parents that that child will eventually take their place. Their own mortality is registered. Even orgasm itself has often been compared with death, for it signifies the death of the ego, a self-oblivion that is both thrilling and frightening for many people. Orgasm is a tiny image of one's own nothingness.

Furthermore, the split between reason and emotion, which has existed in the West since pre-Christian times, has meant that sex, as one of the most passionate and non-rational experiences available to us, has aroused very ambivalent feelings, both delight and horror. The exaltation of reason has made sex a dark shadow experience, since it is made up of intense sensation and emotion.

The Christian onslaught on sex indicates how powerful the yearning for sex is, for repression is often directed against wishes. The confessional tended to dwell on the smallest details of sex, seeking out infringements of the Church's teaching – but surely there is also a concealed fascination for the celibate priest, who wants to poke and pry his way into the mysteries of the marriage-bed. Michel Foucault has argued therefore that Christian 'repression', in bringing about an increased surveillance of sexual activity, actually intensifies sexuality.[47]

One can also bring in notions of subjectivity here, for an obsessiveness about sex brings about a self-consciousness, a self-scrutiny. Again Foucault argues that this self-monitoring actually promotes and articulates a form of knowledge of the self that could be called a Christian psychology – but more than a psychology, a metaphysics, a theory of knowledge, a cosmology.[48]

It may appal us to see how negatively this knowledge was propounded by Christianity, but I suggest that this is not just ruthless propaganda, designed to control people's minds and bodies through sheer terror. Part of the negativity stems from a genuine sense of terror and horror at the uncontrollable nature of the self. The notions of 'will' and 'reason' are crucial here, for sex seems to escape the boundaries of both. That is one reason why sex is seen as so desirable, for it is often believed to take us into a realm where self and other, reason and unreason, mind and body, begin to dissolve into each other. The author of the fourteenth century mystical work, *The Cloud of Unknowing*, describes his abhorrence at this prospect with great eloquence:

> Before man sinned, sensuality was so obedient to will, its master as it were, that it never led it into perverted physical pleasure or pain, or any pretended spiritual pleasure or pain, introduced by the enemy of souls into our earthly minds. But it is not so now. Unless it is ruled by grace in the will ... it will wallow, like some pig in the mire, so wretchedly and wildly in all the wealth of the world, and the filth of the flesh, that the whole of its life will be animal and physical rather than human and spiritual.[49]

The Christian teachings on sex have therefore constituted a massive splitting and projection: for desire, which modern Freudians might see as flowing inescapably from the self in its relations with others, is seen as belonging to 'the Enemy', something alien which must be driven out and conquered in a fierce battle for the soul. Christian theology has therefore analysed the self into constituent parts, much as Freud was to do, but has depicted sexual desire as bestial and evil. It is the duty of the rational part of the self to wage war against it, to denounce it and renounce it.

This is a fantastically dynamic model of the self, continually at war with itself, and in some of the great Christian thinkers, such as Augustine or Luther, one senses the ferocious energy that they devoted to their own internal struggle, and also to teaching others how to fight sin. Desire is placed 'out there', the property of Satan, constantly trying to find its way into the fortress of the devout soul, who must repel it at all costs. This struggle is portrayed by some writers with an intensity that reminds one of the paintings of Hieronymous Bosch – here for example is the Spanish mystic, St John of the Cross, speaking of the 'disturbances of sensuality' that occur whilst undertaking spiritual exercises:

> The second source of these rebellious movements is satan, who, in order to disquiet the soul during prayer, or when preparing for it, causes these filthy movements of our lower nature, and these, when in any degree admitted, are injury enough. ...

This is not all; for he represents before them then, most vividly, the most foul and filthy images, and occasionally in close relation with certain spiritual things and persons, by whom their souls are profited, that he may terrify and cow them. Some are so grievously assailed that they dare not dwell upon anything, for it becomes at once a stumbling-block to them, especially those who are of a melancholy temperament; these are so vehemently and effectually assailed as to be objects of the deepest pity; theirs, indeed, is a sad plight.[50]

This is an awful vision; and no doubt for some medieval and Renaissance Christians it was unbearably real. It threatened the idea of the human being as rational animal, for sex and sensuality in general showed human beings apparently behaving like non-rational animals. The stress by the Church on the procreative function of sex can be seen in this light, for then sex has a rational function, and is not just for pleasure. Pleasure is horrific, for it cannot be subsumed within the definition of the human as a creature who uses reason and will to create order in life.

The Christian view of the human being is therefore schizoid, since it clings to reason and rejects unreason. Ironically, our post-Freudian understanding of repression suggests that it does not simply drive desire underground, but causes the subject to be dominated by the repressed desires, possibly overwhelmed by their eruption into life in the form of extravagant fantasies or actions. Thus Freud argued that 'we are "lived" by unknown and uncontrollable forces', and that those who cannot remember repressed material are compelled to repeat it. Jacques Lacan expressed this more tersely: 'what is forgotten is recalled in acts'.[51] According to this view, the Christian obsession with driving out 'evil thoughts' guarantees their existence and perseverance.

I recall a Catholic priest friend of mine telling me that as a young seminarian, he was instructed, while taking a bath, to sprinkle talcum powder into the water in order to obscure the sight of his own genitals. This bizarre exercise in censorship would surely lead both to a deep guilt about one's body and also to an unconscious fascination with its hidden secrets, just as prohibitions on various forms of sexual activity, for example masturbation, lend them great allure.

One can, of course, reverse this chain of cause and effect. The act of censorship leads to fascination and obsession; but arguably it also stems from them or expresses them. Covering the female breast turns it into a magical or fetishized object, but conversely possibly the act of covering derives from fetishization and fascination. This phenomenon exists in other areas apart from sexuality, for example in religion. There is a tendency in human culture to conceal the most potent symbols, thereby increasing their potency and numinosity. Thus Christianity is not indifferent to sex or the sexual organs: it is obsessed by them.

One must also address the issue of guilt, for Christian teaching has this as one of its foundations. The human being exists in a fallen state – that is the premise for all theological thinking until the twentieth century. But what is the meaning of this all-pervasive guilt? Is it simply a political tool used by Christianity to control people?

Elaine Pagels makes the interesting suggestion, in her book *Adam, Eve and the Serpent*, that the centrality of guilt is not simply referable to mechanisms of control, but also to a desire for meaning.[52] Guilt is an antidote to randomness; Christianity rejected the pagan notion of fate, and the Stoical idea that one must submit to fate.

I find this idea very interesting, for it has a close relation to child psychology. It is notorious that children often blame themselves when something bad happens in their family – for example, their parents get divorced, or a sibling dies. Frequently in adult psychotherapy one has to deal with some long-buried but still ferocious guilt, that derived from such a childhood scenario.

Why does the child blame itself? Partly because it dare not blame its parents, who are idealized, and must remain idealized. But why does the child seek to pin blame on somebody? One can argue that children are brought up in a guilt-laden society, where everything is somebody's 'fault'. But I also connect this phenomenon with Pagel's ideas about Christian guilt: that the guilt felt by the Christian and by the child is preferable to the idea that the universe is meaningless.

Guilt gives meaning: the bad thing has happened as a punishment for my bad behaviour. The alternative is that the bad thing has simply happened for no reason, and human beings seem to find this idea appalling and terrifying. Thus the notion of sin fills the universe with significance, and reduces its randomness, and of course Christians throughout the ages have argued that all kinds of phenomena are not 'accidental', but arise out of one's sin, or as God's punishment.

Incidentally, I have no wish to sound superior about Christianity's attempts to drive desire underground, as if somehow twentieth century culture has solved this problem! In many ways, the Christian stance is a tragic view of human existence, constantly at war with its own wishes, torn between reason and unreason, with peace of mind held out as a far-off promise rather than a present actuality. But the great Christian thinkers did not instigate the duality within which they

were struggling; the drive towards ego-consciousness – which inevitably involves the splitting of the human being into internecine components – was surely something far larger than Christianity itself, and
something within which we still struggle today. That is arguably one
reason why contemporary Western culture seems to be obsessed with
sexuality, since sex appears to offer one way out of the impossible
dualism of mind and body.

Ironically, the image of the crucifixion, so dominant in Christian
cultures, provides a rather haunting symbol for the dismemberment
that occurs in the human self-image within the Christian world-view.
Either the body is renounced, and reason flies aloft, or reason is
drowned out in a fleshly bacchanalia. Is there a middle way?

STRUCTURAL SYSTEMS

It is clear that in Christian theology sexual desire has formed one side
in a series of oppositions. Desire is opposed to reason and will; nature
is opposed to grace; flesh to spirit; corruption to purity. This dualism
can be found in other religious movements, such as Gnosticism, and
fits in with the hypothesis that at some point in antiquity human
consciousness itself had begun to bifurcate into the twin poles of
reason and passion. This suggests that Christianity did not inaugurate
this momentous shift, but it certainly became the main expression of it
within Western culture. Eventually, of course, the split would take
other forms: for example, between religion and science, between madness and sanity, and between 'enthusiasm' and temperateness in the
eighteenth century.

Sexual desire therefore assumes within traditional Christian thought
a highly dangerous allure; it constantly beckons to the man of reason;
yet if he is to stay composed and rational, he must renounce it, or at
least deal with it temperately. I use the phrase 'man of reason' deliberately, for women tend to be obliterated within the scheme of things,
since they are often seen as representative of earthly desire and sensuality, and therefore particularly dangerous to men.

If we look back to ancient Judaism, we find that this fierce dualism
does not exist. Indeed, the Jewish God is a violent, passionate and
arbitrary God, and Satan is his messenger: in this sense, Yahweh is
both rational and irrational. C.G. Jung has argued that Christianity
carried out a grave and dangerous schism by separating the goodness
of God from his evil.[53]

Christian monotheism produced an intense self-consciousness that focused on the human will as monarch of the whole self, defied by insubordinates, of which lust is chief. Whereas Roman paganism had tolerated prostitution, the 'love of boys', bisexuality, divorce, abortion, contraception and infanticide,[54] Christian ethics recoiled at such laxity, and constructed a fierce moral code which *guaranteed failure and guilt*, and therefore subjected the individual to a degree of internal tension and external coercion that can be seen as neurotic, modern and politically sophisticated.

It is interesting to compare such ideas with Eastern religion and philosophy, where the split between reason and nature was not so pronounced, so that the 'problem' of sexual desire did not assume such virulent proportions. For example, in Zen Buddhism it is the search for the individual 'self' that is seen as the ultimate human absurdity, and the separation between self and other that is seen as leading to human craving and unhappiness.

This idea has profound implications for our understanding of sex within Christian thought, for whereas Christian thinking has tended to equate desire itself with a fall from grace, Eastern movements such as Zen suggest that it is the split between 'grace' and 'sin' that is the key problem, and moreover, a problem that is completely insoluble, once the split has been constructed by the mind. Within Zen, therefore, sex is not a problem unless the sexual being starts to believe that there is an originator or instigator of sexual feelings: it is the 'I' that is the real problem.

But it is inadequate simply to posit sexuality as one term within a structural opposition within Christianity. This is too formalist, and ignores socio-political questions. However we estimate the effect of Jewish, Roman and Greek influences on the Christian theology of sex, and however we describe the shift from the eschatological asceticism of the early Christians – sex as an emblem of the old age, which could therefore be renounced in the certain knowledge of the world to come – to the later theological pessimism – sex as the prime index of human insubordination and internal fracturing – the most important conclusion is that it was not 'sex' in isolation that has concerned Christianity, but sex as it is articulated socially and politically.

Christian theology is always a political theology. The early asceticism was in revolt against the tight webs woven in Jewish and pagan society around sex, in the form of marriage, procreation, inheritance, kinship; the Augustinian pessimism over sex was part of a wide-ranging theory of the individual, church and state. Reformation

Christianity produced a theory of individual grace and sin that was ideally suited to the new abrasive ethos of the bourgeois revolutions that were to sweep Europe.

This discussion also has implications for sexuality in the twentieth century, for if for the medieval theologian sex provided a vision of hell, at times in this century it has seemed to promise a new heaven on earth. Sexual prophets such as Wilhelm Reich and Marcuse have argued that orgiastic release is the key to human happiness, and that capitalism is intent on thwarting it, and diverting the resultant energy into production.

If Christianity, in its elevation of rationality, therefore abhorred passion and sex, or grudgingly granted them a limited and tightly restricted place within human existence, the twentieth century has elevated and inflated sex in an attempt to find relief from the cold alienation produced by scientific rationality and capitalism. The structural opposition is similar, but the relation has been reversed. This should give us pause for thought: have sexual 'permissiveness' and radicalness simply rebelled against the old strictures? Has sex become utopia, rather than hell?

3 Freud 1: From Biology to Psychology

It is astonishing how tenacious Christian attitudes to sex have been in Western culture. They still surround us, and no doubt exist in all of us, at least in an unconscious form. But over the last five hundred years or more, changes have occurred in society and in human thought that began the slow disruption, and eventually perhaps the disintegration, of the dominant Christian world-view.

The Renaissance and the Reformation shattered many medieval ideas and many medieval institutions, not least the Catholic Church, whose temporal and spiritual authority was dealt devastating blows by the secession of churches in Northern Europe, and the advancement of new theological ideas by figures such as Luther, Calvin and Zwingli. And the Enlightenment in the eighteenth century (the so-called 'Age of Reason') intensified a trend towards the secularization of human thought from which Christianity has never recovered. The development of rationalism and empirical enquiry meant that many religious dogmas and symbols were subject to a remorseless examination, and the new scientific spirit of enquiry proceeded without looking for approval to prelate or pope.

In relation to sex, a more empirical approach began to emerge in place of the medieval mode of a priori and homologous reasoning. Reproduction began to be examined in terms of a biological framework, as opposed to the standpoint of moral theology. For example, through his accurate drawings of internal organs, musculature and human postures, Leonardo da Vinci made a huge contribution to anatomy, although his work was to remain in manuscript form for a long period. In the sixteenth century, Vesalius published his book on anatomy, which was empirically based on dissection rather than Aristotelian dogma.[1]

Michel Foucault dates the modern explosion of interest in sexuality from the eighteenth century, when disciplines such as criminology, biology and medicine begin to join in the 'steady proliferation of discourses concerned with sex'.[2] In the nineteenth century the study of sexual deviance became a discipline in its own right, as figures such as Krafft-Ebbing and Havelock Ellis published their voluminous studies, laden with newfangled terminology.[3]

It has been argued by Foucault and others that it is at this period that the concept of sexuality itself was invented, and that this concept marks a new development in the study of human sexual relations. For the term 'sexuality' denotes an autonomous force within the human being, and one that acts as a kind of key to the personality. In other words, 'sexuality' partly denotes 'identity'. I shall consider this argument in greater detail in Chapter 5.

It is against this historical background that the emergence of Freud's ideas should be seen, for Freud can be viewed not just as the progenitor of a new way of looking at human sexuality, but also as a synthesizing figure who brought together many ideas that had been incubating for two hundred years. Many influences went into the stream of Freudian thought, including neurology, psychiatry, sexology, hypnosis, and so on.

In this and the following chapter I would like to examine several of the key ideas developed by Freud in relation to sexuality. It would be impossible to attempt a comprehensive study of the Freudian model of sexuality in one chapter, since the research and writings of Freud and his followers are vast, and could not be encompassed in the space of a book, let alone a chapter. It embraces such topics as the sexual drive or instinct; the pleasure principle; the Oedipus complex, including the castration complex and penis envy; the theory of infantile sexuality; the theory of neurosis and its aetiology; and the rich body of techniques used in psychoanalysis.

Out of this massive area, I have chosen to focus on five issues: first, the notion of sexual aetiology, that is, that neuroses stem from some disruption in sexual functioning. This idea also suggests that sexuality lies at the source of human motivation and behaviour in general. This is an astonishing claim, and one that has been largely abandoned in the late twentieth century by psychoanalysts and psychotherapists. None the less it has had a huge impact not just in the domain of psychology, but in Western culture at large.

A second issue is the key shift made by Freud from a biological or organic view of neurosis and sexuality to a psychological one, since this is a major paradigm shift, and can be seen in some senses as part of the move from nineteenth- to twentieth-century ways of thinking, part of the development of modern thought itself.

Third, Freud combined a radical analysis of human sexuality with a model of the unconscious: this produced a very powerful and elegant theory of unconscious desire. This was not seen as a homogeneous phenomenon but as heterogeneous: in the unconscious all manner of erotic desires can coexist. Furthermore, Freud to some extent removed the normative bias common in studies of sexuality: in his famous remark, heterosexuality is as problematical as any other desire.[4]

Fourth, Freud's view of sexuality was heavily masculinist: he embraced a sexual 'monism', which took male sexuality as the baseline and described female sexuality as its derivative. This has had enormous repercussions on psychoanalysis and the analytic theory of male and female sexuality, but as we shall see, contemporary analytic thought has begun to grant female sexuality its own ground.

Fifth, when we consider the biological foundations of Freud's model of sexuality, and its masculinist bias, the important question arises: can one posit a psychoanalysis that has instead a psycho-social basis and that is non-masculinist? In other words, are biologism and masculinism inherent parts of a psychoanalytical theory of sexuality?

I have also spent some time discussing various developments made by other analysts, since sexuality came to enjoy a much less prominent position in psychoanalysis with the advent of pre-Oedipal, object relations psychology. Sexuality also changes its character in post-Freudian thinking – from being an impersonal drive, almost indifferent to its object, it begins to be seen as the most intense expression of the human yearning for relationship with another.

But these later developments are not 'anti-Freudian': they can be seen as developing more fully some of the implications of Freud's own thought. Freud remained ambivalent about the contributions of biology and psychology to the end of his life, but in a sense this can be seen as a positive aspect of his thought, since the tension between the two disciplines gave his ideas their great élan. For Freud, the instincts, particularly the sexual ones, were a great bridge between body and mind. Consciously or not, Freud had found one solution to the perennial debate about the relationship between these two elements in the human being.

SEXUAL AETIOLOGY

From the beginning to the end of his enquiries, Freud never abandoned the notion that there was a sexual root to human neuroses. As I have mentioned briefly, this bias towards sexuality should not be seen as an isolated assumption on Freud's part, for the nineteenth century saw an intense debate about the nature of sexual desire, the differences between men and women, the nature of sexual 'deviation' and so on.

What was original about Freud was that he brought together a nineteenth-century view of sex as a dangerous drive which must be 'civilized', with a sophisticated theory of the psyche, including the notion of the unconscious.

At first, Freud adopted a quite impersonal view of sexual relations – other people seem to function as the means to an end, the end being sexual relief: 'it seems probable that the sexual instinct is in the first instance independent of its object'.[5] However, with the development of the Oedipus complex, Freud's theory of sexuality became more interpersonal. In the Oedipus complex, sexuality is personalized and incorporated into relationships: the infant loves and desires its parents and also identifies with them. The interplay between desire and identification is extremely complex, since while boys, for example, seem to overtly identify with their father and desire their mother, at the unconscious level they have been presumed to desire their father and identify with their mother.[6]

The theory of sexual aetiology therefore goes hand in hand with the Freudian concept of infantile sexuality: for each individual, the basic and enduring template of erotic relationships is established in early childhood. This is a key aspect of the Freudian model, and has many interesting and important corollaries: for example, that in adulthood many people repeat these infantile patterns in the vain hope of seducing the elusive parent (or a simulacrum of them); or that the act of sex itself recapitulates many infantile desires – the wish to suck, to bite, to possess, to be possessed, and so on. Freud's approach to sexuality is very clearly a determinist one: adult erotic predilections are in large part determined by infantile development. Such an approach emphasizes the primitive, one might say, *archaic* or atavistic aspects of sex. There is little doubt that this emphasis has always caused offence to some people, who dislike the 'bestial' aspects of sex.

Another important aspect of sexual aetiology is that it gives to sexuality an importance, not just as a diagnostic principle, but as a means of understanding people. This is the 'hermeneutical' principle: the idea that the sexual feelings and desires of an individual give us the key to their character. In Foucault's words: 'we demand that sex speak the truth... and we demand that it tell us our truth, or rather, the deeply buried truth'.[7]

I should mention at this point one of the interesting problems that confronts all theories of sexuality, and in the case of Freudian psychology, has aroused great controversy: is the theory testable? Is it scientific? The philosopher Karl Popper has argued that psycho-

analysis cannot claim scientific status, since its theses cannot be falsi-
fied. To put it another way, psychoanalytic hypotheses are not predictive in the normally accepted sense of predictiveness in scientific
research.

This is absolutely true, and seems to suggest that psychoanalysis is
not scientific in the sense that biology or physics is: that is, it does not
construct 'laws', defined as predictive generalizations. It cannot do
this, since it is dealing with human subjectivity. Thus although one can
establish as a broad principle the idea that one's parents' sexual
relation will have a powerfully determining effect on one's own sexuality, it is impossible to turn this into a strict cause/effect law.

The arguments about psychoanalysis and science are complicated
by Freud's own predilection for 'hard' scientific subjects such as
neurology and biology. He tended to express his ideas in rather
physicalist terms: sexuality is determined by 'drives', which seek
'detensioning', and so on. At the same time, the practice of analysis
with patients seems to have more in common with an interpretive art
than a science.[8]

It is striking how the study of sexuality has tended to divide into a
more 'scientific' camp, such as sexology, which tries to describe human
sexual behaviour in objective terms, often in laboratory conditions,
and a more 'hermeneutical' camp, which seeks to elicit the meanings
that are conveyed by sexual desires and actions. Psychoanalysis contains both strands of enquiry, and has therefore proved confusing to
those who want to define its 'scientific' or 'non-scientific' standing.

BIOLOGY AND PSYCHOLOGY

Freud's thought does not assume an even and consistent development:
it is full of contradictions, hesitancies, gaps. It is not always easy
therefore to trace the growth of certain ideas, particularly over the
massive span of Freud's writings. But certainly Freud never abandoned the biological basis of the instincts and indeed of psychology.
In *An Outline of Psycho-analysis* (1940), written towards the end of
his life, he still sees physical organs as having a very powerful effect
on the mind: 'the first organ to emerge as an erotogenic zone and to
make libidinal demands on the mind is, from the time of birth
onwards, the mouth'.[9] Clearly this is a dualistic model of body and
mind, which are quite sharply separated, at least in these theoretical or
metapsychological pronouncements.

None the less, the *Outline* is mainly concerned with purely psychological phenomena: the structure of the unconscious, the nature of the ego and its relations with the unconscious, dream interpretation, and the use of transference in psychoanalytic technique. This illustrates the point that analysis or therapy cannot approach patients within a biological framework of reference; nor can one analyse the relationship between therapist and client within a biological model. Thus under the impact of clinical experience, Freud moves towards a more interactive theory of sexuality: the Oedipus complex embodies the idea that erotic energy is something existing between people, taking its form as a result of those relationships.[10]

However, it was very difficult for Freud to take these insights back into the overall theoretical model, the 'metapsychology'. In this realm, Freud remained wedded to a biologically based theory, even though in the practice of analysis biology proved useless. In some senses, therefore, theory and practice, metapsychology and psychology, tended to diverge in Freud.

The most dramatic expressions of the shift from biological to psychological ways of thinking can probably be found in the last years of the nineteenth century, when Freud was wrestling with early formulations of many of his key ideas. The shift was expressed in various ways: for example, in the abandonment of the seduction hypothesis, in the break from his great friend, Wilhelm Fliess, and in the enrichment of his ideas about the treatment of patients. In all of these areas we see the gradual and reluctant abandonment of a physiological approach to neurosis and sexual disorders.

In retrospect, this seems to have been inevitable once Freud made the momentous separation between sexuality and reproduction, and connected the sexual drive with the 'pleasure principle', that is, the aim of 'obtaining satisfaction by means of an appropriate stimulation of the erotogenic zone'.[11] The positing of infantile sexuality demanded such assumptions, since the 'aim' of infantile sexuality could not be seen as a procreative but a pleasure-oriented one, only becoming linked with reproduction with the onset of adult genital sexuality.[12] This gives an indication of the radical stance taken by Freud towards sexuality, and why the notion of infantile sexuality has continued to cause concern and shock, for it implicitly recasts human sexuality in a new non-reproductive frame. It also challenges Christian ethics at its foundations: the pleasure principle is resolutely amoral.

THE BREAK WITH FLIESS

Wilhelm Fliess, an ear, nose and throat doctor in Berlin, became friendly with Freud after attending his lectures at the university in Vienna in 1887. The two men began a lengthy correspondence and a series of regular meetings in German and Austrian towns – meetings which they referred to as 'congresses'. The relationship with Fliess was vital for Freud, for it provided him with 'dialogue and encouragement' at a time when he often felt isolated. Jeffrey Masson comments: 'for many years Fliess was Freud's only audience'.[13] It was also a passionate friendship, and in the correspondence one can sense Freud unburdening himself in a very personal manner, exposing his ambitions, his frustrations, his excitement at scientific discoveries, and also his love for Fliess. It is in fact a very moving correspondence.[14]

The split with Fliess occurred partly over the disagreement over physical (organic) and psychological approaches to neurosis. In the early letters written by Freud to Fliess, we see a concordance between the two men on the organic root of neurosis. Freud seeks to find sexual (physical) causes for neurosis, for example, masturbation, coitus interruptus, use of condoms, and so on. For example, he sees female 'neurasthenia' as caused by male sexual inadequacy.[15] One can imagine that Fliess – obsessed as he was with theories of nasal trauma, and also interested in theories of biological periodicity – believed that he and Freud were co-thinkers in proposing organic, sexual causes for psychological disturbances.

But Freud's abandonment of the seduction hypothesis – the idea that his patients with hysteria had been sexually seduced as children – announced to Fliess in the famous letter of September 1897, must have been an ominous sign for Fliess. In that letter Freud states: 'in this collapse of everything valuable, *the psychological alone remains untouched*. The [dream] book stands entirely secure' [added emphasis].[16] This meant that Freud had abandoned the physicalism of the seduction hypothesis, and was searching for purely psychological causes for neurosis. In fact, Freud was moving from an empiricist psychology – which looks for observable 'causes' in people's behaviour – towards a much richer but more elusive notion of human motivation, in which motivation is as much intra-psychic as extra-psychic.

The reference to the 'dream book' in the above letter is to *The Interpretation of Dreams*, and in a letter written five months later Freud describes his material in that book as 'purely philosophical':

'nothing has come up at the organic–sexual end'.[17] Surely to Fliess this was anathema, and Freud therefore hastens to reassure his friend – who after all had been invaluable to Freud – that he was not at odds with him:

> I am not all in disagreement with you, not at all inclined to leave the psychology hanging in the air without an organic base. But apart from this conviction, I do not know how to go on, neither theoretically nor therapeutically, and therefore must behave *as if only the psychological were under consideration* [added emphasis].[18]

This is an important statement, for it indicates the future development of Freud's own thought, and indeed of 'Freudian thought' itself. Freud persisted to the end of his life in giving the psychology an 'organic base', but the great discoveries in psychoanalysis were psychological ones. *Biological work was a dead-end*, especially in the work with patients, and particularly as the actual relationship between Freud and his patients came to the forefront as a lode-mine of material.

But Freud was reluctant to abandon the organic baseline for his psychological theory, no doubt owing in part to his training as a neurologist, and also to the respectability of biology as a 'hard' science. There may also be deep-rooted political reasons, for if the organic base is abandoned, and a more socio-political theory of sexuality propounded, then society itself might come under fierce criticism for its destructive and repressive attitude towards sexuality. At times, Freud seems to take this line, particularly in his late book *Civilization and its Discontents* (1930). In other words, Freud was ambivalent about the socio-political causes of neurosis, and in this light, biology offered a safe, non-political refuge.

There may well also be deeply unconscious and more personal reasons why Freud clung to a biological view of sexuality, for an out-and-out social or interpersonal theory would force him to confront the erotic tensions and seductions in his own family, particularly in relation to his mother. Such personal details are not out of place when considering Freud's theories, since it was in his own self-analysis that he was able to make many of his key discoveries.

Freud showed considerable ambivalence towards his friend's researches into physiological theories: for example, Fliess developed a theory about the connection between homosexuality and physical bilaterality, suggesting that left-handed people were more likely to be homosexual. Freud was enthusiastic about the notion of bisexuality, but showed coolness towards Fliess's wish to tie it to physiological characteristics: 'where then is the femininity, for instance, in the left half of a man, if it carries a testicle... just like the right one?'[19] Fliess had also apparently suggested that Freud was partially left-handed, so there may well have been implicit suggestions by Fliess that Freud's attachment to him was homosexual.[20]

Freud's disagreement with Fliess on the physiological determination of sexual orientation is a profound one, although it is likely that he concealed its implications from Fliess and perhaps from himself. In a growing number of areas, Freud was beginning to push more and more into a purely psychological enquiry, while Fliess remained mainly concerned with his organic theories. To put it simplistically, confronted with what would be called today a psychosomatic condition, Freud would investigate the underlying psychological causes, whereas Fliess might advocate a surgical operation on the offending area. In fact, this actually happened with Emma Eckstein, one of Freud's patients, and the notorious operation on her shows Freud taking part in a surgical intervention, which he is clearly doubtful of, although he continued to paper over the cracks opening up between him and Fliess.[21]

The split between Freud and Fliess is starkly revealed in an unpublished letter by Fliess, in which Fliess makes an explicitly physicalist analysis of a case of Freud's:

> In this case you are no more responsible for the relapse than your quick and brilliant success: I have often observed that a period of euphoria lasting many months precedes the outbreak of malignant tumours. During that period neurotic symptoms recede as well. Later they return with astounding suddenness.[22]

Fliess comments: 'Freud was appalled by this communication.' Jeffrey Masson's summary of the implications of these statements cannot be improved on: 'It meant, very simply, that there was no need for Freud to engage in psychotherapy; a patient got better or worse according to strictly biological periods. Fliess's view undermined all of Freud's work. Estrangement was inevitable.'[23]

This is the nub of the separation between Fliess and Freud: Freud was searching for a psychological means of investigating neurosis and of alleviating it, whereas Fliess advocated nasal operations, investigations of biological rhythms in the person's life, and so on. In a sense, Fliess remains frozen in a nineteenth-century physicalist universe, whereas Freud is moving on to a new kind of enquiry concerning the mind and its internal operations, and also concerning relations between people. For Freud, sexuality had become *psycho-sexuality.*

THE SEDUCTION HYPOTHESIS

The seduction theory has been the subject of fierce controversy by contemporary therapists and writers, particularly Jeffrey Masson and Alice Miller, who have claimed that Freud basically betrayed scientific truth by abandoning the idea that his patients had been seduced as children, when there was plenty of evidence to back this up. They have also argued that psychoanalysts have subsequently ignored the glaring evidence for actual sexual abuse of children, and have insisted that their patients are indulging in fantasy.

Masson and Miller are right to criticize any analysts or therapists who refuse to take the patient's own story seriously.[24] However, the main line of argument of Masson and Miller ignores a fundamental issue: by turning to the internal structures and processes of the psyche, Freud created a truly *psychological* psychology. Masson, in particular, seems to have gone beyond a criticism of the rejection of child abuse by psychoanalysis, to a point where he himself denies the existence of the unconscious and the inner world. In his book *Final Analysis*, he cites his response when confronted by the board of the Freud Archives:

> I do not believe that children have Oedipal fantasies about their parents, if by that you mean that girls want to sleep with their fathers. On the contrary, I think that parents act upon their children quite literally by hurting them, and in the case of fathers, sexually abusing them.[25]

This statement implies that children are purely passive, and that any sexual wishes or feelings they have must be the result of child abuse. This strikes me as an extraordinary model of human sexuality, for we are left in ignorance as to how sexuality develops in those children who are not 'hurt' by their parents. Are children asexual until puberty? Does this mean that psychotherapists are wrong to see the early mother–infant relation as a prototypical erotic relationship? Are young children intensely interested in their parents' bodies purely because of some abuse they have suffered? Or should we say that this interest is not sexual? In Masson's schema, the inner world seems to disappear completely, to be replaced simply by a world of actual events. In this view, sexuality becomes a very mysterious acquisition, without any infantile origin. In fact, sexuality is *imposed* on children, and does not develop internally at all.

In other words, there is a huge difference between criticizing indifference to child abuse on the part of therapists or analysts, and on the other hand rejecting the whole notion of infantile desires, indeed the *infantile unconscious*. Masson has thrown the baby out with the bathwater, and at the end of *Final Analysis* he rejects the whole notion of psychotherapy: 'there are no experts in loving, no scholars of living, no doctors of the human emotions'.[26]

Masson also tends to be rather imprecise about the meaning of psychological terms: for example, he seems confused about the notion of 'fantasy' compared with 'lying'. This, crucially, collapses the distinction between the unconscious and the conscious, and between the inner world and external reality. Repeatedly in *The Assault on Truth* he argues that Freud claimed that hysterical women were lying:

Fantasy – the notion from Freud that women invent allegations of sexual abuse because they desire sex ...

The early traumas his patients had had the courage to face and report to him he was to later dismiss as the fantasies of hysterical women who invented stories and told lies ...

Freud ... became convinced that the stories of seduction which he had originally believed to be true were lies.[27]

Of course the Freudian notion of 'fantasy' is quite distinct from lying, just as the notion of 'repression' (which creates the unconscious) is quite different from 'suppression' (a reversible conscious act). To collapse them in this way not only destroys the basic premises for psychoanalysis, but those for any non-empiricist psychology. In her book *Psychoanalysis and Feminism*, Juliet Mitchell demonstrates very clearly that many revisions and distortions of Freud attack the very foundations of psychoanalysis, by denying the existence of the unconscious and replacing it with a kind of behaviourism or empiricism.[28]

In fact, the Freudian view amounts to saying that our mental life consists to a large degree of dense and rich unconscious fantasy, which is reproduced (projected) in various ways in our external life. Thus to equate fantasy with 'lies' is an astonishing claim, and amounts to saying that the unconscious does not exist, since lying is usually taken to be a conscious act.

Anna Freud complained to Masson that his ideas would have prevented psychoanalysis ever getting off the starting blocks, and surely this is correct.[29] Freud had the great insight that neurosis is a self-perpetuating *internal self-attack*, and could not be solved simply by locating 'causes' in the past. Neurosis has to be examined as an internal system in the psyche, not simply as a result of childhood trauma. Yes, the failure of caring in childhood – or worse – can often be implicated, but that insight doesn't automatically relieve people of their difficulties. It's what they do to themselves in the present that is critical. This is a repetition or an internalization of what was once done by others, but knowing that in itself doesn't help us to stop our self-flagellation.

Thus a Masson-type empiricism in psychotherapy leads to a total cul-de-sac which refuses to accept that the inner world exists and has a major influence on the external life of the individual. I have had a number of clients in psychotherapy who knew full well that they had been severely abused in childhood, but who still had to explore their own internal self-abuse if they were to begin to live in a more fulfilling way. Masson's arguments provide us therefore, in a back-handed way, with some useful insights into the revolutionary quality of Freud's thought, particularly its anti-empiricism.

A Massonian approach to traumatic injury, in the psychological sense, is rather akin to Hollywood's – as for example, in films such as Alfred Hitchcock's *Marnie* and *Spellbound*. In these films, the tormented protagonist eventually discovers some long-buried secret in childhood – Marnie discovers that as a child she killed a sailor who was sexually molesting her mother. The implication is that 'everything will be all right now', since the trauma has been remembered and is no longer repressed. Indeed, it is possible that this represents a popular view of psychoanalysis and therapy – but nothing could be further from the truth. The main work remains: to unravel all the self-defeating, self-tormenting strategies that are at work in the person's psyche. In that sense, Freud is right: depression, or sexual dysfunction, in the present, is not 'caused' by an event in the past, but by a set of psychological mechanisms which exist now. Those mechanisms may well be connected with traumatic events in the past, but exposing that causative link does not stop them.

A further point to be made in relation to child seduction is that many analysts and therapists today do accept that many patients have been abused, emotionally, physically or sexually. The reconstruction of the past is seen as a vital part of the whole therapeutic process: those who do not remember the past are compelled to repeat it.[30] But one also has to add that remembering the past is not enough to stop us repeating it – one also has to address the compulsion to repeat, which is often addictive.

INNER AND OUTER WORLDS

In this sense, from the standpoint of contemporary psychotherapy, one can argue that Freud did go too far in his internalization of neurosis. The external environment became a shadowy world, seen as having little effect on the psyche. This approach is dramatically illustrated in Freud's case-study of 'Dora', in which he expresses surprise that the young girl, approached seductively by her father's friend, does not experience desire towards him. This comment tends to arouse revulsion in contemporary commentators, as it sounds inhuman, and ignores the mystification that Dora was subject to, and the fact that she was being used by her family as a kind of sexual bribe. Freud, on the other hand, declares that her neurosis has its roots in an internal blockage of her sexual feelings.[31]

This turning away from external events is shown very starkly in the seminar notes written by Freud's disciple Lou Andreas-Salomé. After a seminar on infantile sexuality, she notes laconically:

> On traumas of childhood. Not important in themselves. An unsheltered child exposed to all manner of traumas might often remain healthier if his later way of life is untroubled than a protected one, who in later life is confronted by greater cultural renunciations.[32]

I doubt if contemporary child psychotherapists would agree with that statement.

The controversy over seduction has great metapsychological implications, for the respective roles of external reality and internal psychic reality are brought into question. Freud's position changed from seeing neurosis as having external causes – child sexual abuse – to a much more intrapsychic one. Thus the reported acts of abuse were seen as the child's fantasies, used to defend against the child's own erotic wishes and masturbatory acts. According to this model, neurosis became very much an internal conflict, occasioned not by external trauma but by forces within the psyche opposing each other.

This philosophical debate has continued during the remainder of this century, and positions have been taken at each extreme and in the middle. Thus, Melanie Klein at certain stages of her career took a very 'internal' position, and relegated external reality – particularly the influence of parents – to a minor position. However, as with most analysts, Klein does not show an absolute consistency on this.[33]

One can refer to D.W. Winnicott as an analyst who tended to see external factors as very important. He cited deprivation as crucial in the ego-integrity of the growing child. Many psychotherapists today do take child sexual abuse seriously, but the contemporary furore over 'false memory syndrome' shows how the conflict between external reality and internal fantasy is not an obscure footnote in psychology, but in fact arouses very intense feelings.[34]

From the point of view of the study of sexuality, two very different concepts are revealed in this debate. In one version (roughly speaking, Freud's), sexuality is a force operating *within the organism*, both physically and mentally. It comes into conflict with other forces in the psyche, and also with the demand of society for some form of self-control, this idea being internalized in the superego.

From the other point of view (which can be loosely termed an 'object relations' one), sexuality arises as an *interactive energy or force*. The mother–child relationship is the prototype of an erotic relationship, for it is intensely physical, concerned with gratification and touch; this is not reducible to some kind of stimulus–response model, but centres on a relationship between two persons.

Of course the two views are not incompatible. One can adhere to the position that sexual energy is endogenous or innate, but requires social contact to give it impetus and direction. One can draw an interesting parallel here with language, which clearly needs social contact to facilitate its development. Yet there is also compelling evidence that speech and language have a biological, that is, innate, base.[35]

These two concepts of sexuality can be related to a political division between those who stress the environment, and its effect on individuals, and those who see individuals more as 'lived' by internal structures. One can also link this division to the philosophical divide between materialism and idealism, for it is likely that psychoanalysis has been heavily influenced by Hegelian thought, with its emphasis on the development of self-consciousness and the realization of the worldwide Idea or Spirit. One can also adduce Hegel's formulation of dialectical logic, and speculate how much this has influenced the Freudian division of the psyche into the three entities of ego, id and superego. It is striking how, just as Marx 'turned Hegel upside down' by giving matter precedence over thought, so various revisions of Freud have striven to give the environment much more importance.[36]

POLYMORPHOUS SEXUALITIES

The contemporary arguments over seduction, sexual fantasy and infantile sexuality show that Freud's ideas still arouse controversy and hostility. His ideas still seem radical in the 1990s, for Freud refused to identify sexuality with heterosexuality, reproduction, genitality or adulthood. He assumed a sexual instinct, or rather, instincts, that are heterogeneous, that aim for pleasure in many parts of the body, and that originally have no specific object. The effect of the Oedipus complex is to 'train' these amorphous sexual drives towards definite objects – in the form of one's parents; later, puberty brings about the potential genital fulfilment of sexuality, without, however, entirely erasing the pre-genital drives. The unconscious is timeless, Freud argued, and therefore all the primitive desires of infancy are retained there, and still exert their influence. Indeed, arguably human personality itself is largely constituted by such ancient patterns of relating and desiring.[37]

This model of sexuality is an extraordinary one, for it does not begin with a normative scheme of adult genital heterosexuality. Indeed the first forty pages of *Three Essays on the Theory of Sexuality*, written in 1905, are devoted to 'Sexual Aberrations', and the next forty to 'Infantile Sexuality', before the author moves on to puberty and the 'primacy of the genital zones'. By structuring the book in this way, Freud is concerned to show that sexuality has many 'component instincts' and body zones, which are originally neither unified nor genital.

In a sense Freud has deconstructed the prescriptive concept of heterosexuality, and has shown how much human sexuality is shot through with 'perverse' currents:

a disposition to perversions is an original and universal disposition of the human sexual instinct and . . . normal sexual behaviour is developed out of it.[38]

Our sexual drive is not therefore for Freud a unity: it is made up of different components and different body zones which are eventually amalgamated by the force of the genital aim, but which are still likely to appear in adult sex in the form of foreplay, non-genital sex (for example, oral sex), and in fantasy. Freud does see aberrations in adult sexuality as examples of 'infantilism'; none the less he accepts that 'polymorphous perversity' remains a factor in everyone's sexuality.

Jeffrey Weeks makes the comment that Freud combined a normative prejudice in favour of heterosexuality with an openness to different kinds of sexuality that is liberal and non-condemning.[39] Thus
psychoanalytic ideas about sexuality can be used by 'sexual radicals'
in the contemporary era to grant validity to their own sexual tastes
and practices. The gay movement, feminists – particularly feminist
lesbians – and others who enjoy non-genital sex are able to cite Freud
as an authority who, if he did not sanction such practices, showed that
they are not exotic or in fact unusual.

One striking example concerns masturbation, which was seen as
morally degenerate in the nineteenth and early twentieth centuries,
and even in the early psychoanalytic movement was seen as injurious
to mental health. However, eventually analysts argued that learning to
masturbate is a necessary and healthy part of a child's development:
'autonomy, the definition and elaboration of oneself, occurs in the
self-experience of masturbation'.[40]

Freud must be distinguished from later psychoanalysts, some of
whom seem to exhibit strong conservative prejudices. For example,
homosexuality was seen by some analysts as something to be cured.[41]
This normative strain of analysis has been particularly strong in
America, and invokes Lacan's scorn for the way in which patients
were seen as requiring adaptation to the goals and norms of bourgeois
American society.[42]

UNCONSCIOUS DESIRE

The intersection of the theory of non-genital, non-reproductive and
infantile sexualities with the Freudian theory of the unconscious produces a remarkable synthesis, for, as I have already pointed out, the
unconscious does not recognize the boundaries of time, space and
stable identity. In a sense, the Freudian unconscious is infantile,
perverse and solely interested in its own desire for pleasure. The
notion of *repressed unconscious desire* is therefore the foundation
stone of psychoanalysis, and disrupts all notions of settled identity
and personality, and all notions of 'self-knowledge'.

And these ideas are not esoteric or rarefied: they have direct practical consequences in people's lives. Frequently in psychotherapy one
meets people who are at war with themselves: their social persona is
subverted by their unconscious desires, which are compelling them to
go in a totally different direction from the rest of their life. But the

unconscious does not speak in a clear voice: its messages are garbled, and often take the form of 'symptoms'. The task of therapy is then to translate symptoms into symbols, so that the communications of the unconscious can be understood.

But what is the unconscious? Is it simply that which is not known? This would be a critical misjudgement of the terms 'unconscious' and 'conscious'. For the unconscious is not simply topographically distinct from the conscious – that is, situated in a different position in the psyche – but is qualitatively different. However, some critics of the Freudian unconscious have attempted to identify it as the unknown. A clear example of this can be found in the work of R.D. Laing, who was extremely critical of the Freudian unconscious. For example, in his book *Self and Others* he subjects Freud's notion to a critique from the existential and phenomenological point of view. Laing argues that 'the "unconscious" is what we do not communicate, to ourselves, or to another'.[43]

This explanation of the unconscious fits in with Laing's interpersonal theories, but it has nothing to do with Freud's concept, which posits an unconscious that is primitive, irrational, amoral, contradictory and devoted to the pleasure principle without any regard for the 'reality principle', that is, 'the real circumstances in the external world'.[44] James Strachey gives an excellent summary of the strange characteristics of the 'primary process' in the unconscious:

> In the unconscious, it was found, there is no sort of organization or coordination; each separate impulse seeks satisfaction independently of all the rest; they proceed uninfluenced by one another; contradictions are completely unoperative, and the most opposite impulses flourish side by side. So too, in the unconscious, associations of ideas proceed along lines without any regard to logic: similarities are treated as identities, negatives are equated with positives. Again, the objects to which the conative trends are attached in the unconscious are extraordinarily changeable – one may be replaced by another along a whole chain of associations that have no rational basis.[45]

The implications of this model of the unconscious are considerable, and go way beyond the notion of the 'unknown' or that which we do not communicate. In the Freudian unconscious, desires can exist side by side that at the adult rational level would be seen as cancelling each other out: for example, one can have both heterosexual and homosexual desires; one can feel active and passive; one can feel both masculine and feminine. Such desires do not obey any social prescriptions whatever: one can simply desire anyone and anything. Desire knows no boundaries of time, death or space: one's infantile desires – for mother's breast or father's penis – still exist in this zone, if in repressed form.

Thus there is a profound gulf between this primitive world and the adult rational persona that most of us habitually wear, and this gulf causes massive problems for many people, for the primitive desires are repressed, unsatisfied and indeed unrecognized, but still exert considerable influence.

However, psychoanalysis does not propose that our primitive desires should simply be satisfied in action, but that they be recognized in consciousness. Indeed we cannot simply abandon ourselves to the unconscious: for one thing, it also contains murderous feelings directed both at other people and at oneself. Furthermore, as pure unconscious, I do not exist, I have no identity. It is through the splitting of the unconscious, and the emergence of the ego from it, that my own sense of identity develops. Thus one should not romanticize the unconscious as the repository of primitive energy: it is the struggle between ego and id that constitutes the individual's existence and identity. The task of human maturity is not to elevate the unconscious to the status of a guru, but to achieve a balance between unconscious and conscious, something that Jung conceived of as a kind of 'inner marriage'.

In fact, so far from treating the unconscious as holy, Freud considers it as a dangerous part of the psyche that must be treated with caution. He states: 'in neurotic anxiety the ego is making an attempt at flight from the demand by its libido, that is treating *this internal danger* as though it were an external one' [added emphasis].[46]

Furthermore, Freud's concept of pleasure and unpleasure has a rather austere flavour, for 'pleasure' consists of a draining of the tensions created by the sexual instincts. There is an odd kind of aversion to sex here: as the psychotherapist Estelle Roith comments,

> There is a bleak and bitter quality that is striking not least because the *pleasures* of successful adult sexuality – the need to give pleasure to the loved one and indeed the whole notion of tenderness – are virtually absent from Freud's account.[47]

One can also cite in this context Freud's various remarks that human genitals are ugly, that a repugnance to sex may be quite natural, that menstrual odours put people off sex – taken all together it is possible to detect within Freud's 'scientific' attitude to sex a rather defensive approach to its pleasures.[48]

Furthermore, one could argue, as some object relations theorists do, that he got things back to front. Instead of seeing human beings as subject to bodily excitations, which makes them seek 'objects', so that their sexual tension can be given relief, it is possible to reverse this: we are attached to other people, and this attachment causes bodily excitement and pleasure. In other words, Freud's view of sexuality has a rather positivist, dehumanized and, one might even say, autistic, flavour.

On the other hand, Freud's detachment of sexuality from reproduction; the flexibility of the sexual drives, and the interchangeable objects which they aim at; his description of sexual perversions as a consequence of infantile sexuality – these aspects of Freud's theory of sexual desire potentially provide a very liberal, not to say liberating, model of sexuality. For example, Freud was quite willing to accept that homosexual desire was not bizarre or deviant, but in fact universal. Of course, Freud also did prioritize heterosexuality as the least neurotic outcome for adult sexuality, but his model of sexuality is a remarkably open one.

And the Freudian model is not an abstract or philosophical one: above all, it is a practical one, designed to be used in close work with people. This is clear enough in psychotherapy, where in-depth work includes the recovery of 'forbidden' desires. As one of my clients said to me: 'I can now accept that my wish to anally rape you, urinate over you and suck your penis are valid desires; although I also know I don't really want to commit them, and they really express my love for you.' That comment for me sums up some of the value of the Freudian theory of unconscious desire in practical terms.

ANTI-EMPIRICISM

The theory of the unconscious has further implications: in particular, the notion that the unconscious is unknowable. Of course, this is not absolutely true, since the unconscious communicates its desires, admittedly in a distorted manner, but none the less in a manner that can be deciphered. But it is one thing to patiently decipher the symbolic manifestations of the unconscious, and another thing to say that we have a clear knowledge of the unconscious. The plain fact is, we do not.

We can add the further corollary that the unconscious has a will of its own, separate from our normal sense of will-power. Thus quite frequently one finds people doing something that goes completely against their conscious moral or emotional sense of 'who they are'. In this respect, the unconscious is very powerful, and can dominate people's lives. Indeed, in psychotherapeutic work, one grows accustomed to the paradox that it is the repressed contents of the psyche that 'speak' very loudly, both in symbolic ways and in the actual content of people's lives. For example, one of the characteristics of hysterical symptoms – found in both men and women – is that a denied and unspoken sexuality shrieks from the individual's body.

When we connect these ideas about the unconscious with sexuality, we are faced with a most dramatic idea: that sexuality, in its unconscious state, is itself unknowable and uncontrollable.

Again, we have to make necessary qualifications to this statement. For example, it is possible to make some inroads into the unconscious domain of sexual desires; it is possible to arrive at a point where one is more aware of them, and hence not inexorably driven by them. None the less, we are still left with the uncanny sense that one's own sexuality is something other than oneself; it seems to belong to a stranger, one might even say, to an alien being – for this is how the unconscious is often viewed by people.

The psychoanalytic theory of sexuality therefore presents a stern challenge to all models of sexuality, for it proposes that our unconscious desires are inaccessible, elusive and willed by another. In particular, to argue that one has 'choice' over one's sexual orientation, or to suggest that one can 'invent' or 'reinvent' oneself sexually – such ideas directly contradict the psychoanalytic notion of the unconscious.

But a further inference can be made: if we accept that sexuality is both unknowable and uncontrollable, it is likely that this makes it both very exciting and very frightening for human beings. It is precisely the sense of 'losing myself', going out of myself, finding myself in a quite different experiential universe, that makes sex so alluring and so terrifying. Hence, we try to control sex in many ways, precisely because it feels uncontrollable.

In terms of scientific methodology, Freud's approach to the psyche can be described as an anti-empiricist one: that is, he refused to simply accept what lies on the surface, or what can be seen. Thus when he worked with Charcot at the Salpêtrière Clinic in Paris, Freud refused to accept the clinical definitions of 'hysteria', with its visible and behavioural signs, and worked instead to penetrate behind these to what the woman in question was trying to say through her symptoms – or rather, what her unconscious was trying to say. This early work therefore can be seen as the beginning of the breakthrough to a new paradigm: 'it is perhaps this early and now mostly forgotten moment which can give us the strongest sense of the force of the unconscious as a concept *against a fully social classification relying on empirical evidence* as its rationale' [added emphasis].[49]

Freud's concept of the unconscious is an anti-empiricist one since it penetrates beneath the surface of behaviour, and seeks motives and causes which are unseen and not explicit. Thus it has frequently caused offence and bewilderment to those who adopt empiricist and behaviourist methodologies. In her critique of certain feminist critics of Freud, Juliet Mitchell argues that they all deny the unconscious, and adopt instead a 'descriptive' empiricist approach:

> Desire, phantasy, the laws of the unconscious or even unconsciousness are absent from the social realism of the feminist critiques. With Millett, as with the other feminist studies, empiricism run riot denies more than the unconscious; it denies any attribute of the mind other than rationality. As a result it must also end up denying the importance of childhood experience. The feminist's children are born directly into the reality principle; not so Freud's.[50]

These arguments strike me as crucial ones in the study of sexuality. Irrespective of the criticisms that can be made of Freudian thought – and in the next chapter I shall attempt to show how rooted in masculinist assumptions it is – it marks a highly significant turning point in intellectual history. Jacqueline Rose argues in her article 'Femininity and its discontents' that the radicalism of psychoanalysis lies in its recognition that identity is always a 'failure': 'Because there is no continuity of psychic life, so *there is no stability of sexual identity*, no position for women (or men) which is ever simply achieved' [added emphasis].[51] The 'social realism' which Mitchell refers to, which might argue that boys and girls are 'taught', 'trained' or 'educated' to adopt certain assumptions and ideas about gender and sexuality, is confronted therefore by the Freudian 'failure' – the idea that this 'education' does not, and cannot, work. In other words, patriarchal ideology is not, and indeed *cannot be*, internalized in a linear and simple manner.

And this is not simply a speculative or fanciful idea: working as a psychotherapist gives one ample confirmation that many people are confused about gender and sexuality – they are not sure who they are supposed to be, or what they are supposed to do, and above all, they are not sure what they want. The 'internalization' of 'social norms' has not worked – but this is predicted by the theory of the unconscious, which argues that unconscious desires are inevitably in conflict with the outer social persona, and furthermore, that those desires are not harmonious, but are also in conflict with each other.

These ideas obviously have great implications for the study of both male and female sexuality, for in place of any notion of homogeneity or uniformity the theory of the unconscious proposes instead a heterogeneity, an inevitable psychic conflict, around gender and sexuality. In this sense, it predicts that no-one is simply 'masculine' or 'feminine', 'heterosexual' or 'homosexual'. The mask which we habitually present to the outer world is only part of the whole complex person that we are, large parts of which are unknown to the outside world, and indeed unknown to ourselves.

4 Freud II: Male and Female Sexuality

Over a period of forty years, Freud's model of sexuality changed considerably, and it is impossible in the brief space available to give a full account of these developments. One of the most important shifts is from the 'drive model' of sexuality towards a model that is concerned more with 'sexual objects', and particularly the triangular relationship between people in the Oedipus complex. It is this latter model that contains the seeds of the development of 'object relations psychology', which has become an important school of psychoanalysis and psychotherapy. To demonstrate some of the shifts in Freud's own thinking, I would like to compare an early and a late publication of Freud's, and outline briefly some of the significant changes that have taken place.

At this point, it is important to point out that the English word 'drive' is a literal translation of the German 'Trieb', which is usually translated as 'instinct' in the standard edition of Freud's writings, and also in the Penguin Freud Library. This use of 'instinct' has been criticized by many subsequent analysts, since Freud rarely uses the German word 'Instinkt', which denotes a more biological notion than 'Trieb'. In some ways, the distinction between 'drives' and 'instincts' corresponds to that between psychology and biology.[1]

The *Three Essays on the Theory of Sexuality* (1905) is one of Freud's most important works, as it drew together in a comprehensive form many of his current ideas about infantile sexuality, the various component instincts that form part of the sexual drive, and their expression in various neuroses and perversions.

In fact, Freud's connection between the various components of infantile sexuality and their outcome in adult perversions is a brilliant piece of theorization. He argues that if normal sexual development is repressed for some reason, the sexual instinct 'flows' into 'collateral' channels already dug by the components of infantile sexuality, which, as we have seen, are not united in a genital aim but have 'polymorphous' aims. Thus, as a model of infantile sexuality and its connections with adult neurosis and perversion, the *Three Essays* is supremely elegant.

This line of argument leads Freud to the famous statement that we are all perverse, since perversion is 'innate in everyone'.[2] The sexuality of neurotics is similarly seen as a regression to an infantile state. Freud does not deny that the environment plays a part in deciding whether sexuality finds its adult expression in neurosis, perversion or 'normal sexual life', but the *Three Essays* spends very little time discussing the forces existing in the environment, particularly what the impact of the child's parents have on its sexual development. Perhaps the key word in the *Three Essays* is 'constitutional': for example, when discussing fetishism, Freud explicitly argues that this is only partly caused by environmental factors, and is also 'constitutionally determined'.[3]

Freud's description of puberty gives a fair flavour of his approach in the *Three Essays*:

> With the arrival of puberty, changes set in which are destined to give infantile sexual life its final, normal shape. The sexual instinct has hitherto been primarily auto-erotic; it now finds a sexual object. Its activity has hitherto been derived from a number of separate instincts and erotogenic zones, which, independently of one another, have pursued a certain sort of pleasure as their sole sexual aim. Now, however, a new sexual aim appears, and all the component instincts combine to attain it, while the erotogenic zones become subordinated to the primacy of the genital zone.[4]

What is fascinating about the language of this passage is how the human subject, and its relations with others, almost seem to disappear: it is 'instincts' that find 'objects', the sexual instinct itself is made up of 'independent' instincts and zones which 'pursue pleasure'. With puberty, the various instincts 'combine' to 'attain' the new sexual aim of genital intercourse. The picture of the human being is of someone essentially passive, subject to the influence of various instincts, zones and aims, which decide for themselves what they want and what they shall do. Thus, there is a strong 'separatist' view here: not only are mind and body seen as separate, but the sexual instinct itself is broken down into separate sub-instincts and zones. Sexual development goes on as an apparently independent biological process, quite separate from the person concerned.

The same point can be made about Freud's discussion of female sexual development. This is analysed very much in terms of 'zones': the clitoris gives way to the vagina, hence, masculinity gives way to femininity.[5] Again it is striking how the woman herself inevitably submits to this biological process, and how the process appears unaffected by relationships with others. It is also clear that Freud sees female sexuality as a shadow or derivative of male sexuality.

Freud does make some comments in the *Three Essays* on the 'finding of an object', including the fascinating idea that the loss of the breast forces the male infant, first to focus on itself as an erotic object, and later to 'refind' the breast in adult sexual activity.[6] However, Freud is silent about the problem of how girls find a heterosexual object and move away from their mother.

In short, the *Three Essays* plays down the effect of social ties – particularly parent–child relations – in favour of 'endogenous' forces, particularly the 'component instincts' and the 'erotogenic zones', which are seen as compelling forces. In one sense, this gives Freud's theorization a distinctly radical tinge, since he is able to claim that 'perversion' is a universal, because innate, part of human sexuality. Thus, *inter alia*, he argues that homosexual desire exists in all children and adults. On the other hand, even though the *Three Essays* is an intellectual and theoretical *tour de force*, its biologism perhaps represents a cul-de-sac in the history of psychoanalytical thought, since much of the subsequent research on sexuality has been directed towards the interpersonal aspect.

FEMALE SEXUALITY

Freud's essay, *Female Sexuality* (1931), provides a fascinating comparison with the *Three Essays*. From the outset, Freud firmly indicates that it is the world of 'objects' that concerns him: the Oedipus complex – which had been formulated in the 1920s – presents a particular problem for the understanding of female sexuality: how does the girl transfer her affections from her mother to her father? Freud still alludes to the clitoris/vagina issue, but his chief concern is clearly with the change in relationships for young girls. In particular, Freud is obviously struck by the intensity of the pre-Oedipal attachment of the female infant to her mother, and this idea points forward to the massive amount of work that would be done by analysts such as Klein and Winnicott on the mother–child relation. Freud also makes a fascinating comment about how the mother-attachment is revealed and re-enacted in the analyst/patient relationship: he had difficulty with this, whereas some women analysts found it easier.[7] One could suggest here that the 'shadowy' nature of the pre-Oedipal phase, which Freud imputes to the patient's repression/resistance, might also be due to his own shying away from the mother–child relation.[8]

There is a sense of confusion and hesitancy in this essay that is unusual in Freud. He himself comments: 'this account will very probably strike the reader as confused and contradictory'.[9] Even more striking is the coda, in which Freud, very unusually, discusses the contributions of other analysts to the discussion of female sexuality. Thus he briefly cites Karen Horney's claim that little girls do have vaginal sensation, but dismisses this tersely: 'This does not tally with my impressions.'[10]

Freud is being unusually defensive, since without doubt he was aware that the theoretical elegance of his theories of sexuality, and the Oedipus complex in particular, were muddied by the problem of female sexuality. He cites many reasons for the girl's turning away from mother: disappointment at not being given a penis; the loss of the breast; prohibitions on masturbation, and so on. There is a sense of uncertainty and confusion that is rather uncharacteristic of Freud; as he comments: 'all these motives seem nevertheless insufficient to justify the girl's final hostility [to her mother]'.[11]

There are two important issues here: there is a tension between the Oedipal theory of personal relationships and the long-held drive theory; and material about female sexuality is beginning to prove an awkward thorn in the side of the phallocentric model of sexuality. The elegance of the model is beginning to look rather dishevelled.

Drive theory and object relations sit side by side rather uneasily in this essay: the little girl witnesses a shift in erotic interest from her clitoris to her vagina – a shift which is perfectly explicable within drive theory as a biologically determined change – but she also undergoes a shift in erotic interest from her mother to her father. Here we are not dealing with instincts or zones but other people, and there is perhaps a sense of strain in Freud's attempt to yoke the two theoretical models together. Of course, it is remarkable that Freud managed to formulate these issues at all in such an explicit and coherent manner. The fact that we can in retrospect see certain ambiguities and contradictions does not detract from this: indeed the reason we are able to do this is because of Freud's honesty and clarity.

DRIVES AND OBJECTS

Later analysts took up and developed the theme of object relations in greater depth and detail, and while homage was still done to drive theory, there is little doubt that it was the relationships between infants and their parents that became the central theme of psycho-analysis. Melanie Klein is particularly interesting since she incorpo-rated the idea of the 'object' into drive theory, and suggested that the infant has an innate propensity to form relationships. In other words, the drive moves towards objects: this is inherent in its nature – 'Drives, for Klein, are relationships.'[12] Klein also saw drives in a much less biological or physiological way than Freud.

Klein's position is complicated and enriched by the central role of fantasy, which is able to create objects, internalize them, and so on. Thus the notion of 'internal objects' assumes great importance in Kleinian theory, and has considerably influenced many currents in analysis and psychotherapy.

But these shifts mean that sexuality assumes a quite different char-acter. Instead of being a source of physiological tension that demands relief, whether through masturbation or interaction with someone else, sexuality comes to be seen as the most intense means of relating to others. In Freud's schema, the object exists, but partly as a place for sexual instincts to relieve themselves. There is therefore a rather autistic flavour about Freud's portrayal of the human infant, and indeed of human sexuality, whereas for other analysts the infant is immediately and passionately *involved* with other human beings. This difference is summed up neatly in a statement by the British analyst W.R.D. Fairbairn: 'It is not the libidinal attitude which determines the relationship, but the relationship which determines the libidinal atti-tude.'[13] This argument also has the interesting corollary that 'plea-sure-seeking' in isolation is considered to be neurotic, in the sense that 'pleasure' has replaced relationship. In other words, people seek plea-sure in itself when relationships seem to have failed them.[14]

The shift from drive theory to object relations was a momentous and traumatic one within psychoanalysis, and later analysts were conscious that they might be betraying Freud's theoretical legacy. Various solutions were found to this dilemma, including the fervent avowal of loyalty to drive theory, while in fact simultaneously and covertly major revisions were being carried out.

At times, in the psychoanalytical literature, one can see the process of change at work. A paper by the Hungarian analyst, Michael Balint, 'Changing therapeutical aims and techniques in psycho-analysis' (1949), argues very clearly that psychoanalytical *theory* had been built up on the basis of the study of individuals, with their internal drives and conflicts, whereas psychoanalytic *technique* had been built up on the basis of the actual work with patients. This meant an increasing focus on the transference and counter-transference, in other words, the examination of the relationship between analyst and patient. It proved impossible to base analytic technique on biological principles: as soon as one sets up the analytic situation, where two people talk to each other and relate to each other, one is implicitly conceding that psychological work is best done via a relationship and through the analysis of that relationship: 'What we need now is a theory that would give us a good description of the development of object-relations comparable to, but independent of, our present, biologising, theory of the development of instincts.'[15]

Balint shows clearly the gap between theory and the actual practice of analysis, and calls for the reconciliation of the two. In fact, his clarion call was already being answered by different figures, for example, by Melanie Klein who made object relations the cornerstone of her work, and Harry Stack Sullivan in America who openly rejected drive theory.

With these developments, the notion of sexuality also begins to broaden, for if the relation between analyst and patient was seen as an erotically charged or 'libidinous' one, then this was often interpreted as involving the patient's need for love rather than sexual gratification. Balint argues in many papers that patients need – in a phrase of his that became famous – to make a 'new beginning', that is, to give up old self-defeating ways of relating to people, that were shrouded in suspicion and paranoia, and to begin to relate in ways that were optimistic and life-enhancing. But the new beginning could only begin in the actual analytic situation, in the relationship between analyst and patient. And Balint describes how his patients began to expect small signs of affection, signs that they were important to him, and began to admit how important he was to them. Again, interpretations as to the biological or 'drive-derived' source of such impulses would be insulting and probably damaging to patients, who are going through an extremely vulnerable phase, when they are gingerly trying out life without the old defences.[16]

These shifts in psychoanalytic thought are particularly momentous for the theory of sexuality: the sexual drive was no longer seen as an end but a means, no longer the prime motive for human behaviour, but the most dramatic expression of the fundamental societal identity of human beings. This also meant that the conflict between 'instincts' and 'civilization' itself was seen quite differently. Whereas for Freud there was an inevitable conflict between society and the instinctual needs of the individual, for later analysts the individual was inherently a social being, who was born into relationships, and acquired identity in and through them. Individuality itself can therefore be seen as societal through and through, and sexuality can be seen, not as an individualistic search for pleasure, but as a means of bonding with others. The instincts themselves can be seen less as primitive biological urges than as expressions of the fundamental relatedness of human identity. The 'sexual drive' itself can be seen as societal.

Of course these arguments are not abstract philosophical ones: they also reflect the differing social and political contexts in which they were formed. The growing 'socialization' of sex found in later analysts must surely be read against a general intellectual context in which nineteenth century individualism was being challenged by more radical sociological and political views, as found, for example, in the work of the 'left wing' of psychoanalysis, including such figures as Erich Fromm, Karen Horney and Wilhelm Reich.

THE CASTRATION COMPLEX

But I would like to return to the 'classical' formulations of Freud, at the heart of whose mature thought on sexuality is the Oedipus complex – and at the heart of the Oedipus complex is the castration complex. According to Freud, it is the *threat* of castration that impels boys to renounce their desire for their mother and identify with their father, and the *actuality* of castration that impels girls to turn away from mother to father. In fact, as I have already indicated, the Oedipus complex is much more complicated than that, since the reverse processes go on: children also identify with the opposite sex parent and desire the same sex parent.

The history of the castration complex in this century has been an odd one. Freud came to see it as the core of his psychological theory; yet some later theorists and analysts seem to have discarded it. On the other hand, the French psychoanalyst Jacques Lacan has reinstated it as the key to the theory of sexuality and the human subject.

In Freud's 1905 publication *Three Essays*, the castration complex has a vestigial presence, and its connection with the Oedipus complex is absent, and therefore the distinction between the sexes is ascribed to biological causes: in particular, both sexes are 'masculine' until puberty, when girls undergo a shift in their 'leading erotogenic zone' from the clitoris to the vagina.[17]

Yet Freud was also unhappy with such biological or naturalist theories, since they were non-psychological. If the distinction between males and females really was determined biologically, then psycho-analysis need have nothing to say about it. But in fact gender and sexuality seem to be highly contentious areas, involving much personal struggle and suffering. And people often do not seem at all clear about their own identity in terms of gender and sexuality: Freud refers to the 'vicissitudes of the tributary streams of sexuality springing up from their separate sources'.[18] What was lacking in these early theories was a psychological explanation which could account for male and female sexuality, and the difference between them, within a unified theoretical schema.

Freud eventually developed the idea of the castration complex, which not only leads to the separation between males and females, but in part to the notion of human identity itself. That is, it is partly through our sexual differentiation that we emerge as individuals. It also, in conjunction with the Oedipus complex, gives human beings that sense of loss that Lacan was to develop into his notion of 'lack', and leads to the setting up of symbolic surrogates for the 'lost object'. For example, the theory of fetishism is revolutionized by the theory of the castration complex, since the fetish could be seen as a symbol for the missing female penis.[19] On the other hand, women could be said to spend their lives searching for their own 'lost penis'.

As is well known, the castration complex has different routes for boys and girls. The boy is forced to renounce his desire for his mother under the threat of castration; he begins therefore to identify with his father (his rival) and look to other females to satisfy his desires. The girl, on the other hand, realizes that she is already castrated, and therefore turns from her mother to her father in search of the penis, which her mother has failed to give her.

But the intrusion of prohibition into sexual relations has greater significance than just a turning from one sexual object to another. It represents the notion of law itself: law which is internalized in the form of the superego, which then begins to regulate the internal affairs of the psyche. What Lacan was to call the 'name-of-the-father' makes its entrance upon the stage, and the symbiotic relation between mother and child is shattered irrevocably.

Lacanian theorists have given immense significance to this law of prohibition, seeing in it the foundation of human identity, indeed human culture, itself. Feminists have been able to argue that patriarchy is founded at this moment for each child, as it imbibes the 'rule of the father'.[20] Other schools of analysis have treated it with less reverence, particularly object relations, which has tended to focus more on the mother–child dyad. None the less, most schools agree that the intrusion of the 'third figure' of the father into the maternal symbiosis is supremely important.

Freud's own conception of the castration complex is quite complicated, as one would expect of someone struggling to formulate it for the first time. In particular, Freud seems undecided between a biological and a psychological standpoint. Thus the notions, first, that boys perceive that women are without a penis, and secondly, that girls perceive that boys have a 'bigger penis' than they do, are both highly contentious. If this is left as a unadorned perception of differences between physical organs, Freud would seem to be suggesting that there is a direct transmission belt between such perceptions and certain attitudes and personality traits.

Such a direct link between biology and psychic structure leaves the symbolic meaning of the organs still in question. Why is a 'bigger penis' or a 'missing penis' of such consequence to boys and girls? Why doesn't the presence or absence of beards have such massive consequences? In other words, what the theory has yet to explain is the symbolic meaning of the penis and its absence: in other words, the penis perceived *as a phallic symbol*, the carrier of all manner of stipulations as to authority, the right to speak, the making of law, and so on.

Freud was aware of this dichotomy between biology and psychic symbolism, and struggled to show that 'the penis' was not simply a physiological organ, but a key sign within a symbolic order, that is, the phallus. None the less, Freud's biologism keeps breaking through.

This confusion can be seen clearly in his 1925 article 'Some psychical consequences of the anatomical differences between the sexes'. In relation to the boy's perception of the female's lack of a penis, Freud makes this comment:

When a little boy first catches sight of a girl's genital region, he begins by showing irresolution and lack of interest; he sees nothing or disavows what he has seen, he softens it down or looks about for expedients for bringing it into line with his expectations. It is not until later, *when some threat of castration has obtained a hold over him, that the observation becomes important to him*: if he then recollects or repeats it, it arouses a terrible storm of emotion in him and forces him to believe in the reality of the threat which he has hitherto laughed at [added emphasis].[21]

Thus the raw observation of female genitals does not at first have symbolic, or one might say theoretical, importance; but does so once it takes place within the ambit of the castration complex. Then the missing organ, the 'anatomical distinction', takes its place within the child's own theorization, 'the observation becomes important to him'. The girl's missing penis 'proves' that the threats of castration are not idle ones: it could happen to him too. Being without a penis assumes massive symbolic importance, as evidence for a prohibitive law regulating sexual desire itself; possessing a penis is a mixed blessing – it gives the male authority and prestige, but he is also haunted by the possibility of losing it.

In relation to male development, Freud has therefore set out a fairly clear distinction between isolated observations (of human beings without penises) and observations taking place within a field of knowledge. In a sense, the little boy *develops a theory of sexuality*, based on the triangular configuration of child–mother–father, and the prohibition of his own desires. But in the same article, Freud's account of the little girl's experience is quite perfunctory:

A little girl behaves differently. She makes her judgment and her decision in a flash. She has seen it and knows that she is without it and wants to have it.[22]

The problem for Freud – and for all later theorists of sexual difference – is how does the little girl 'know' that she is without something? How does she know that differences in size in the genital region have such momentous consequences, not only for being male or female, but for many aspects of being human? Freud leaves this unexplained, which perhaps indicates the greater uncertainty which he consistently betrays towards female sexuality. But it also indicates his straddling of the boundary between biology and psychological symbolism. Later in the same article, Freud makes this interesting comment on the different fates of boys and girls within the castration complex:

The difference between the sexual development of males and females at the stage we have been considering it is an intelligible consequence of the anatomical distinction between their genitals, and of the psychical situation involved in it; it corresponds to the difference between a castration that has been carried out and one that has been threatened.[23]

Here Freud indicates precisely the difference between boys and girls in terms of the symbolism of the castration complex, but he does not really expand on the notion that for girls castration 'has been carried out'. We still need to know how girls 'know' that their own diminutive penis (the clitoris) has such momentous meanings: that they have been castrated, that they belong to the castrated sex. As we shall see, Freud is quite hostile to socio-political arguments on this score – for example, that girls are aware that women are treated as inferior beings in society at large. Freud explicitly rejects such a tying in of political meanings, but this leaves him rather theoretically threadbare. The problem is that having a 'smaller penis', or in fact 'having no penis' does not automatically lead to a supposition that one is 'castrated': the first experience is a raw perception, the second is a theoretical inference. It is clear that boys obtain a 'theory of castration' from the threats that they receive; but where does the little girl obtain it from? Freud remains silent on this issue.

THE LITTLE GIRL IS A LITTLE MAN

The discussion above has brought into focus the relentless masculinism of Freud's model of sexuality. Freud's papers on female sexuality never abandon their assumptions as to the masculine nature of human sexuality in general. Thus Freud's last written statement about 'femininity' states baldly that

> The discovery that she is castrated is a turning-point in a girl's growth. Three possible lines of development start from it: one leads to sexual inhibition or to neurosis, the second to change of character in the sense of a masculinity complex, the third, finally to normal femininity.[24]

The penis assumes prime importance in Freud's model of sexuality: the sexes define themselves by its presence or absence. Women are therefore gripped by a sense of inferiority and lack, which they never entirely escape, and have to compensate for in various ways, such as having babies, possessing their husband's penis, pursuing masculine ways of life ('penis envy'), and so on.

Freud's analysis of female sexuality is a very odd one, since the little girl does not turn away from her mother to her father out of a desire or need for him, but because of a desire to have a penis for herself. Thus somehow female desire, and indeed 'feminine' character, is formed negatively, not out of a positive desire for one parent, or a positive identification with another, but out of pique at the refusal of the girl's mother to give her a penis. What is most striking about this account is that sexual organs seems to take precedence over people: the little girl turns to her father, not for a relationship, not because she desires *him*, or loves him, but because she has been thwarted in her attempt to obtain a penis off her mother, and now realizes that he is the sole repository of such an organ.

The oddness of this theory is not necessarily an argument against it, since human motivation seems to be full of strange non sequiturs. But the disjunction between male and female sexuality is quite striking: the little boy has his mother from the beginning as his desired object. The maternal and the seductive seem to follow on from each other, or blend into each other, not of course without massive strain, since the boy must renounce his incestuous desires, yet must retain sufficient of them to be able to transfer them onto other women.

But since Freud rejects the notion of a 'primary' or innate feminine sexuality, he has to find a way of accounting for the little girl's shift from her mother, usually the first caretaker, to her father. This involves disappointment in the mother, chagrin at the discovery of being castrated, and the turn to the only person who seems to possess a penis – the father. Femininity and female sexuality therefore assume the character of second prize: consolations for the disgruntled little girl, furious with the discovery of her castratedness, and determined to find a penis somehow or other, from her father, or from her own male baby. Femininity is driven by the penis, or its absence; of course, this seems to relegate female sexual organs or female sexual processes to the category of 'also-rans', or purely derivative phenomena.

Freud is also forced to carry out some rather strained pieces of analysis in order to preserve his theory. For example, many little girls play with dolls, and this is often taken as a typical example of 'feminine' behaviour. However, since Freud has determined that little girls are masculine, he has to argue that playing with dolls is not feminine, since the girl is taking an active, implicitly masculine, position towards her doll.[25]

Critics might argue, on the contrary, that the little girl's playing with dolls is a sure sign of her identification with her mother, and the acquisition of feminine traits – this is roughly the argumentation of R.J. Stoller, the outstanding postwar psychoanalytic specialist in gender.[26] Furthermore, if we accept Freud's claim that 'the little girl is a little man',[27] in other words, that little girls and boys are the same, why do boys not play with dolls? Of course, one can argue, depending on one's philosophical and political position, either that boys and girls *are trained* to play with trains and dolls respectively (as part of their training in gender/sexual positions); or alternatively, that they 'instinctively' take to such different toys. In either case, Freud's monism collapses.

Again, on the question of the 'masculinity' of little girls, and the precedence of the clitoris (the 'inferior clitoris' Freud calls it)[28] as a sexual organ, a number of analysts have argued that young children seem to have an unconscious knowledge of the vagina, and very young girls seem to have vaginal sensations. This tends to demolish Freud's model, since the little girl's 'masculinity' is predicated on the clitoris, taken as a minor model of the boy's penis. Freud therefore has to deny that vaginal sensation or knowledge exists, even though his own case histories seem to suggest otherwise. Thus in the Little Hans case, it is striking that the boy Hans seems to know that his penis must find a receptacle. Freud has to ignore such evidence if his penis-based model is to be preserved.[29]

One must also question Freud's assumption that the clitoris is a 'masculine' organ, and the vagina a 'feminine' one. Freud's argumentation from quasi-biological premises to psychological generalizations seems highly dangerous, and takes as an assumption what is to be proved. Again, the question arises: why should the little girl compare her clitoris with the boy's penis?

Many of these objections were raised by analysts in the 1920s and 1930s, such as Ernest Jones and Karen Horney, who also pointed out that little boys (and grown men) also exhibit signs of deep envy of women, and their procreative and sexual powers, and specifically, envy of their sexual organs. Thus penis envy is matched by breast and womb envy.

However, for the opponents of Freud, the problem of innateness raises itself: for those who speak of a 'primary femininity' are in a sense solving the problem of sexual difference by ascribing it to biology.

Psychologically speaking, it is tempting to assume that Freud's insistent masculinism is defensive, that he had carried out a massive denial of female sexuality as an independent force, and had thereby – as many men are compelled to – blotted out the force of his own mother as a seductive and overpowering figure. Freud's phallocentrism bears all the hallmarks of a defensive denial, in this case of the male identification with the female, and particularly with the maternal body. Freud turns this round and makes female identity contingent upon the male body, and the perception of the female body as deficient, wounded.

There is also some suggestion that Freud's thinking was coloured by the primacy given to the father in Jewish thought, and the ambivalent role of the Jewish mother, both powerful in the home, and powerless outside the home.[30]

In this sense, psychoanalysis as a whole is a narcissistic psychology, exalting the masculine at the expense of the feminine, which is both feared and hated. To put it starkly, *women are wounded by psychoanalysis itself*, which obliterates them by casting them as half-men.

SEXUALITY AND PATRIARCHY

However, Freud's masculine bias has been seen by some feminists, not as a manifestation of Freud's own anti-female prejudices or, more subtly, his intense fear of female sexuality and his own feminine identity, but as a faithful description of the construction of sexuality under patriarchy. Juliet Mitchell's book, *Psychoanalysis and Feminism* (1974), brilliantly pulled the rug from under the feet of the many anti-Freudian feminists, since she argued that Freud was not justifying or recommending the phallic bias in Western sexuality, merely recording it.

Mitchell's argument seems rather shaky at times, since she has to find a way round Freud's attempts to provide a biological bedrock to these views. Freud consistently argued that the little girl is biologically masculine. In a sense, female sexuality *does not exist* in its own right until the shock of the castration complex forces girls to abandon masculinity and seek femininity – since she cannot have a penis for herself, she must try to 'receive' one from a man. Vaginal sexuality is therefore a means to an end: the acquisition of a penis. Hence Freud is saying that female inferiority is inevitable, since it is biologically, not socially, constructed. Freud seems generally hostile to sociological explanations of gender and sexuality – for example, in his refutation of Alfred Adler's theories, he dismisses sociological accounts of the sexual theories of young children:

> Children have, to begin with, no idea of the significance of the difference between the sexes; on the contrary, they start with the assumption that the same genital organ (the male one) is possessed

by both sexes; they do not begin their sexual researches with the problem of the distinction between the sexes, *while the social under-estimation of women is completely foreign to them* [added emphasis].[31]

I am sure Freud is wrong – it now seems unlikely that children do not absorb socio-political information at a very early age, since their surrounding culture is saturated in it. But this passage seems to make crystal clear his hostility to any attempt to derive women's 'inferiority' from social as opposed to biological causes. Freud even claims that women come to despise themselves because of their biological inferiority, that is, their smaller 'penis'.[32]

It strikes me that Juliet Mitchell has to exercise some rather dazzling footwork to get round this biological bias in Freud. However, Mitchell's main thesis still stands, and is surely crucial in any contemporary use made of psychoanalytic thinking: whether or not Freud is seen as having his own masculine prejudices and fears, the psycho-analytic paradigm, and particularly the psychoanalytical model of sexuality and the unconscious, can be utilized in a non-masculinist manner. Simply enough, as a model of phallic sexuality, the Freudian paradigm can be divested of its biological base and viewed as a psycho-social model. In other words, the primacy of the phallus is not biologically but socially ordained.

In some ways, Lacan does socialize psychoanalysis, with his theory of the 'Law of the Father', and the fundamental importance of the phallus in culture. None the less, Lacan's formulation still leaves one wondering how the whole thing is set up in the first place: is the primacy of the phallus socially constructed, and therefore subject to change, either through evolution or revolution? Or is the phallus somehow built into the human condition for all time? Lacan's argument that language itself contains a phallic bias pushes the argument back one stage: how does language acquire this bias? In fact, Lacan is very shy of talking about 'origins' and 'causes'.

But, as with Freud, Lacan can be utilized even by those who are wary of his rather 'imperious, metaphysical and universal style'.[33] In particular, feminists are able to synthesize the Lacanian notions of language, the symbolic order, and the 'name of the father' into a socio-historical account of patriarchal sexuality.

What I am saying is that while Freud and Lacan, and indeed many other psychoanalytic thinkers, can be seen as subject to an unconscious masculinist bias, stemming in part from the patriarchal context of their theories, and also no doubt from a deep fear of female sexuality and creativity, psychoanalysis itself is not inevitably masculinist. The question hinges on the foundations of the discipline: if one rests the phallic bias of psychoanalysis on a biological base, then female inferiority is inevitable and eternal. However, if one argues that the 'primacy of the penis' is a social product of patriarchal society, psychoanalysis can be seen as a psycho-social, rather than a bio-psychological, discipline. No doubt the orthodox might argue that such a psychoanalysis is not psychoanalysis as Freud intended it, but that is an argument akin to theology not psychology.

NATURALISM

The above arguments concerning Freud's unconscious masculinism point to the contentious issue of the ideological bias of scientific method. Of course, many scientists and others have claimed that ideology is precisely that which science abjures: it is 'neutral', 'objective', concerned only with 'the truth'.

However, Michel Foucault, and other workers within 'social constructionism', have provided us with a barbed retort to this:

'Truth' is centered on the form of scientific discourse and the institutions which produce it; it is subject to constant economic and political incitement ... it is produced and transmitted under the control, dominant, if not exclusive, of a few great political and economic apparatuses.[34]

In other words, there is no neutral truth exempt from somebody's ideological pressure or ownership.

The orthodox Freudian can deny vehemently that there is any ideological or political bias in his views: they are simply based on certain hypotheses backed up by empirical observation. However, the Foucaultian reply to that is that all hypotheses contain unconscious political messages, and empirical observation is also unconsciously biased. One might argue that perception itself is shaped by certain expectations. Notoriously, scientists see what they want to, or what they set out to. Nobody can begin in a position of neutrality: for one thing, we wouldn't even know in which direction to look!

This argument has particular import with regard to Freud's hostility to the social explanations of the oppression of women. For this involves him in the thesis that there are areas of human experience exempt from socio-political significance. Thus penis-envy arises because the little girl perceives that the male penis is bigger than her 'penis'; Freud denies categorically that this has anything to do with the social and economic position of women, which, he claims, children can have no knowledge of: 'the social underestimation of women is completely foreign to them'. This can be taken alongside Freud's statement that 'children have, to begin with, no idea of the significance of the difference between the sexes'.

Freud is therefore giving children, their perceptions, and their relations with others, an extraordinary status within human society. They may be sexually precocious, but they are politically innocent. There is a kind of virgin territory within human existence, which is untainted by any political or social or cultural message. The adults around children do have ideas about the difference between the sexes, and the social underestimation of women – but somehow these ideas are not transmitted to children, not even unconsciously. This is a rather remarkable position from the man who revolutionized the theory of the human mind with his model of the unconscious! It also seems to be contradicted by Freud's own case-study about Little Hans, for Hans is saturated with material from his father, all of which contains many 'ideological' messages.

These arguments not only apply to the Freudian theory of female sexuality, but to his approach to gender and sexuality as a whole. Freud is in effect stating that for children these issues are free of political influence; but since it is infantile sexuality that is the cornerstone of the Freudian paradigm of sexuality, this amounts to saying that sexuality *per se* is free of political values. In retrospect, this seems an extraordinary statement, since in the age of post-feminism and post-modernism we have become habituated to the idea that everything is part of a political structure or construction. Freud argues in similar fashion that aggression is an innate drive, and does not arrive from social deprivation. In an explicit reference to Marxist theories, he comments: 'Aggressiveness was not created by property'.[35]

But of course Freud is not alone in proposing such 'natural' areas of human experience. The nineteenth century had an orgy of 'naturalization': that is, it was proposed that certain human and social phenomena simply existed in nature and are therefore unchanging. For example, the notion that women are maternal was heavily 'naturalized', and women who did not feel maternal were considered to be almost non-human.[36]

Of course naturalization still goes on – used by right-wing politicians, to indicate that people are 'wicked', not socio-economically deprived, when they commit crime, have illegitimate children, and so on. 'Naturalism' is usually a conservative position, which implicitly argues that reality is unchanging, and one can only submit to it. But it is striking that Marxist thought was itself shot through with naturalism in relation to sexuality.[37]

However, Freud is a very complex and dialectical thinker, and he also argues, for example, that heterosexuality is not 'natural', but is as problematical as homosexuality. In many ways, Freud exposed the flaws in Victorian naturalism, by arguing that many aspects of the psyche are not at all predictable, natural or trivial. He also proposes a transmission belt between the psyche and society at certain points – particularly in relation to the superego, which is an internalized condensation of social messages. Freud's thought is therefore a patchwork of 'naturalist' and 'non-naturalist' ideas.

PSYCHOANALYSIS AS A POLITICAL INSTITUTION

The subsequent history of psychoanalysis has tended to play down the more radical currents in Freud's thinking. For if much of Freud's theoretical exploration is potentially liberating, in the sense that 'perversion' is seen as normal, and 'normality' itself is seen as highly problematical, none the less psychoanalysis as a political institution came to adopt a conservative, even punitive standpoint. This is particularly true of American psychoanalysis, which became much more centred on 'ego-psychology' than Freud had been. This seems to fit in well with the pragmatism and extroversion of American society, but it turns analysis and psychotherapy into forms of adaptation to the norms of bourgeois society – this particularly excited Lacan's scorn, and led him to split from the mainstream analytical movement in France.

The conservative attitudes of analysts are revealed most clearly in relation to homosexuality, which has been heavily stigmatized by many analysts, particularly in America. In his book, *The Psychoanalytic Theory of Male Homosexuality*, Kenneth Lewes shows conclusively how punitive and negative American analysts were towards gay patients, particularly in the postwar period. Furthermore, theoretical studies of homosexuality often had a deep methodological flaw: they were often based on studies of patients who were admittedly emotionally disturbed, but then results from such studies would be extrapolated to the homosexual population at large.[38] However, such flawed methodology was underpinned by the belief that homosexuality is *ipso facto* pathological, and had to be 'cured'.

Such attitudes on the part of analysts and therapists are little short of scandalous, and show an arrogance that is breathtaking, since psychotherapy is, after all, self-referring. That is, it is not the therapist who determines what is wrong with the patient, but the patient.

A similar judgemental conservatism has existed towards women patients, underwritten by the orthodoxy of the vaginal orgasm and the equation of mental health with active heterosexuality and child-bearing. No doubt, such attitudes still persist amongst the super-orthodox, although there is little doubt that feminism has had a considerable impact on psychoanalysis and psychotherapy.

In short, some branches of psychoanalysis have shown a profound distrust towards 'deviations' and diversity in gender and sexuality, and have maintained a conservative position that is politically suited to conformity rather than radical self-expression. Overall then, there is an enormous paradox about Freudian thought and its aftermath: many radical ideas and approaches can be found within it, but they have often been disregarded by later analysts, who have abandoned any claim to objectivity or neutrality, and instead have operated with a set of implicit socio-political norms against which people are measured. Of course, all of us operate with a set of such norms, but the hope is that these can be made conscious and allowed for.

SUMMARY

It is difficult, then, to come to an overall estimation of the psychoanalytic approach to sexuality. One has to balance the radicalism of some its ideas against its political conservatism.

In the first place, psychoanalytic ideas have extraordinary implications for any theory of gender, sexuality and personality. The notion of the unconscious implies that any stable identity can be, and is, subverted; that every gender position inevitably contains its opposite, and probably positions in between; that heterosexual and homosexual desire exist side by side; that there cannot be a unitary sense of the individual; that 'perverse' desires are universal. Psychoanalysis is in part a theory of psychic *incoherence* in the individual.

Admittedly, the unconscious is unconscious – that is, it is not visible, it speaks with a distorted and bizarre voice, it has to be inferred from the 'gaps' in conscious behaviour. In Lacan's phrase, it is the 'censored chapter'.[39] None the less, its influence on our everyday existence appears to be palpable and considerable – and this does not apply simply to 'neurotic' or 'psychotic' people. I have already cited Freud's comment that we are 'lived' by the unconscious.

Let me give some simple examples. It seems pretty clear that many homophobic people are fascinated by homosexuality – arguably the homophobic male is bitterly refuting his own homosexual desires in projected form. He hates himself above all, but his self-hatred is also unconscious and projected.

Another example concerns male impotence. Jim informs me that he is so terrified of women he cannot 'manage it in bed', as he puts it. In particular, female genitals strike him as eerie and bizarre. After some considerable work around this area, we discover something else: Jim also sees female genitals as intrinsically fragile, 'like Dresden china', in his words, and his penis, in comparison, is a sledge-hammer. Thus his fear of female genitals conceals a further fear of the damage he could wreak with his own genitals.

Of course, it is likely that this fear in turn conceals a sadistic *wish* to damage women. This also connects with Jim's disbelief that women can also feel powerful, aggressive and sadistic during sex, and that these feelings can be enjoyed safely by both partners.

Another very clear example of the influence of the unconscious can be found in Freud's writings. Discussing the 'primal scene' – children who see, or fantasize about, their parents making love – Freud states that the boy who watches identifies both with his father and his mother. Freud comments: 'the second [identification]...is the one that will become the more important in the subsequent neurosis'.[40] In other words, the wish to be female and be penetrated by the male is normally repressed in the young boy, but may well exert its influence in later life.

I was reminded of this example by several male clients who commented, with some surprise, that they now realized that their female partners reminded them, both psychologically and physically, not of their mother, but of their father. In other words, their own feminine identification and homosexual desires could operate within a heterosexual relationship. The reverse seems equally true: that some women find in their husband or boyfriend an image of their mother.

For those familiar with such work in psychotherapy, these examples will seem well-worn. However, for those unfamiliar with these ideas, they may seem over-ingenious or over-elaborate. However, it seems likely that the human psyche is remarkably ingenious at concealing its own motivations and desires, and constructs multi-layered edifices that hide one feeling beneath another: a wish beneath a fear, or behind its opposite, and so on.

The main point I am making is that the Freudian theory of unconscious desire is a very radical theory, since it strips down the surface appearance of things to much deeper foundations, where opposites exist side by side, and nothing is as it seems. As we have seen, Freud also had various prescriptive attitudes and assumed that heterosexuality was the best of all possible worlds; but that is neither surprising nor prohibitive. One can work within the psychoanalytic model without accepting some of Freud's attitudes, just as one can work within it whilst excising some of its biologism.

Freud shattered any notion of a unitary and uniform human sexuality; he posited a sexual heterogeneity instead, that eventually entered into the main river of heterosexuality, but survives in the unconscious as a kind of opposition voice, or set of voices, from where it may exert considerable influence. The word 'deconstruction' was non-existent in his era; but if anyone can claim to have deconstructed human sexuality, it is Freud.

At the same time, as we have seen, psychoanalysis became in part politically conservative and negative, and discouraged diversity and experimentation in relation to gender and sexuality. There have therefore been many rebellions against its perceived tyranny – for example, the rise of the 'new therapies' in America in the sixties and seventies, or the breakaway led by Jacques Lacan in France – so that the psychoanalytic movement as a whole is by no means monolithic in the late twentieth century. If we enlarge our perspective to take in the whole of the psychotherapeutic world, we are confronted with a 'buzzing confusion': many splinters and schools have emerged in the last thirty years, varying enormously in their radicalism/conservatism *vis-à-vis* sexuality. In retrospect, such a fissiparous tendency seems inevitable: human psychology can never aspire to being monolithic, since human beings are most definitely not so.

5 Lacan: Lack and Desire

Probably the most important non-British 'revisionism' within psycho-analysis has been provided by Jacques Lacan, the French analyst, who separated from the mainstream psychoanalytical movement in 1953, and has produced a dazzling if difficult body of work.

Ironically, Lacan claims that his ideas directly connect with Freud, and it is other analytical thinkers who have distorted the latter – but then this claim to fidelity has been the cry of every rebel and revision-ist in the psychoanalytic movement.

Lacan has enriched psychological theory in many areas, including the fields of language, desire, the notion of the ego – which Lacan is quite dismissive towards – sexuality, and the unconscious itself. His writings are particularly difficult to assess – many of them are tran-scripts of talks, they are often elliptical and couched in a rhetoric that is both flamboyant and opaque. Indeed, Lacan's attitude towards the reader (or listener) is not a benign one; he sets out to be difficult and disdains comprehensibility.

I have therefore selected several of Lacan's key ideas, and I have tried to elucidate them, and also to extemporize upon them a little, since they are such fertile areas.

LACK

The notion of lack is at the core of Lacanian thinking, for it is through the experience of lack that the human being begins to use the imagi-nation, and constructs symbols, fantasies, desires and even the image of his/her own identity. Furthermore, Lacan argues that the human subject is fundamentally split, that being an 'I' itself constitutes a cleavage in being. In order to be aware of myself, or to 'know myself', I become an object to myself, and in that sense become alienated from myself; I therefore have to continually seek images of myself, identi-fications that enable me to comfort myself with my own existence. Yet I am forever haunted by the underlying knowledge that these images of myself are evanescent, that there is no one stable or permanent thing that provides me with a solid sense of self.

Desire itself flows from loss: for example, it is the original loss of the breast that compels the infant to imagine a fantasy breast. Here are the seeds of symbolization as well as fantasy: human beings are forced to invent imaginary realities, since actual realities constantly let them down.

Furthermore, many primitive infantile desires – for example, the desire to possess the mother completely – have to be repressed, and form part of the unconscious. The unconscious therefore consists of part of myself that is disowned: again, there is a fundamental split in my being. Part of me has to repress another part of me, if I am to assume my identity as human.

Desire therefore fills the gap left by the disappearance of the 'object' and the repression of the need. In this sense, Lacanian thinking is quite pessimistic compared with some object relations theorists, who are quite prepared to accept that 'good parenting' leads to a solid and positive sense of self that will prove a haven amidst life's vicissitudes. For Lacan this is a pipedream, and covers up the fundamental human loneliness and alienation.

We can express the Lacanian sense of loss another way: if the human infant found that all its needs were instantly gratified by the environment, there would never be any need for it to think that it had 'needs', that there was 'an environment', or indeed, that there was a 'self' or an 'I'. A perfect fit between self and environment renders the distinction between self and not-self meaningless: it is precisely in that lack of fit that the 'I' comes into being. It is not that the I is permanently dissatisfied, but that the I is constituted *by, and as, dissatisfaction*: 'This ego, whose strength our theorists now define by its capacity to bear frustration, is frustration in its essence.'[1]

Sexuality for Lacan is therefore less a search for pleasure, or a search for 'contact' – Lacan is scathing about the 'cream puff' that contact has become in contemporary psychology[2] – than a search for meanings by people who feel bereft of meaning, and a search for themselves by people who feel bereft of themselves. But, Lacan argues, this is not some 'depressive' position that can be rectified by well-meaning psychotherapy – Lacan is particularly scornful of such remedial measures – but is the exact truth. I had to be bereft of myself in order to become an I.

The search for meaning is therefore endless, for one cannot find any ultimate meaning that will be absolutely fulfilling, in sex, religion, or anything else, since the human being is founded in loss and separation. The I exists precisely because it has separated out from everything else, and therefore permanently longs to 'go home', to become one again. Sex is one very powerful means of attempting to do this, but it is fundamentally illusory: we have to try over and over again to find an ecstatic reunion, but such experiences are transient and hollow.

Although Lacan can be accused of pessimism, I think he has highlighted something very profound about human sexuality and its connection with human identity. The massive value given to the sexual orgasm in contemporary culture is not simply because of the pleasure involved, but also because orgasm seems to provide a blending of me and not-me that for many people is ecstatic, and for some terrifying.

Of course orgasmic experience involves many other feelings – for example, quite commonly it seems to intensify a sense of domination or mastery over the other, or alternatively a sense of being dominated – but even this domination seems allied with a feeling of union. Some such connection may also exist in the psychology of rape, which at times seems to represent a perverted attempt to 'become one' through force. This is a very primitive idea – and seems akin to infantile fantasies of subjecting the maternal body to its absolute control and destruction.[3]

REPRESSION AND THE UNCONSCIOUS

Lacan's claim of fidelity to Freud seems borne out in relation to 'lack', for Freud's ideas about fantasy and unconscious desires are predicated upon the premise that reality fails, desire is repressed, and hallucination acts as a surrogate. Freud's notion of the dream rests on this thesis:

> The shutting off of mental life from reality at night and the regression to primitive mechanisms which make this possible enable this wished-for instinctual satisfaction to be experienced in an hallucinatory manner as occurring in the present.[4]

Thus the whole notion of repression, which is instrumental in creating the unconscious, rests on the notion of a split in the human being. One part of the psyche – in Freud's later formulations, the ego – is identified with the 'reality principle' – and seeks control over the id – which is consumed by the 'pleasure principle'. In other words, our deepest and most primitive wishes – many of which are erotic – are continually blocked by the ego, which argues that these wishes are not realizable in ordinary reality. Furthermore, Freud argues that 'the character of the ego is a precipitate of abandoned object-cathexes and ... it contains the history of those object-choices'.[5]

This is a very condensed and profound idea: we *internalize* both the prohibitions that were first externally presented to us and the people who made those prohibitions. This backs up Lacan's claim that each human individual is fundamentally divided against itself – and must be so, if it is to be human. To be human is to be split – there is no escape from this equation. I have to be permanently at war with my own deepest and most primitive wishes, if I am to exist as a human being.

None the less Lacan has considerably enlarged the notion of 'lack' far beyond Freud's own formulation, and he has also turned it into a much more metaphysical thesis than Freud did. Freud after all tended to see psychoanalysis as a practical discipline.

But Lacan has highlighted something very profound within the psychoanalytical paradigm, and something which he is correct in saying has been played down or diluted in ego-psychology, which has tended towards an 'adaptionist' stance: psychotherapy as a means of fitting people into society. For Lacan, this is both absurd and impossible, since the whole idea of 'being a person' is an alienation without cure. Lacan is surely correct in saying that part of the true radicalism of psychoanalysis rests on this devastating analysis of human beings. Indeed, Lacan argues that it is this which made Freudian thought seem scandalous, not its sexual orientation:

> If we ignore the self's radical ex-centricity to itself with which man is confronted, in other words, the truth discovered by Freud, we shall falsify both the order and methods of psychoanalytic mediations...
>
> The radical heteronomy that Freud's discovery shows gaping within man can never again be covered over without whatever is used to hide it being profoundly dishonest.[6]

ON THE EDGE

Lacan brings up a further idea which offers a profound contribution to the study of sexuality: the notion that the so-called erogenous zones have a 'rim-like structure'.[7]

At first glance this seems rather trivial, but Lacan is making a connection between human sexuality and the boundaries of the self. Generally, sex goes on in or around certain bodily orifices: the mouth, the vagina, the penis, the nipple, the anus. We should not forget the eye, which is also deeply involved in sexual excitement. These orifices form boundaries, exits and entrances, between the I and the not-I, boundaries which during sexual activity are often breached.

Most of them have other physiological functions, concerned with taking in or expelling substances such as food, excrement and so on, the oral and anal functions being of great importance during infancy. Of course this is part of Freud's thesis concerning infantile sexuality: for example, in relation to oral eroticism, 'sexual activity has not yet been separated from the ingestion of food'.[8] The sexual organs tend to have other non-sexual functions, which are eroticized for the primitive human infant, and which remain eroticized for adults – this can be seen for example in the many eating disorders which now exist in Western society. Eating provides a primitive erotic comfort for people who feel lonely and empty.

Thus the points of entrance and exit to the body are sites of great excitement in children and in adults: sexual energy seems to play along the edges of the body, seems to derive its charge from the oscillation between the I and the not-I. Furthermore, when two people have sex, each brings his or her own boundaries into contact with the other's: momentarily we face each other edge to edge, and even allow each other's edge to slide over the other's edge, whether this is in terms of penis to vagina, or penis to anus, mouth to genitals, or mouth to mouth, or mouth to breast, and so on. Our orificial boundaries collide and mingle.

But Lacan is less concerned with such semi-biological observations. He argues, in a typically complex chain of ideas, that the sexual drive emerges over the 'rim', apparently finds an object, but then returns to itself. For Lacan, this suggests that the object is really not the point of the exercise: the sexual drive is *only interested in itself*. If you like, people are not turned on by other people, but by their own being turned on. For Lacan, there is a fundamental alienation and narcissism within sexuality itself: the other is always a mirage, and a refraction of something in myself that I have lost and can never find.[9]

These ideas have many implications. For example, the 'breaching' of the body's boundaries can be looked at in several ways. First, something is filled: lack is apparently satisfied. The mouth is filled; the rectum is filled; the vagina is filled; the eye is filled by a fabulous vision. Alternatively, one can say that something is inserted: the breast is put into the mouth; faeces (or the penis) enter the rectum; the penis penetrates the vagina. Again, one can say that something is expelled: the penis expels semen; the vagina expels the new-born baby; the breast expels milk.

The not-me fills the inside of me, and causes massive excitement, until at the moment of orgasm, there is a shudder in the body – a shudder of ecstasy, or a shudder of horror? Perhaps both. What seems to be going on here is both a fusion of me and another, and a turning inside out, so that the inside of me temporarily contains part of another, or alternatively, a part of me now forms the inside of another.

Sexual excitement is therefore very much concerned with the traversing or dissolution of the normal boundaries that exist between me and the rest of the world. I allow myself to be penetrated by another; or I penetrate another. Even in a kiss, many people penetrate the other's mouth with their tongue.

One can see why orgasm has often been compared with death, for example in the literature of the seventeenth century. In John Donne's words:

> The Phoenix ridle hath more wit
> By us, we two being one, are it.
> So to one neutrall thing both sexes fit,
> Wee dye and rise the same, and prove
> Mysterious by this love.
> 'The Canonization'[10]

Donne's metaphors are apposite: each sex dies inside the other sex, since its boundary walls are breached, the distinction between inside and outside is dissolved, the distinction between me and not-me is exploded. The orgasm for both sexes seems to encapsulate this explosion of boundaries: at the point of orgasm, one may not be very sure who is who, or who is doing what. Isn't that part of the delight?

Of course, it might be argued that this is a very male view of sex, all to do with penetration and loss of boundaries, and that there are other forms of sexual pleasure to do with the surface of the body, gentle affection, and so on. Certainly, it is true that in the dialectic of 'filled' and 'filler', women and men have been stereotyped as 'receptive' and 'penetrative'. In fact, Lacan gives us an acid definition of sex: 'the act of love is the polymorphous perversion of the male'.[11] However, this is a product of the social dynamic of gender, not the biological nature of human bodies. It seems likely that in the contemporary ferment over gender and sexuality these stereotypes can be, and are being, dismantled.

It strikes me that this formulation of sexual excitement and pleasure goes further than the normal sexological analysis of sex, since it takes us to the root of selfhood, and suggests that sex plays around with identity and loss of identity. Sex can be so delightful, because we are allowed to play with those boundaries and orifices that are normally stopped up and sealed against the outside world, and thereby give us our sense of separate existence. Sex shows us the relative nature of these boundaries, and of our sense of self.

It is easy to see how 'perversions' involving urine, faeces, blood, semen and so on arise, since again the normally prohibited secretions of the body become charged with wonder, as signs that my normal social identity is undone. Exhibitionism can be seen in the same light: I uncover what is supposed to be covered up – and here I include not only the display of the penis, but women's display of the breast and other parts of the body.

Sex can therefore be seen as *an ontological dismantling*, in the sense that it unpacks the apparatus of social identity, and transforms it into a pleasurable form of play. I open myself up to you, and show you what normally is unshowable and unseeable. I become something quite different from what I normally am: during sex I deconstruct myself in the same tempo as you deconstruct yourself. I go to the edge of myself and fall off, and meet you, who have also fallen off the edge of your being: at this point, we meet inside each other's edgelessness. No doubt this is a very idealized view, and does not often happen – but this also fuels our desires, since we sense the possibility of meeting in a place that is outside time and space, and outside normal ego identities. This also seems to return us to a state of paradise, such as we recall – or imagine – was the state of innocence in our childhood, before the burdens of being an I assumed their full weight. It may also evoke uterine feelings: being inside another person, sealed against the hazards of independent existence.

Sex is a pleasurable playing with selfhood itself, but of course this also makes it very frightening for many people. The idea of being inside someone else, or someone else being inside them, is literally unspeakable and provokes extreme terror. This is not particularly to do with sex *per se*, but with the dissolution of boundaries which sex can involve.

Without doubt Lacan would object to the rather positive interpretations I have given to the notion of the 'rim' of the body: in fact, Lacan's radical interpretation of Freud leads him to the famous statement that 'there is no sexual relation'.[12] In other words, desire always fails in its attempts to attain its object, for desire is illusory and its object is illusory. Sexual desire is saturated in fantasy, and therefore actual sex is frequently disappointing since 'reality' cannot match up to fantasy.

This argument seems particularly applicable to romantic love, which seems to be very clearly founded on 'hallucinatory' wishes, which no real human being can fulfil. Hence the 'honeymoon' stage in relationships – including psychotherapy itself – has quite a short time span, after which comes the more difficult task of relating to somebody real. The fantasies involved in romantic love are very complex, but certainly one element of them seems to involve a projection of lost elements of oneself: that is, in the beloved I seek aspects of myself that have been repressed. Thus, it is quite common to find that womanizers are completely out of touch with their own feminine side – and are therefore compelled to seek it in others.

Having said that, I think Lacan's pessimism in relation to sexual desire and passion is excessive. Granted, that heady combination of romantic infatuation and sexual passion which often marks the beginnings of relationships does not last, or at any rate, its intensity does not last. But is it really true that desire inevitably fails, that sexual passion is doomed to ignominy and the disappointment of reality?

I have met people who claimed to feel sexually and emotionally fulfilled with a long-standing partner, and I have no reason to doubt them. Without doubt, Lacan has perceived something in the core of the human being that is disturbing: that there is no essential core. But from this brilliant perception, Lacan constructs a series of metaphysical generalizations which at times seem ahistorical and unempirical.

LANGUAGE AND THE UNCONSCIOUS

For Lacan, language is absolutely central to notions of human identity and meaning. He argues that the unconscious is structured like a language,[13] and once one accepts that startling thesis, it follows that our desires, our sense of self, our basic orientation to the world – all of which can be assumed to flow from the unconscious – are discursive, or linguistic, in nature. Lacan reverses the normally understood relation between the individual and language: so far from seeing speech as the 'expression' of the human person, Lacan argues that language is 'prior'. Thus, the *pre-human* infant is confronted with speech and language, and it is through them that he comes to acquire human identity: 'the psychoanalytic experience has rediscovered in man the imperative of the Word as the law that has formed him in its image'.[14]

Once this idea is accepted, it leads to a whole series of startling corollaries. For example, arguably perception itself is linguistic, since the coming into being of the individual is coextensive with the coming into being of the comprehensible universe. That is, the infant learns to categorize reality, so that in the end it can accept the category of the I, that is, its own existence; the categories are what make it human, and the categories are derived from language:

> It is not only man who speaks but in man and through man that it (*ça*) speaks... his nature is woven by effects in which we can find the structure of language, whose material he becomes, and... consequently there resounds in him, beyond anything ever conceived of by the psychology of ideas, the relation of speech.[15]

Thus, if the unconscious is seen as language-like, then the desires that exist in the unconscious are forms of speech, and the repression that holds them down is yet another form of speech.

How does this relate to sexuality? In the Lacanian paradigm of alienation, sexual desire always seeks a 'lost object', which can never be found. But this lost object is a hallucination, which is itself part of the ongoing 'speech' of the unconscious. If you like, I am driven by unconscious desires which 'speak' to me, like Scheherazade, continually bringing before me another tantalizing vision, yet forever postponing the day of fulfilment.

Furthermore, since my own status as an 'I' is constituted in and through language, and since this lonely I seeks to overcome its isolation through the 'joys of sex', and since 'the other' whom I may encounter in sex is itself a mirage formulated in the discourse of the unconscious – then we arrive at the dazzling, if lugubrious, notion that in sex one fictive entity meets another fictive entity in a meeting that is itself a mirage!

At this point, one might want to pause, and register feelings of disbelief, awe, excitement, and so on. Lacan's philosophy certainly takes us towards conclusions that are both exciting and disturbing. There is, however, a nagging suspicion that the emphasis on language has resulted in a kind of idealist Hegelian paradise (or hell), where nothing exists except ideas and speech. The body itself seems to disappear in the Lacanian dialectic, or it becomes yet another 'alienating identification' to which I submit in order to prop up my shaky belief in my own existence.

At the same time, Lacan has certainly thrown a grenade into any cosy sentimentality that we might be tempted to adopt in relation to human relationships, intimacy and sexuality. I see the Lacanian position as quite an extreme one, but one that is very useful, as a kind of razor's edge, with which one can test conceptions of desire, love and sex. Certainly, much human sex seems inauthentic and narcissistic, as Lacan would predict. For many people, the other is only a mirage, a reflection of their own needs. However, one might want to demur at a global analysis along Lacanian lines. One is left indeed with the tantalizing question: is authentic and intimate sex possible?

A further interesting concomitant of the linguistic nature of the unconscious is that sexual desire itself becomes less a desire for pleasure than a desire for meaning. It is the meaninglessness of the isolated ego that compels it to find solace in sex, through the illusion of 'contact' and completion.

THE PHALLUS

With the notion of the phallus, many of Lacan's preoccupations come together. In his system of ideas, the phallus is a purely symbolic entity. It definitely does not refer to the penis, but is an abstract 'signifier', whose meaning is signification itself within patriarchal society.[16]

Lacan traces his use of the term 'phallus' to Freud's delineation of the 'phallic' stage in children, at which point both boys and girls seem to be the same, and seem to assume the existence of only one sexual organ. However, as we have seen, this genealogy is complicated by Freud's frequent reference to anatomy, wherein the penis does seem important. After all, it is the sight of the female genitals that is supposed to traumatize the little boy with the realization that there are penis-less beings.

In the Lacanian system, both sexes lack the phallus: women, because they are designated as the castrated sex; men, because they go through the castration complex, which simultaneously assigns them to the masculine gender and destroys their elementary desire for their mother. But at the same time, through the constellations of patriarchal society – which are embedded in language – men seem to be rewarded with the phallus as the signifier of meaning itself: that is, it is men who speak, who create meanings, who designate and categorize reality.

The phallus therefore has a strong linguistic element, since as a 'signifier', that is, a sign, it is part of human language. However, there are problems here associated with Lacan's use of the term 'signifier', for in linguistics this term has very precise meanings. For example, in de Saussure's formulations, signs only have meaning in relation to each other.[17] It is puzzling then to imagine what other signifiers the signifier of the phallus is related to. Lacan defines the phallus as the signifier of all signifiers, which seems to mean that it is the sign of meaning itself, reserved for men.

Lacan also seems reluctant to give language and signs in general any socio-political provenance. For even if we accept that the 'phallus' is embedded in human language – men are speaking subjects, women are receptive objects, if you like – is this an eternal state of affairs, or is it tied up with a historically evolving form of society, that may one day disappear?

These questions have been of particular importance to feminists, who have been strongly influenced by Lacan, but who have been less enthusiastic about this 'eternalizing' streak in him, which seems to accept that patriarchy is an inevitable state of affairs.[18]

ALIEN DESIRES AND DESIRES FOR THE ALIEN

Although many of Lacan's ideas seem highly metaphysical and hyper-logical, some of them also seem to have a direct relevance to many people's sexual problems. For example, it is common in psychotherapy to meet people whose desires appear to be damaging to themselves. One common example of this is the desire for someone remote. This can lead to a string of broken relationships, each one leading to another. Eventually (it is hoped) the sheer repetitiveness of this can lead the person to seek help.

But in such a situation we are faced with something quite bizarre. I desire someone remote, 'frozen'; in fact, I am excited by such people. They turn me on. But I can't really relate to them; sex with them is exciting but not fulfilling; I can't live with them in a spirit of companionship.

As Lacan points out, it is worse than useless to enlist the 'healthy' part of the person, and hope to strengthen this against the 'unhealthy' side. In my experience, this can simply reinforce the civil war going on, or can actually increase the longing for the frozen prince or princess. No, one has to take this desire seriously: rather than striving to repress it, one has to bring it out more. In fact, it is because it is partly repressed that it is so urgent, and will not brook compromise. If we are lived by the unconscious, the task is not to say no to it, but to make it conscious (which is a kind of saying yes to it), so that we have some choice over it.

The desire for the exciting and depriving partner has to be fully exhumed, and traced back to its infantile roots, where invariably it will be found to connect to an exciting and depriving parent. This work does not end the desire, but it can give it a different place within the psyche, so that the individual concerned is not driven by it. In other words, one can restore choice, so that when I am tempted to go off and chase another frozen goddess, I am able to have the feeling without acting on it.

None the less, the basic psychic structure here is a stunning confirmation of the Lacanian analysis of desire. The desire for the remote partner is in a sense 'the desire for desire'. What I want is *to be unfulfilled*, to be perpetually desiring, eternally excited, without ever finding completion. I seek a partner who will keep my desire burning brightly by frustrating it; in that sense, I am not interested in that person at all, but simply in my own desire. That is what I am fascinated by; the other person is a kind of mirror into whom I throw the beam of my longing, hoping to see a true reflection of it coming back to me. Far from hoping to see my own 'lack' filled up, I deliberately seek those people who will not fill it, and I shun those people who might. It is my own lack that I jealously guard and preserve: in some ways, it seems to be who I am. It is a commonplace in psychotherapeutic work that it is love – apparently most cherished of all human aspirations – that many damaged people shun like the plague. As the psychoanalyst R.J. Stoller argues, these psychological mechanisms are essentially conservative ones: 'we inflict punishment on ourselves in order to avoid change'.[19] This paradox can make therapeutic work extremely difficult, since it is the success of the work that some clients are most afraid of, since that success will bring them love – which they dread. Hence, such people tend to sabotage their own development and self-fulfilment.

But Lacan's view of desire is quite global: he argues that all desire is like this. It is all based on a fundamental lack, a lack which cannot be satisfied, since its object is a hallucinatory one.

My own view of this is complicated: I think Lacan is partly right, but also he seems too pessimistic to me. There seems little doubt that we all retain infantile desires which were not met; on the other hand, I think some people have happy childhoods! I am not saying that all their desires were satisfied – in fact, that would not constitute a happy childhood – but they had 'good enough' parents. In such cases, it is quite likely that in later life relationships will prove to be satisfying, and specifically that sexual relations will be 'good enough'.

None the less, if we accept the Freudian thesis that the unconscious consists largely of infantile desires, then clearly such desires are unrealized. That is why we still dream of them, hoping to fulfil them in fantasy. Desire in the unconscious is therefore by definition a nodal point of frustration; in fact, the unconscious can be regarded as a repository of forbidden wishes. Hence the relation of the ego to the unconscious is always an uneasy one, since the 'reality principle' of the one clashes directly with the 'pleasure principle' of the other. The ego is one of the forces holding down repressed wishes, but it also gains its own energy and élan from them – a genuine case, perhaps, of biting the hand that feeds you.

It is likely that many images of horror in popular culture – especially in the horror film – are references to the dark and subterranean desires which fill the unconscious, and which tantalize us yet appal us. So much of this horror is to do with sexuality and gender, for example in the figure of Dracula, whose oral sexual excesses seem to blend categories of gender: Dracula is simultaneously oral, phallic and vaginal. In relation to the rapacity of the vampire, Lacan makes the interesting comment that 'since we refer to the infant and the breast, and since suckling is sucking, let us say that the oral drive is getting sucked, it is the vampire'.[20] I take this to mean that in the unconscious, notions of subject and object tend to collapse: the one who sucks also wants to be sucked. Dracula embodies therefore our hidden desires both to suck and 'get sucked'.

Reference can also be made to the trilogy of *Alien* films, which centre around a terrifying monster, which is both phallic and vaginal, and in the first *Alien* film (1976) spectacularly bursts out of a man's stomach, in a ghastly parody of childbirth. In these films, the alien also seems to represent an image of the maternal body, seen as grotesque and murderous: but it is equally an image of our own desires, which in their most primitive form terrify us with their rapacity and destructiveness.[21]

This train of thought reminds me of the old joke about the psychiatrist who takes down details from a new patient, and finally enquires as to his sex life. Having previously recounted a long list of woes, the patient replies brightly, 'Oh, that's one thing that is good in my life', whereupon the psychiatrist groans: 'Hell, we are in trouble.'

The joke is only partly true, but it is astonishing how often one meets with an inverse correlation between good sex and a happy life. That is, there are plenty of people who seem to have an energetic, exciting – and yes, orgasmic – sex life, but who otherwise seem discontented, unable to find intimate relationships, and so on. The Lacanian thesis predicts this: it is the discontent that makes for a 'good sex life', since sex is always aiming to overcome a gap or a discontinuity within oneself. At the same time, such people do not seem satisfied in the least with their sexual exploits: they are true addicts, who continually need a fix in order to put off the recognition that the last fix didn't fix things at all.

Is the reverse true? Does a contented life lead to a dull sex life, since it lacks the frisson of frustration and lack? This is the complaint of many married people, especially middle-aged ones, and the temptation then is to have an affair: the illicit nature of this of course produces great excitement. None the less, I remain optimistic: I have met people who are middle-aged, contented, and still seem to have good intimate sex.

In that sense, I have to stop short of an extreme Lacanian position. Lacan is so scathing about the 'healthy ego', so caustic about 'adaptionist' psychologies that try to help people to make compromises, that it becomes rather alarming to suggest that there is something to be said in favour of 'benign desires' that are adequately satisfied. However, like many prophets, Lacan has exaggerated his position, and positively revels in his destruction of humanist and liberal views of humanity.

Lacan has presented a brilliant – if opaque – picture of twentieth century angst and alienation. To suggest, as he does, that his picture of human beings is trans-historically true is less convincing. After all, as the ex-psychoanalyst Alice Miller never tires of saying, our contemporary child-rearing practices are so cruel, so depriving, that it is not surprising that our society is full of discontented people, who perpetually seek excitement but never find fulfilment.[22]

LACAN, HEGEL AND MARX

Lacan has without doubt taken some of the insights of psychoanalysis and deepened them considerably. His investigations into language and the unconscious, the nature of human lack and the compensatory fantasy life that ensues, the nature of the phallus as a key symbol in human existence – these offer many brilliant if difficult insights.

However, we have seen that certain problems arise with Lacanian psychology. In the first place, it is curiously asocial and trans-historical. Lacan does describe the social relationships that are embedded in language, and that the human infant has to absorb if it is to become fully human. But there is an absence of any wider socio-economic background, so that we are left wondering how language itself emerges. This criticism of Lacan has been made forcibly by Julia Kristeva, who develops many of his ideas, but insists that the human subject is a social and historical one. This criticism is particularly relevant to the topic of sexuality, since it is likely that sexual manners are not trans-historical but vary widely from culture to culture. Such a critique of Lacan is also particularly apposite within feminism, which has been disenchanted with the 'eternalizing' aspect of psychoanalysis.[23]

This also means that Lacan does not consider the role of psychoanalysis itself as a socio-political instrument within certain social contexts. He tends to treat it as a rather disembodied procedure, without historical roots or development.

A third criticism one can mention is that Lacan seems rather gender blind in much of his writings. While some feminists have been eager to avail themselves of his theoretical developments, since they offer a means of describing patriarchy that is not biologically based, other feminists have felt critical of his own rather overbearing and masculinist attitudes.[24]

Fourth, the objection can be raised that Lacanian sexuality is curiously disembodied: it is a matter of logic, language and lack, not of actual bodies in contact with each other. Of course, there is an instant Lacanian riposte to this criticism, that human sexuality is inevitably disembodied, since it continually seeks something that has been lost. In other words, sex is inevitably shrouded in, and expressed through, fantasy.

But these criticisms also belong to psychoanalysis as a whole. If it has provided a brilliant picture of the psychic configurations connected with sexual development in human beings, it tends to treat the psyche in isolation from society. Particularly in relation to gender and sexuality, psychoanalysis is open to the criticism that it tends to abstract and universalize, so that the Oedipus complex, the castration complex, the sexual drives, and so on, seem to become processes outside history and political discourse. At its most extreme, Freudian thought can even claim that history is determined by intra-psychic structures and processes: this is another version of idealism that seems to take us back to Hegel, in whose philosophy the mind is not a product of history, but its agent.

It seems likely that Lacan was heavily influenced by Hegelian thought, and there seem to be close correspondences between Hegel's vision of a World Spirit which lives through individuals and Lacan's view of the individual as created by pre-existent forms of discourse.[25] Thus there is a tendency to 'globalization' in Lacanian thought which has attracted some readers and repelled others. One can also cite the rather disembodied flavour of Lacanian sexuality: sex seems to be a logical rather than an emotional connection. Lacan's emphasis on the phallus rather than the penis seems indicative here: while this seems to provide a greater explanatory power, it also seems to take us one step back from sex as we experience it concretely.

Lacan's 'Hegelian' bent has caused great excitement amongst some groups of Western intellectuals, including some feminists, for it seems to provide an escape from Freud's biologism or from a crude mechanical form of Marxism. On the other hand, Lacan's very abstract and abstruse explanation of sexuality can prove quite alienating in itself for some readers, for it does not seem to capture the concrete excitement and pleasure of sex. Lacan is therefore very much an intellectual's intellectual.

One can direct towards the Lacanian view of sexuality the same criticisms made by Marx towards Hegel that he is both idealist and positivist.[26] For example, in relation to the state, Hegel saw it as an expression of an absolute Idea, whereas Marx saw it as a product of socio-historical evolution (since many societies have no state). To put it crudely, Hegel had made absolute and eternal certain specific and historically relative aspects of society – the state, the monarchy, science, even philosophy itself – and had changed them from being the relative products of history to being the absolute agents or god-like Ideas of history. Or as Marx puts it succinctly: in Hegel, 'the soul of an object, in this case of the state, is established and predestined prior to its body which is really just an illusion'.[27]

Marx also describes this as the inversion of the historical subject and object: 'The mystical substance therefore becomes the real subject, while the actual subject appears as something else, namely the moment of the mystical substance.'[28] This means that human society and human activity always appear in an alienated form: 'human activity, etc. necessarily appears as the activity and product of something other than itself'.[29]

In the same way, Lacan turns certain aspects of human existence – desire, language, the unconscious – into forces which dominate and tyrannize us, and indeed create us. Sexual desire, rather than being a means whereby human beings relate to each other, is defined as a sign that they are lost in illusion and cannot communicate. Everything seems to turn into its opposite: 'contact' turns into the impossibility of contact; desire is haunted by its own hallucinatory nature; sexuality is a dream from which we never wake up.

But Marx also made the profound observation that Hegel had not *invented* the inversion of 'object into subject', for the alienation and reification of the state was not imaginary, but actual. As Lucio Colletti argues:

> It is no longer accurate to say only that the concept of the state Hegel offers us is a hypostatized abstraction; the point becomes that the modern state, the political state, is itself a hypostatized abstraction.[30]

In other words, Hegel had correctly perceived the alienated nature of the modern (bourgeois) state, but had transformed this alienation into a trans-historical absolute, a kind of World Idea of statehood which is incarnated in actual states, and whose final and climactic realization is the nineteenth century Prussian state. Thus, Marx's criticism of Hegel was that he transformed this 'estrangement' – which Marx saw as a historical phase in the evolution of human society – into something eternal and inevitable. This is the sense in which he accuses Hegel of positivism.

In the same way, Lacan is surely correct to point out that desire – so far from being an organic human expression and relation – has become an alienated lack which haunts us and drives us, and never gives us fulfilment. The question that must be asked is whether this is an inevitable aspect of human existence, or one created by modern society, which has tended to alienate and fetishize many useful things and turn them into our gods and dictators, for example money.

It is relevant at this point to cite Marx's comments on the estrangement of social bonds, which appear as external and hostile forces:

> Only in the eighteenth century, in 'civil society', do the various forms of social connectedness confront the individual as a mere means towards his private purposes, as external necessity.[31]

It is striking that the historical period cited by Marx as that in which social bonds turned into 'external necessity' – the eighteenth century – is also the period given by Foucault as the birthplace of the concept of 'sexuality'.[32] One can argue then that 'sexuality' is itself a form of 'social connectedness' that has been externalized and reified, so that it now confronts us as an alienated force.

In other words, is the Lacanian view of human alienation simply true for all time, an inescapable part of being human, or is it a contingent product of human history at one specific time?

Of course one's views on this are subjective: my own view is that Lacan is pessimistic and idealist. Perhaps most crucial here is the lack of historical relativization in Lacan, for as we shall see in the next chapter, the notion of 'sexuality' is arguably itself a modern invention. Thus it is possible that 'sexuality' is an alienated and reified concept, which has been 'abstracted' from social existence, and which now tantalizes and haunts us. If this is true, then the impossibility of desire is not an inescapable part of the human condition, but part of our modern historical development.

Furthermore, I would argue that the human predicaments described by Lacan can be, to a greater or lesser extent, overcome: by grasping the fantastic and unrealizable nature of some of my desires, I am able to distinguish them from my realistic desires. It is possible therefore to meet someone in a real way, and not simply see them through a veil of projections; it is possible to be sexually intimate with someone and to feel content with that. Sex can be real and good enough.

6 Sexuality as a Modern Concept

It seems necessary, after spending three chapters discussing the psychoanalytic contribution to the study of sexuality, that we now turn to a more sociological and historical view. For if psychoanalysis has been probably the most important theory of sexuality in the twentieth century, its drawbacks are palpable. I have already described some of them: the pervasive masculinism; the biological bias; the conservatism of psychoanalytic institutions; and above all, the trans-historical tendency to reify certain categories of sexual relations, for example the Oedipus complex.

In this chapter I want to consider a thesis that is diametrically opposed: that 'sexuality' itself is a modern concept with a historical origin and line of development. Many people find this idea surprising, if not bewildering. At first glance it seems unthinkable that other cultures – indeed, all other cultures – have not found ways of talking about, thinking about and analysing sex, sexual behaviour and feelings, and so on. No doubt this is true, but this is not what the word 'sexuality' refers to. When I use phrases such as 'my sexuality' or 'sexuality in Western culture', there are all kinds of implications: that there is a discrete entity within me, or within society, which can be labelled in this way; that somehow it is separate from other aspects of me, as for example, my emotions, my social status, and so on; and that it is closely connected with my identity. There is also the notion that through sexuality I become manifest as I really am; sex is seen in the twentieth century both as a revelation of the self, and as a means of salvation. In the eloquent words of Michel Foucault, 'we have placed ourselves under the sign of sex'.[1]

Most strikingly, sexuality is seen as an autonomous force, both socially and individually. It seems to have become split off from other aspects of human existence, and has acquired a life of its own. The body of ideas known as 'social constructionism' therefore argues that sexuality is a historical concept that came into being at a certain time and in certain cultures, and that in many previous times and cultures it has not existed:

Sexuality must not be thought of as a natural given which power tries to hold in check, or as an obscure domain which knowledge tries gradually to uncover. It is the name that can be given to a historical construct.[2]

The most straightforward way of testing this hypothesis is by comparing modern Western culture, and its concept of sexuality, with another culture's approach to sex. In his article 'Is there a history of sexuality?', David Halperin does this in relation to classical Athenian society, and his argument is highly persuasive. He argues that Athenians were not interested in an individual's 'sexuality' as a separate entity, but in the way his sexual life interrelated with his social status. Thus men of a high social status had sexual relations with women, boys, slaves and foreigners, who were all considered to be of a lower status. These men could not be therefore described in modern terms as 'heterosexual' or 'homosexual', or even 'bisexual'. Quite simply, a different socio-sexual system operated in Athenian society. But we can say more: not only were sexual distinctions different – the emphasis we place on object choice is absent – but 'sexuality' is not considered in isolation.[3]

It strikes me that a similar comparison can be made with the ancient and medieval European world after Christ. Of course, sexual issues were discussed extensively, but 'sexuality' as an autonomous phenomenon was unknown, since sex was inextricably tied up with other domains, particularly a moral–philosophical framework which saw 'passion' as a relinquishment of self-control and reason. We saw in Chapter 2 that in Christian sexual ethics, sexual desire is subsumed within the wider categories of 'disobedience', self-will and pleasure. No doubt sex in itself offends Augustine: but he fulminates mainly about the implications that sexual desire has for the rational integrity of human beings.

What is striking about the modern Western notion of sexuality is that first, it is understood to be an independent entity, and second, it is seen as so important in the life and the identity of the individual. Halperin describes it as a key to the 'hermeneutics of the self' in the West.[4]

MARXISM AND SEXUALITY

In considering the historical development of ideas about sex, one of the surprising lacunae is the dearth of theorizing about gender and sexuality within Marxism. One might imagine that, with its materialist and historical approach to social developments, Marxism would have developed interesting theories of gender and sexuality, but classical Marxism generally paid lip-service to Engels' *The Rise of the Family* (1884), and left the matter there. Only in the postwar period of 'revisionist' Marxism have attempts been made to link its materialist class-based analysis with an examination of the family, heterosexuality and 'perverse' forms of sexuality, as for example in the writings of Marcuse and Wilhelm Reich.

The importance of Engels' *The Rise of the Family* was that he described the oppression of women as a historical circumstance, not a biological one. The family was not seen as frozen in amber for all time, but shown to have a historical development. In this sense Engels provided a kind of proto-constructionism: phenomena such as the family are social constructs rather than biologically given.

Furthermore, Marxism does not start from the individual: in fact, individualism is itself seen as a social product, as Marx states in the famous words of the 'Theses on Feuerbach': 'the human essence is no abstraction inherent in each single individual. In its reality it is the ensemble of the social relations'.[5] According to Marx, it is through alienation that the individual begins to be regarded as separate from other people, and the social bonds between people are fetishized and projected in the form of money, God, property and so on:

> In this society of free competition, the individual appears detached from the natural bonds etc. which in earlier historical periods made him the accessory of a definite and limited human conglomerate... Only in the eighteenth century, in 'civil society', do the various forms of social connectedness confront the individual as a mere means towards his private purposes, as external necessity.[6]

While in Marx's *Grundrisse* this argument is used towards the profound analysis of money as an estranged form of social relationship, it can also be applied to sexuality, which in many bourgeois forms of thought has been seen as an individualized 'instinct', having little connection with other people, and having no societal origin. Freud shows this trend clearly: in his early writings, the sexual instinct exists without an object, and only seeks an object under the impact of puberty. Individual sexuality is reified and detached from socio-historical contexts, and even from interpersonal relations.

But in fact, Marxism, while analysing the socio-economic under-pinnings of the family, monogamy, kinship, and so on, has generally ignored sexuality itself. Marx seems to have accepted that heterosexuality was the 'natural' human relationship: 'the immediate, natural, necessary relation of human being to human being is the relationship of man to woman'.[7] And Engels' separation of production from reproduction – defined as 'the production of human beings themselves' – has aroused suspicions, particularly amongst feminists, that reproduction has been treated as an autonomous and 'natural' process, about which Marxism has little to say, except that it flows from the biological division between the sexes. In the words of Donna Haraway, 'the root difficulty was an inability to historicize sex itself'.[8]

Thus while Marxism can be used to criticize the reification and isolation of individual sexuality, in fact very few Marxists, certainly in the 'classical' period of Marxism, attempted to do so. One of the few who did was the Bolshevik Alexandra Kollontai, who in a number of articles, such as 'Sexual relations and the class struggle', went beyond Engels and considered the nature of human sexuality outside the tyrannical grip of the family.[9] But Kollontai's views were considered heretical in the Soviet Union in the 1920s, and, as the right wing increasingly took control, anticipating the coming Stalinization, she was branded an 'ultra-leftist' for her ideas of free love and women's rights.[10]

The conservatism of Soviet leaders on issues of sexuality and morality can be illustrated by referring to Trotsky's comments on marriage:

> A long and permanent marriage, based on mutual love and cooperation – that is the ideal standard.... Freed from the chains of police and clergy, later also from those of economic necessity, the tie between man and woman will find its own way, determined by physiology, psychology and care for the welfare of the human race.[11]

MICHEL FOUCAULT

It was partly as a critique of such ahistorical and rather crude analysis in Marxism that Michel Foucault wrote his massive *History of Sexuality*, published in three volumes between 1976 and 1984. In a short autobiographical sketch written for a French encyclopedia, Foucault describes his whole lifetime's work as a significant 'break' from Marxism, and as a particular riposte to the looming figure of Sartre.[12]

From the early sixties, Foucault, along with other postwar French intellectuals such as Derrida and Deleuze, had mounted a devastating attack, not just on Marxism, but on Enlightenment rationalism and all notions of 'continuity' and 'progress', which they saw as fig-leaves covering up massive oppression, complacency and hypocrisy. In a series of astonishing 'histories', (*Madness and Civilization* (1961), *The Birth of the Clinic* (1963), *Discipline and Punish* (1975)) Foucault argued that rationalism, and indeed modern society as a whole, could only constitute itself by excluding those who were non-rational, 'perverse', or unwanted, for example the mad, the poor, the criminal, the homosexual. Furthermore, Foucault argued that the notion of the subject itself – the stable rational centre of experience and decision making – so beloved of political and philosophical thinking since the Enlightenment, was itself a fiction, vital to the myth of a progressive and rational social order, but kept in place only through enormous oppression and deceit.

In rather general terms, Foucault's thesis is that 'the Other' is constructed or reified in order to bring into place and to consolidate the 'self', or the rational being. Thus unreason is placed outside the ambit of reason, but in fact is required in order to define it. Homosexuality is constructed as a definite category (or 'species') of sexual identity partly to help delimit and reinforce heterosexuality. Colonial peoples are defined in certain ways – 'primitive', 'infantile', 'indolent' – so as to define the colonizers as naturally superior. Deviance must be described and analysed as a kind of buttress for the non-deviant. One can cite as an example Foucault's argument, in relation to prisons and other forms of punishment, that their function is not to isolate and restrict the criminal, but in a sense to create 'delinquency': 'Delinquency is the vengeance of the prison on justice.'[13]

Foucault has therefore described a massive exercise in splitting and projection that goes on historically, whereby a dominant group utilizes, and, one might even say, *constructs*, a subordinate group in order to define itself, and also to act as a depository for aspects of itself that are unwanted. The great example of this – which significantly Foucault ignores to a large extent – is the patriarchal use of women as 'the Other', thereby defining 'men' as all the things women are not – rational, orderly, temperate, constructive, and so on. Foucault did not pay much attention to the patriarchal nature of sexuality, and this has troubled feminists, who have been interested in Foucault's historical and political deconstruction of sexuality, but are less enamoured of his obliteration of female sexuality.[14]

Some of Foucault's ideas are quite Nietzschean – for example, the deconstruction of the self seems to echo Nietzsche's description of the 'synthetic concept I', the I that is effect not cause. And Foucault's thesis that liberalism, while appearing to offer freedom to people, actually constitutes a subtle form of control, is akin to Nietzsche's castigation of democracy: 'the democratization of Europe is at the same time an involuntary arrangement for the breeding of *tyrants*' [original emphasis].[15] Foucault describes his researches as taking place 'under the sun of the great Nietzschean quest'.[16]

In this light, Foucault believed that one important task was to retrieve those 'transgressive' experiences and individuals which had been cast out by bourgeois society. Like a number of postwar French intellectuals and artists, he was fascinated by excess, deviance, a Sadean eroticism of cruelty and death. Foucault allied himself with such avant-garde figures as the writer Bataille and the composer Barraqué, and his first great work, *Madness and Civilization*, which argues that madness is a social construct needed to delimit the rational, also reveals his lifelong personal obsession with madness and death as 'limit-experiences'.

Many postwar French intellectuals were disillusioned by both Marxism and humanism, which they saw as vitiated by a stale rationalism and a naive idea of progress. Sartre's existentialism was seen by some as a warmed-up humanism, relying in the end on notions of freedom and authenticity, which for the avant-garde were hypocritical and complacent.[17]

Foucault is critical not only of Sartre, but of both Marx and Freud, first, for relying on a rational view of human beings and of history, second, for using normative criteria for judging people and history, and third, for proposing solutions that lead to yet more forms of social control over people. Foucault argues that attempts to 'liberate' people from oppression or repression are themselves a form of policing. In the words of the philosopher David Ingram:

> The ... redemption of repressed desires, sensibilities, and productive powers sought by Freud and Marx itself contributes to ever greater objectification and repression. Ultimately, hope for a rational reconciliation of ethos and eros unwittingly becomes a pretext for increased domination.[18]

Foucault's position is therefore that of philosophical anarchism, not to say nihilism, for all hopes of 'progress' or emancipation seem doomed to failure, in the sense that the emancipators come to acquire a subtle form of power themselves. In this sense, Foucault proposes a subtle and paradoxical theory of repression and liberation, which, when applied to sexuality, produces a dazzling and provocative contradiction of liberal thought. Sexual 'liberation' can be seen as a subtle form of social control, and sexual 'repression' in fact goes alongside a 'veritable discursive explosion' about sex.[19]

Foucault's scepticism is far-ranging – for example, he rejects the Marxist notion of ideology or false consciousness, for it suggests that there is a 'truth' lying concealed behind illusion. Foucault denies that there can be an underlying truth in this way, for this 'truth' has itself been constructed by certain groups of people. This suggests that science itself is always ideological, and cannot be 'neutral' as is often claimed. There is no objective truth, detached from socio-political power, and science is always contained within political parameters.

Foucault's prose style contributes to the surprising, even shocking, force of his arguments: in turns ironic, sarcastic, learned, using brilliant series of images, it tends to bewitch and seduce the reader. Here is truly an erotics of style, or an erotics of thinking. One can cite for example his enjoyably malicious description of psychoanalysis: 'yet another round of whisperings on a bed'; or one of his great perorations on the absurdity of the notion of 'repression':

> Is sex hidden from us, concealed by a new sense of decency, kept under a bushel by the grim necessities of bourgeois society? On the contrary, it shines forth; it is incandescent. Several centuries ago, it was placed at the center of a formidable *petition to know*. A double petition, in that we are compelled to know how things are with it, while it is suspected of knowing how things are with us [original emphasis].[20]

Foucault is therefore one of the great French prose stylists, and style is important in his understanding of sexuality: through one's sexual practices, one can develop an 'aesthetic' of the self.

Foucault did modify his nihilistic position towards the end of his life, and this shift can be seen taking place within the three volumes of *The History of Sexuality*, which is therefore a difficult and contradictory work to assess. While the first volume is an elegant theoretical dissertation on the explosion of 'sexual discourses' in the modern age and the use of sexuality to deploy power, volumes 2 and 3 take an abrupt change in direction, focusing on the sexual mores and ethics of ancient Greece and Rome. Foucault's original linkage of discourse–

power–sexuality seems to fade, to be replaced by a new interest in the cultivation of the self via sexuality.

The History of Sexuality is not really a history, but rather expounds a certain theory of sexuality, part of which is that sexuality indeed has a 'history' whose development can be studied. *The History* is written in a much cooler style than Foucault's earlier works; none the less it presents certain ideas that are bold, arresting and provocative. I propose to outline four of its main themes: sexuality as discourse; the concept of repression; sex as power and knowledge; and the relation between sexuality and the subject.

Speaking of Sex

Foucault is not alone in granting language a privileged position – for example, Lacan's radical shift within psychoanalysis stems in part from his emphasis on language as the central mechanism both of analysis, and of the unconscious itself, and Roland Barthes' view of myth stems partly from his view of it as a 'form of speech'.[21]

Foucault's application of discourse theory to sexuality produces a radical overturning of traditional concepts. Foucault argues that sexuality is actually 'produced' by the 'sexual discourses' that have been inaugurated in the modern age. It is the 'speaking of sex' that creates sexuality.[22]

This connects with Foucault's sarcastic onslaught on the notion of 'repression' – the idea that Christianity, and Western culture in general, had placed sex in a dark and hidden place. Foucault retorts: 'A censorship of sex? There is installed rather an apparatus for producing an ever greater quantity of discourse about it.'[23]

Not only through the religious confessional, but in medicine, psychiatry, the criminal justice system, biology, psychoanalysis – many disciplines and institutions have joined in the 'great sexual sermon' that has swept across Western culture in the past three hundred years. Foucault's use of the word 'sermon' suggests that a comparison can be drawn with theology, which can be described as 'speaking of God'. But speaking of God not only creates theology, but creates, or consolidates, the concept of God itself. Thus, it is discourse that creates fields of knowledge.

Foucault also argues that this 'incitement to discourse' permits a great deployment of power and control:

Sex ... was at the pivot of the two axes along which developed the entire political technology of the body. On the one hand, it was tied to the disciplines of the body: the harnessing, intensification, and distribution of forces, the adjustment and economy of energies. On the other hand, it was applied to the regulation of populations.[24]

Foucault cites the example of confession in the Christian Church, which by extracting 'the truth' from people, regulated both their sexual practices and their concept of who they are. One can also return to the example of psychoanalysis, which, while on the one hand offering people a means of understanding and alleviating sexually rooted neuroses, in effect, according to Foucault, ends up policing their desires. I have already pointed out in Chapter 4 how this is clearly true in relation to homosexuality, towards which American analysts in particular adopted a tone of contempt and negativity.

However, problems can arise with the theoretical prominence given by Foucault to discourse in the 'production' of sexuality, and indeed of other aspects of human existence. In particular, it is not clear what status non-discursive reality has in relation to discourse – how do material objects fit into Foucault's theory? This is particularly relevant to sexuality, since after all human beings do have bodies, and sex does take place on, around and in bodies, as well as through people's imaginations and through their speech.

Tracing Foucault's complex theory of discourse is beyond the scope of this book – suffice to say that he originally gave discourse a primacy over other aspects of reality. This view is summed up by Lois McNay: 'the social–institutional field only acquires a meaning or a unity once it is articulated within a particular discursive formation'.[25]

But Foucault did adapt his radical stance, and to a degree dissolved the priority given to discourse over other factors. Thus in *The History of Sexuality* he argues that 'it is in discourse that power and knowledge are joined together'.[26] This seems a less contentious claim. Moreover, Foucault was alive to these criticisms – that he might be positing a 'sexuality without sex' – and responds by accepting that 'deployments of power are directly connected to the body'.[27]

The importance given to discourse in the 'production' and maintenance of 'sexuality' has many ramifications. For example, it can be related to the idea that the mind itself is made up of 'scripts', largely unconscious, which actually determine the ways in which we perceive and act. This idea is of great value in psychological work, since our sexual life seems to be shot through with such scripts, some of which may contain very damaging or negative prescriptions.[28]

Furthermore, the notion of 'sexual discourses' need not be confined to the academic: as well as the vast mountain of research, theorizing and publications about sexuality, there is also a large amount of material in popular culture, ranging from the advice column in the woman's magazine to pornography, from the 'sexploitation' film to the serious art film, 'containing some nudity', as the TV guides helpfully tell us. Sexual images pervade advertising, pop videos, cinema, romantic fiction, the theatre and so on. Thus both academic and popular cultures join in the continual stimulation of discourse concerning sex.

Repression

Foucault argues that the 'repression' which seems to have existed towards sex since the seventeenth century is in fact an 'intensification' of sex. This paradoxical idea can be seen at work in other areas, and can be defined as the tendency to hide that which is most valuable. Examples abound in religious practice: for example, in Judaism, the holy of holies was seen only once a year by the high priest; in Christianity, the communion wafer is hidden and exposed in the monstrance. The concept of *revelation* in religion brings out the dual quality of concealment and exposure.

In relation to sexuality, one of the clearest examples concerns incest. The incest taboo exists precisely because incestuous desires are universal and intense, but the 'repression' of incest does not simply forbid but also magnifies, inflates and underlines that which is repressed. Foucault comments: 'incest...is constantly being solicited and refused; it is an object of obsession and attraction, a dreadful secret and an indispensable pivot'.[29]

Another example can be found in the furore over masturbation in the nineteenth and early twentieth centuries. This attempted to root out masturbation practices amongst children, and included the invention of devices that made it physically impossible. But this whole moral panic also has the effect of making masturbation supremely important as an index of depravity on the one hand, and perhaps more unconsciously, as an autoerotic pleasure.

There is an excellent example of the paradoxical relation between repression and intensification in Aline Roussel's book *Porneia*, concerning the Desert Fathers, who went to the desert to renounce sexual desire and the body as a whole, and found that they were compelled to talk about sex a lot, in order to vanquish it. As one monk said: 'If you do not think about it, you have no hope, for if you are not thinking about it, you are doing it.'[30] Many of the Desert Fathers report that their days and nights were filled with sexual fantasies, and these did not diminish with time.

One can put this idea rather crudely: human cultures prohibit those ideas and forces which are considered important, attractive and dangerous. If something is trivial or uninteresting, why bother to prohibit it? Furthermore, the actual act of prohibition involves 'talking about', legislation, moral dissertations, learned research, and so on, so that a process of magnification has occurred. A very clear example of this concerns pornography – the 'anti-pornography' movement has in fact raised the profile of pornography considerably, and has probably made many people think about pornography who never used to. In an article critical of feminist anti-pornography campaigns, Carol Vance describes how the American Meese commission on pornography was compelled to devote many hours to the screening of pornographic films, so that this ostensibly anti-porn conference became a cornucopia of pornography: 'The atmosphere throughout the hearings was one of excited repression: witnesses alternated between chronicling the negative effects of pornography and making sensationalized presentations of "it".'[31]

A famous example from the 1960s concerns the *Lady Chatterley's Lover* trial for obscenity. The trial involved huge amounts of testimony from 'expert witnesses', testifying to the artistic merit of the novel, and to its 'moral' or visionary approach to sexuality. Literary critics, bishops, and other distinguished figures jostled with each other to pay tribute to Lawrence's work. The trial was extensively publicized, and the result was a kind of in-depth public seminar on the Lawrentian view of sexuality. One might say simply enough that the attempt to suppress the book back-fired, but the trial illustrates exactly Foucault's linking of repression and intensification.[32]

However, the Foucaultian thesis regarding repression can be taken too far – actual repression does also take place. For example, gay men have been savagely persecuted at certain periods in this century in Britain; homosexuals were gassed in the Nazi concentration camps; women with illegitimate babies were placed in mental hospitals up to the 1950s in Britain; single mothers have been frequently scapegoated by Conservative governments in the eighties and nineties; Black men have been lynched in America for suspected sexual relations with White women. One can of course still argue that Foucault's thesis holds: for example, the tie-up between racism and sexuality found in lynching reveals both a fascination with 'Black sexuality', and an attempt to destroy it. Psychoanalysis might comment that the process is one of collective projection: the lynch mob is striving to destroy its own lurid desires, yet is also highlighting them.

There is a danger, then, that Foucault's dazzling sense of paradox might inure us to repression as something that is practised systematically by many governments and regimes. Furthermore, the feminist argument that heterosexuality itself has been repressive to women is formidable, and indicates again that a genuine repression is at work.

Power/Knowledge

Foucault argues, particularly in volume 1 of *The History of Sexuality*, that sexuality is an important means of acquiring and maintaining power over people, and also a means of acquiring knowledge of oneself and others. This is a crucial layer in the Foucaultian thesis, for otherwise we might be rather perplexed as to why the massive 'production of sexuality' has been going on since the eighteenth century. Foucault argues, with a characteristic historical sweep, rather lacking in empirical evidence, that since the Renaissance the means of deploying power has shifted dramatically:

> The old power of death that symbolized sovereign power was now carefully supplanted by the administration of bodies and the calculated management of life... there was an explosion of numerous and diverse techniques for achieving the subjugation of bodies and the control of populations.[33]

This is what Foucault variously calls 'bio-power' and 'the political technology of life'. In one of his most famous passages, he argues that this wielding of power was achieved in part through the creation of four key figures: the hysterical woman, the masturbating child, the Malthusian couple and the perverse adult.[34] Thus women's bodies were controlled through the creation of the concept of 'hysteria', children were sexualized, the fertility and birth control measures of couples became of great interest to the state, and the 'perverse' desires of adults were both psychiatrized and criminalized.

This line of argument strikes me as a compelling one, for which there is plenty of concrete evidence. Thus, feminism has been able to mount a counter-assault on the notion of 'female hysteria' and has demonstrated how that functioned as a constraint on women and their sexuality; the notion of child sexuality is a burning issue in the 1990s, faced with an ice-berg of abuse of children; population growth remains one of the main concerns of the United Nations and other bodies; the concept of 'perversion' continues to be fiercely debated in relation to homosexuality and other sexualities.

Within this 'political technology' psychoanalysis and psychotherapy have an important role, and an ambivalent one. On the one hand, these therapies do help individuals unknot themselves; on the other hand, some critics have argued that they also embody an unequal power relation between therapist and patient. Furthermore, the whole of the 'mental health' field often seems to involve ways and means of controlling and silencing wayward voices.

However, I find Foucault's concept of power to be one of the weakest areas in his argument. He specifically rejects a 'top-down' theory of power:

> I do not have in mind a general system of domination exerted by one group over another, a system whose effects, through successive derivations, pervade the entire social body.... Power is everywhere; not because it embraces everything, but because it comes from everywhere.[35]

This seems to be a straightforward attack on the notion of 'hegemonic' power, and an attack on the Marxist concept of class power and class revolution: 'there is no single locus of great Refusal, no soul of revolt, source of all rebellions or pure law of the revolutionary'.[36]

It is understandable that Foucault wanted to get away from the crude theories of power that had been propounded within Stalinist varieties of Marxism, or the very fuzzy left-wing arguments that 'capitalism controls sex in order to make people work harder'. Yet his replacement thesis suffers from its notion of 'ubiquity' and 'multiplicity'. If power is everywhere, if 'points of resistance' are everywhere, it strikes me that the concept of 'power' itself has become trivial and rather empty.

In particular, such a concept of power relations militates against any notion of patriarchy and patriarchal power – the notion that men have generally wielded power over women. This shows again Foucault's lack of interest in – or perhaps his resistance to – the study of gender as a relation of dominance and subordination.

The Subject

It is clear that a dramatic shift took place between the writing of volume 1 and volume 2 of *The History of Sexuality*. Foucault describes his new direction as follows:

> It seemed appropriate to look for the forms and modalities of the relation to self by which the individual constitutes and recognizes himself *qua* subject.[37]

This also seems to involve a shift away from Foucault's earlier nihilism, for the 'aesthetics of the self', as practised by the ancient Greeks, seems to offer some means of authentic self-affirmation which had seemed impossible in the radical scepticism of Foucault's earlier thinking, in which the self itself was derided as a myth of the Enlightenment.

Foucault argues that sex permits a relationship to the self to develop, since desire and pleasure are intense, and therefore have to be monitored, which involves a self-monitoring. In Greek thought, this seems to imply a self-mastery, in Christianity a self-renunciation. But self-renunciation or -denunciation still involves a heightened sense of self, an intensification of subjectivity: 'the individual is summoned to recognize himself as an ethical subject of sexual conduct'.[38]

In a sense, Foucault's thesis concerning sexuality is broadening: through reflection upon sexual conduct, morality and aesthetics, the self itself comes into being. Foucault is not saying that sex happened to be one of the means by which 'the self' was explored, but that it was as 'subjects of desire' that human beings began to arrive at a new self-consciousness, a new sense of subjectivity. Furthermore, by means of the ascetic practices of Christianity, a topography of the self was elaborated, involving a close scrutiny of every thought, every wish, and a burning zeal to return to a state of purity. The will, reason, desire, evil – a psychology of the self is articulated, all within the overarching concern to drive out desire.

However, volumes 2 and 3 of *The History* are specifically concerned with pre-Christian 'sexual discourses' as indicative of certain attitudes towards sex and the self quite different from the Christian one. None the less, through reflections on sex, Greek and Roman cultures were able to reflect upon the self, and the relations of the self to others.

It is interesting to speculate as to what led Foucault to take this different direction in relation to 'the history of sexuality'. One of his biographers, James Miller, argues that although the scholarly discussion of Greek and Roman aesthetics seems rather distant and calm after the fireworks of volume I, in fact Foucault was involved in a profound examination of himself and his own sexuality. It is perhaps significant that in the 1970s Foucault became more involved in the gay community, experimented with sado-masochism, and enjoyed the gay leather scene in San Francisco.[39] In a sense, Foucault was giving up his former scepticism towards notions of 'the self': 'the self that he spent a lifetime trying to unriddle, renounce and reinvent, he was never quite able to escape: he is always there, right before our eyes, lurking in the pages of his books'.[40]

APPLICATIONS OF SOCIAL CONSTRUCTION

Although Foucault's *History* is one of the most elegant formulations of social constructionism, its ideas are not entirely original. At the time of the publication of its first volume (1976), social constructionism had already begun to attract many thinkers within feminism, gay studies, and radical social science. For example, the British writer and academic Jeffrey Weeks had been writing about the 'history of sexuality' before Foucault's *History* was published.[41]

The basic ideas of social construction can be applied to many areas. For example, biology – often seen as a neutral, objective and scientific approach to sex – can be unpacked into a covert set of discourses that embody certain views about bodies, sexuality and gender relations. For example, many biology textbooks have traditionally described human fertilization in terminology that is loaded: the sperm are 'active', the egg is 'passive'.

Similarly, one can argue that while Freud described the psychic deep structure of sexuality, he left in place many socio-political assumptions, for example, the active/passive distinction, and the primacy of the penis. If you like, Freud did not uncover the ideological ramifications of sexuality, but took them to be eternal biologically based formations.

In the remainder of this chapter, I would like briefly to consider several areas of sexuality that seem to be illuminated by social construction theory.

One-Sex/Two-Sex Models

A number of writers on sexuality have pointed out that before the eighteenth century, most descriptions of the human body assumed that male and female bodies were similar. Thomas Laqueur, in his book *The Making of Sex*, argues that women's bodies were seen as 'turned inside out', but were homologous with men's. Thus the ovaries were seen as testicles; the vagina as an inverted penis, and so on. More accurately, we should say that women's bodies were similar but inferior to men's.[42]

According to this view, a huge shift took place in the eighteenth century, whereby men's and women's bodies were perceived to be radically different. The important point about this is that this change did not flow from empirical discoveries, but articulated certain ideological currents, which began to separate male and female reproduction and sexuality. For example, whereas ancient medicine had argued that female orgasm was as essential to conception as male orgasm, the nineteenth century saw the rise of ideas of the 'passionless' nature of women. Clearly, one effect of the theory of 'difference' was a greater suppression of female sexual desire.[43]

But the relation between 'similarity' and 'difference' is a complex and shifting one. For example, embryology, with its discovery of the original bisexuality of the foetus, seemed to help corroborate the ancient view. Likewise, Freud, with his theory of girls as 'little men', their clitoris a miniature penis, constructed a kind of sexual monism. The nineteenth century as a whole saw a very complex interplay between notions of similarity and difference: although Victorians constructed a fairly rigid separation between male and female sexuality, they were also aware – and concerned about – the possibility of interplay between the two. For example, one of the common claims about prostitutes was that their sexual excesses led to a 'masculinization', and specifically, an inability to have children.[44]

One can also cite the fascination with drag in contemporary culture: cross-dressing seems to provide certain insights into the artificial binary nature of gender. As Judith Butler argues, parodies of gender seem to show that gender itself is parodic, or is certainly a performance, and can be transcended or reversed.[45]

Clearly, then, single sex theories did not die out in the eighteenth century: rather, the notions of one sex and two sex collide with each other, negotiate with each other, and are used in different ways by different thinkers, writers, artists and performers.

What is most striking about this discussion is the clear inference that theories of sex and sexuality do not simply follow empirical discoveries in biology or psychology. This is a traditional view of science: that it pursues neutral and value-free goals, untrammelled by the personal prejudices of the experimenter or observer, that it 'discovers' the 'secrets of nature', which somehow exist 'out there'.

The constructivist view argues against this that science always operates within an ideological ambit, and selects its goals and its methods according to certain philosophical and political parameters. Thus one-sex and two-sex models alternate according to ideological ebbs and flows, and not scientific 'discoveries'. The 'truths' about sex are not 'discovered', but invented according to the political climate.

Clitoral/Vaginal Orgasm

Also relevant here is the debate about the relative merits of clitoral and vaginal orgasm, which has raged during the twentieth century, and which seems to hinge very much on the act of male penetration: the advocates of vaginal orgasm see female pleasure as contingent upon male thrust.[46] Clitoral orgasm has seemed very threatening then, since it dispenses with the thrusting penis, and indeed, often finds the man guilty of insufficient attention to the woman during intercourse, or argues that women can enjoy better sex without men and their penises. The clitoris itself therefore seems to be highly threatening to patriarchal models of sexuality, partly because its sole function (unlike the penis) is sexual pleasure. Patriarchal control of female sexuality has therefore frequently condemned female clitoral masturbation, and in some cultures has gone as far as removal of the clitoris.

What is interesting about this debate is that both sides are able to adduce various items of scientific knowledge to back them up. Those who support clitoral orgasm find their champion in Masters and Johnson, and their book *Human Sexual Response* (1962). They demonstrated in their laboratories that women were capable of many orgasms through stimulation of the clitoris, and also threw considerable doubt on the existence of the vaginal orgasm.

The chief advocate of the vaginal orgasm has been Freud, who saw it as one of the main hallmarks of a successful attainment of 'femininity'. In a sense, Freud argues that to be truly feminine, a woman must find penetration by a man's penis pleasurable. The frequent use of the clitoris in the adult woman is seen as regressive and infantile.

Of course, it seems relatively easy to expose the ideological currents concealed in Freud's 'scientific' examination of female sexuality, but then Freud is not alone in this: in fact it is impossible to 'do science' without an ideological bias. Thus there cannot be an 'objective' resolution to the controversy over clitoral/vaginal orgasm. In the end, none of us selects a theoretical position simply because it has better empirical backing, but also because it accords with our own beliefs. Thus, some feminists have speculated that women who enjoy intercourse with men are revelling in their own masochistic obliteration – but again, this is very much a loaded interpretation.[47]

Incest and Social Structure

One can approach incest from many different viewpoints: morally, psychologically, mythologically, genetically, and so on. Generally such approaches explain why human beings appear to have an abhorrence of incest, and have therefore created incest taboos. However, many commentators, including Freud, have noted that the intensity of the prohibition seems to correspond to the intensity of the desire. In fact, incestuous ties between parents and children, expressed sexually and emotionally, are very common. Consequently other factors are adduced as to why incest is forbidden: inbreeding produces mutant children, and so on.

However, a social construction approach can reverse this argumentation, and can claim that the incest taboo *helps to create society itself*, in that movement outwards from the immediate family of parents and siblings is guaranteed by the prohibition on sex or marriage with close kin. Instead of claiming that there is an 'instinctive' or innate rejection of incest in human beings, which leads to the setting up of incest taboos, the constructivist approach might suggest that the emotional and moral abhorrence is secondary to, and derived from, the social function of the taboo.

In particular, exogamous marriage guarantees a continual network of relationships with non-kin, and therefore a spreading outwards of the social group. The anthropologist I.M. Lewis argues that exogamy is found in cultures which are 'already strongly united and feel little need for further social integration'.[48] Furthermore, warfare and marriage become intimately connected through exogamy: brides are taken from other groups with whom the 'home group' are habitually engaged in warfare. Thus: 'the northern Somali nomads deliberately marry their daughters to men of distant lineages to establish alliances with hostile or potentially hostile groups'.[49] Thus one of the principles of exogamy is not the Christian 'love your enemy', but 'marry your enemy', or more accurately, 'marry your enemy's daughter'.

There are also forms of endogamous marriage, whereby marriage outside the group is forbidden, as seen for example in the Indian caste system, or in certain cultures where marriage with cousins is strongly favoured.[50] Endogamy therefore tends to reinforce the internal bonds within the group, and specifically keeps property at home. However, even endogamous marriage systems do not countenance marriage with close relatives: cousinship is the closest degree of kin permitted in such cultures.

This hypothesis explains why incest is viewed with such abhorrence in many cultures, for a denial of the taboo is in effect a denial of the core social structuring of the culture in question. One can argue therefore that the various moral, emotional and scientific arguments against incest are in fact rationalizations of a much deeper (and unconscious) social function. To reject the incest taboo is to reject society.

Incest provides an outstanding example of the deep unconscious connection between sexuality and social structure, and demonstrates how closely everyone is identified with the structured form of sexuality that exists in a particular culture.

The undoubted deleterious effects on children of incestuous sexual relationships with either parent brings up a fascinating question concerning social structure, sexuality and punishment. Do individuals suffer from incestuous relationships because incest is simply and inevitably a bad thing psychologically? Or is it because in patriarchal cultures incest must carry a heavy punishment if the incest taboos are to be preserved? The punishment is as much internal as external, in the form of massive guilt and self-hatred. But is this society's means of enforcement? It is striking that Freud argued that parent/child incest was not in itself harmful, just as eating human flesh was neither good nor bad, but that since human culture has given it such a heavy taboo, those who commit incest are subject to massive guilt.[51]

The whole complex issue of incest also provides a powerful argument against voluntarism – that one can 'choose' one's sexuality. Someone who is suffering from the effects of an incestuous tie cannot 'choose' to be free from it, except by much arduous and painful exploration and working through, which will probably take many years.

'Men' and 'Women'

One of the fascinating implications of social constructionism is that since all aspects of social existence are taken to be invented, the categories of 'men' and 'women' are themselves artificial. This might be seen as a position of extreme scepticism, but there are arguments in its favour.

The phenomenon of transsexualism shows that it is possible to literally deconstruct sex and gender categories. The male transsexual wishes to change his body to that of a female, as far as possible, since he feels irrevocably like a woman. Thus the transsexual illustrates a profound clash between the social definitions that are imposed on people according to their body shape, as against their own feelings and wishes. Of course a Foucaultian approach would insist that these feelings and wishes are themselves socially produced.

One can mention again in this context the phenomenon of drag – such a parody of gender indicates that gender is itself a parody. Or in the words of Judith Butler, 'gay to straight is not copy to original, but copy to copy'.[52]

The extreme deconstructive approach has been of interest to some lesbian theorists, who have argued that the category 'woman' is irrevocably defined in relation to 'man', and that being a lesbian enables the individual to escape both categories: 'a lesbian has to be something else: a not-woman, a not-man, a product of society, not a product of nature, for there is no nature in society'.[53] However, this statement by Monique Wittig ignores the fact that until recently biology was important in gender/sex distinctions: the fact that 'women' give birth to children, for example, has been very significant in many cultures for whom the production of large numbers of children was of great economic and social importance. Thus Elaine Pagels states, in relation to the Judaic emphasis on procreation, that 'Jewish communities had inherited their sexual customs from nomadic ancestors whose very survival depended upon reproduction, both among their herds of animals and among themselves'.[54]

The radical deconstruction of gender/sex categories may also prove distressing to many feminists and gay activists, since it is precisely the identities of being a woman, or being gay, or being a lesbian, that are important, and there is no desire to have them taken away. I shall return to this dilemma in Chapter 8, in a discussion of feminism, since there has been a fierce debate within feminism between those who tend towards an essentialist view of 'women' and 'female' virtues, and those who take a more socio-historical stance, and therefore reject all traditional categories of gender and sex.

Maternity

One of the driving forces in the Victorian study of sexuality and reproduction was the attempt to define the female body as an essentially maternal one, not concerned with sexual desire except as a means to an end – woman's reproductive destiny. In other words, the reproductive aspects of women's bodies were 'naturalized', treated as an inevitable part of nature, not as an ideological/political construct. The process of 'naturalization' in such cases was also one of mystification, since once a subject has been removed from the domains of political or social struggle and placed within the parameters of 'nature', it becomes unchallengeable. The fact that women might contest this can then be portrayed as 'perverse'. In fact, such contestation did occur over issues such as infanticide, about which the Victorians had frequent moral panics. For if maternalism was inherent in women, how could certain women defy it and kill their babies?[55]

Various solutions were found to this problem, but most Victorian commentators were careful to avoid a socio-political analysis that might argue that mothers killed their babies when they were desperately poor. That too was mystified: instead the 'moral depravity' of certain mothers was highlighted. But this had to be linked with class, since middle-class infanticide was generally glossed over: it was the depravity of the working class that lay at the root of child-murder.

Further problems arose with the issue of prostitution, again involving the hidden agenda of poverty and economic necessity, and the socially oppressed status of women. Instead, the Victorians preferred to conduct their discussions of prostitution on a more elevated and moral plane. Prostitutes had debased the exalted status of womanhood.

But of course societies are not monolithic, and Victorian society least of all. These issues were contested by feminists, by early socialists and other reformers.

It is striking how these issues are still alive in the late twentieth century. In Britain, the issue of 'single mothers' has been repeatedly raised, mostly by Conservative politicians, but also by Labour ones. The single mother has become an icon of working-class fecklessness, dependence on the state and sexual irresponsibility. Remedies have ranged from making fathers pay for their children to having the children taken into care or adopted. In America the 'Black woman on welfare' seems to fulfil the same slot for the right wing.

Conservative politicians in both Britain and America seem infuriated by the notion that such women are mothers without men – that is, they have refused to accept the patriarchal bargain: bear our children, and we'll pay the bills. Of course the right wing also hopes to whip up fear and anger amongst the middle classes that their money is being used to support layabouts.

What is striking about these contemporary controversies is how sexuality, class and gender are fused together in the image of the single mother. She is generally presented as living on a council estate – when in fact many single mothers are divorced middle class women. She is working-class, and hence ignorant of birth control, and breeds like a rabbit, thus tying in the notion of sexual irresponsibility.

Such political bouts of hysteria and 'outrage' demonstrate quite conclusively the mythological and ideological status of many 'facts' about sex.

Sexual Practices

It might be tempting to separate 'sex' – as a raw biological 'fact' – from 'sexuality', as a cultural construction. But this is too polarized. Clearly sex does have a biological basis – after all, human bodies are biological! But those bodies are enveloped in meaning; their postures and actions are not 'instinctive' or 'natural', but function as signs in a complex communication system.

We might say that descriptions of sex are political and psychological metaphors, but also that acts of sex are too. This is very clear within a psychotherapeutic context, where people discuss their sexual activities in some detail. The widely varying preferences that exist amongst men and women for certain sexual practices, even certain sexual organs, are not accidental or value-free choices, but are replete with symbolism and meaning. Thus some men are terrified of intercourse with the woman on top; yet there are others for whom it is the preferred form of sexual activity. Masturbation is not simply a solitary pleasure, but often signifies to the masturbator quite complex meanings: for example, one of my male clients would masturbate the minute his wife had left the house. Eventually he was able to see how the act of masturbation summarized a cluster of feelings and ideas: that he was lonely, felt abandoned, but also that he was relieved to be alone, and glad to reclaim his own body, which somehow seemed to be stolen from him by women.

Contemporary Hollywood films show a fascinating use of sex acts as an emotional and political language: for example, the film *Basic Instinct* (1992) describes an intense power struggle between men and women very much in terms of sexual position during intercourse. Frequently in this film the woman is shown on top of the man, and she also often ties his hands to the bedstead. The film begins with this image, and the woman kills the man with a knife.

The major act of intercourse in the film is portrayed very much as a duel with many reciprocal actions. The man sucks the woman's breast; has oral sex with her, and then intercourse. Then the woman sucks the man's breast; has oral sex with him and gets on top during intercourse. There is a contest here!

These images therefore seem to articulate a male sense of rage against feminism: if women are handed too much power, they become dangerous psychopaths. One scene of intercourse in the film reinforces this interpretation: the enraged detective has sex with his girlfriend violently and from the rear. She complains to him about his brutal treatment – in fact, he made love to her in this way as an act of revenge.

The most celebrated scene in *Basic Instinct* shows the main female character (played by Sharon Stone) exposing her genitals to a group of detectives, who are questioning her. She taunts them provocatively during the interview: 'I have nothing to hide'; 'I like hands and fingers'; 'have you ever fucked on cocaine, Nick?' This scene is particularly interesting since it became the main image associated with the film. Yet its meaning seems ambiguous: does it signify female sexual liberation, or does it perpetuate an image of the female body observed by men?[56]

Sex acts themselves therefore act as a 'signifying system', a set of signs by means of which human beings communicate to each other. What is remarkable is that through sex we are able to communicate about non-sexual matters, such as power, hatred envy, domination, and so on.

Theorization

It is interesting to apply social constructionist theory to theory itself – by which I mean the frenzy of theorization that has gone on in relation to gender and sexuality since the 1970s. What is its significance?

In part, we can refer to the break-up of old paradigms concerning sex and gender, particularly the moral paradigm of Christianity. New social forces, particularly feminism and the gay movement, have turned upside down many traditional ideas, and have therefore been forced to theorize intensely about the nature of gender and sexuality. The process of 'deconstruction' demands new theoretical underpinnings.

At a more mundane level, it can be argued that academic theorizing is a capitalist industry like any other: people obtain jobs by specializing in it, and a whole subculture grows up around 'gender studies'.

Does this indicate that theorization is the preserve of an affluent and leisured middle class? That would be a rather harsh judgement maybe, but it should serve as a reminder that theories are not neutral in the socio-political arena, but often serve the interests of one particular group. This issue has come up very sharply within feminism, since White middle-class feminists have sometimes found their ideas are not all that relevant or welcome to non-White working-class or peasant women.[57]

Another aspect of theorization that interests me is the control aspect. Sexuality is a very frightening phenomenon for many people, precisely because it is something out of control: it is spontaneous and climactic. Thus, one cannot control who or what turns one on; one cannot feel sexually excited simply through will-power; orgasms are famously out of control experiences – this is why they are considered so ecstatic, but also so terrifying.

Most human cultures seem to devise various ways of controlling sexuality, and therefore lessening the anxiety it provokes. For example, stipulations as to the 'perversity' of certain desires and acts form a tight boundary around the permissible forms of sex, and exclude the impermissible. Guilt, shame and embarrassment are emotions that serve to control our own sexual feelings; and of course repression itself is a key mechanism.

But *theorization itself* can be seen as a form of control of sex. By defining and describing various sexualities, one might have the illusion that one has somehow 'captured' or 'tamed' them, or reduced their problematical status. In other words, theorization gives a sense of mastery.

I am not saying that control is the only function of theorization – for one thing, theorizing about sex is also quite sexy! – but it surely plays a part. I have already referred to Jung's intuition about Freud – that he was so disturbed by sexuality that he had to defend the notion of sexual aetiology against all comers, and in the process adopted a quasi-religious attitude to sex: it was sacred, untouchable, unquestionable.

Of course arguably the whole of science, philosophy, and the humanities are attempts to 'control' human existence by providing descriptions and explanations. There is nothing malign in this process, unless it gets out of hand, but it is arguable that control by means of theorization is one of the chief mechanisms of patriarchy itself.

SUMMARY

Social constructionism provides a keen scalpel with which many traditional and unchallenged ideas can be dissected. Foucault demonstrated this brilliantly in the first volume of his *History of Sexuality*: one can almost sense his enjoyment as, one by one, he demolishes many of the accepted shibboleths concerning sex and sexuality. In particular, Foucault demonstrates that the notion of 'repression' – the idea that post-Renaissance culture began to conceal sexual desires, feelings and representations is only a partial truth, and that in fact 'repression' went hand in hand with an 'intensification' of sex.

Foucault also refers to the 'production of sexuality', the idea that sexuality is not 'discovered' as some inert entity existing in nature, but is actively constructed by the frenzy of discourse which has surrounded sex during the last two centuries. It is this 'speaking of sex' which constitutes sexuality. This idea throws a fascinating light on Freudian thought, for example, for instead of assuming that Freud made 'discoveries' about a pre-existing human 'sexuality', it can be argued that Freud set about creating a new field of theory and practice, and actually invents a new human activity – the self-conscious scrutiny of one's sexuality as a key to one's identity. In this process, 'sexuality' is reified as an apparently solid and permanent entity.

It strikes me that Foucault has offered a partial solution to the puzzlement that often surrounds the concept of 'sexuality', which in comparison with the word 'sex', seems to denote something very abstract, even artificial. 'My' sexuality is in fact a product of my self-consciousness: it is my own sexual feelings, thoughts and acts as I think about them and speak about them. Hence it would be quite odd to suggest that animals – which are undoubtedly sexual beings – have a 'sexuality', since we tend to assume, wrongly or rightly, that animals are entirely unconscious beings. That is, they do not 'know' that they are sexual, and therefore cannot think and speak about sex.

Furthermore, the notion of 'speaking of sex' is rooted in history. It is possible to trace back the origins of this discourse to a certain period in the Enlightenment, and also to argue that although the Greeks and Romans, and medieval philosophers, often referred to sexual desire and sexual practices, they did not really develop such a notion of sexuality.

One can make specific criticisms of Foucault's own approach – as I have pointed out, his notion of power seems very fuzzy, and specifically rejects any quasi-Marxist attempt to link social control to class politics, and also seems to argue against the feminist critique of patriarchy as the institutionalized rule of men over women.

A more general critique of social constructionism might point to its corrosive ability to dissolve all categories, including the categories 'men' and 'women'. However, this must involve radical activists in a contradiction, for there is nothing left to defend or advance. No identity can be sustained, since all identities are in the end illusory, or symbols of oppressive power practices.[58] But if everything is deconstructed, how do individuals cope amidst a chaos of floating signifiers, signs that instantly dissolve? This strikes me as an impossibility, or possible only as an intellectual exercise.

7 Sexuality, Spirituality and Alienation

Many approaches to sexuality tend to see sex as *appetitive*, that is, as some kind of bodily need or craving. Within such models, sex and sexuality are seen very much in materialist, or, one might even say, mechanistic, terms. For example, within Christianity, sex is often seen as part of the wretched life of the body, acting as a prison to the human soul, which yearns to take flight.

Within the Freudian paradigm, sexuality is explicitly defined in terms of the 'sexual instincts', derived from the body, and impinging on the mind. Although Freud constructed a psychological model of sexuality, his researches took place very much within the biological framework which dominated the nineteenth century approach to sexuality, and he never abandoned his wish to place psychology upon a firm biological basis.

The rise of sexology in the late nineteenth century was seen as the construction of a 'science of sex', and commonly used biological or behaviourist ideas.[1] For many sexologists, the orgasm tends to be seen as a 'goal' to be attained, and in cases of sexual dysfunction can be achieved through improvements in sexual technique.

These approaches can be criticized therefore, first, for being so mechanistic, and second, for a certain reductive parochialism or ethnocentricity, since they tend to ignore those sexual practices and theories in non-Western cultures which have seen sex much more as a transcendental or spiritual exercise, for example the tantric tradition within Hinduism. Such approaches seem at odds with the Western, Christian approach, which has counterpoised sexuality and spirituality. However, it is also possible that part of Christianity's hostility to sex has stemmed from a fear of a powerful rival, an alternative means of becoming one with life, one with the universe, and even one with God.

CHRISTIAN EROTICISM

Yet the connection between sexuality and spirituality is not unknown in Western culture. For example, Christian mysticism contains a fascinating strain of quasi-erotic thought and feeling, which seems to betray deep-going and unconscious links between sexual experience and spirituality. That this is an ancient connection can be seen in the language of the biblical Song of Songs, whose erotic language has often been interpreted symbolically as a description of the relation between a people and their God, or the relationship between an individual and his soul.

A very famous example of 'erotic spirituality' can be found in Teresa of Avila's spiritual autobiography, in those sections which describe certain mystical experiences, which she calls the state of 'union', defined simply enough as 'two separate things becoming one', in this case the human being and God.[2] Her own experiences seem to have attained a great intensity, described graphically and most famously in the 'penetration' passage, illustrated so superbly by Bernini's baroque statue:

> Beside me, on the left hand, appeared an angel in bodily form, such as I am not in the habit of seeing except very rarely. Though I often have visions of angels, I do not see them ... He was not tall but short, and very beautiful; and his face was so aflame that he appeared to be one of the highest ranks of angels, who seem to be all on fire ... In his hands I saw a golden spear, and at the iron tip there appeared to be a point of fire. This he plunged into my heart several times so that it penetrated to my entrails. When he pulled it out, I felt that he took them with it, and left me utterly consumed by the great love of God. The pain was so severe that it made me utter several moans. The sweetness caused by this intense pain is so extreme that one cannot possibly wish it to cease, nor is one's soul then content with anything but God. This is not a physical, but a spiritual pain, though the body has some share in it – even a considerable share. So gentle is this wooing which takes place between God and the soul that if anyone thinks I am lying, I pray God, in His goodness, to grant him some experience of it.[3]

Teresa's experiences are not unique within Christianity: for example, other female mystics, such as the thirteenth century Mechtild von Magdeburg, and the Flemish mystic Hadewijch of Antwerp, also described union with God very much in sexual terms.[4]

An example from English poetry can be found in the writings of Richard Crashaw, the seventeenth century 'metaphysical' poet, whose religious speculations are both lurid and highly eroticized. Thus his 'divine epigram' on the Virgin Mary:

> Suppose he had been Tabled at thy teats,
> Thy hunger feels not what he eats:
> He'll have his Teat ere long (a bloody one)
> The Mother then must suck the Son.[5]

Significantly, Crashaw wrote several long poems about St Teresa, and seems to exult in her mingling of pleasure and pain:

> How kindly will thy gentle Heart
> Kiss the sweetly-killing Dart!
> And close in his embraces keep
> Those delicious Wounds that weep
> Balsam to heal themselves with.[6]

Although extravagant, such imagery is characteristic of the 'metaphysical' style, which brought together associations normally seen as divergent. The poet John Donne is of great interest in this context, since he used religious imagery in his love poetry, and erotic imagery in his religious poems.

SEXUALITY AND TRANSCENDENCE

One's approach to Teresa's experiences, and her description of them, depends very much on one's theoretical position. A Freudian approach would tend to view them as sexual experiences couched in, and denied through, religious language, following Freud's adumbration that 'religious ideas ... are illusions, fulfilments of the oldest, strongest and most urgent wishes of mankind'.[7] Within such a model, the religious framework for Teresa's ecstatic experiences is seen ultimately as a denial of their erotic roots.

On the other hand, a more sympathetic approach, such as that of Carl Jung, would grant greater validity to such experiences as erotic/spiritual events, and might suggest that sexuality and spirituality are not all that separate, and specifically that sexual orgasm can be experienced as a quasi-religious experience. Thus, the idea of sexual orgasm taking place during religious rituals such as the Christian communion is not unfamiliar to psychotherapists, and suggests that sexual excitement and release cannot be simply defined in physiological terms.

In fact, this was one of the important issues over which Freud and Jung became estranged, and Jung argued, in relation to this split, that

Freud was fascinated and gripped by the theme of sexuality as if it were a religious dogma:

> It is a widespread error to imagine that I do not see the value of sexuality. On the contrary, it plays a large part in my psychology as an essential – though not the sole – expression of psychic wholeness. But my main concern has been to investigate, over and above its personal significance and biological function, *its spiritual aspect and its numinous meaning, and thus to explain what Freud was so fascinated by but was unable to grasp* ... Sexuality is of the greatest importance as the expression of the chthonic spirit. That spirit is the 'other side of God', the dark side of the God-image [added emphasis].[8]

Here Jung aims a telling blow at Freud, for Freud *physicalized* sex, and described it very much in terms of tension and relief. Freud also expressed his revulsion at the 'foul mud of the occult', which Jung was drawn to irresistibly. Freud's attitude could be described as a type of philosophical ethnocentricity: a predilection for rationality and science over 'superstition', religion and spirituality, which Freud saw as outmoded illusions, yet which, according to Jung, he was secretly fascinated by.

Freud therefore treats sex in an austere manner, and neglects sexual *passion*, and focuses on the sexual 'instincts' and the drive to 'detensioning'. However, it is the passion present in sexual desire and sexual relationships that often overwhelms people and seems to act like a drug. How can this passion be described?

Here we find an interesting connection with spiritual passion ('consumed by ... great love' in Teresa's words), which aims to overcome feelings of separation and alienation from a universal Other, and aims to merge with that Other. One might suggest therefore that in this respect sexual and spiritual passion have the same roots: the drive to overcome one's own selfhood and immerse oneself in an experience that is transcendent.

The idea of sexual and spiritual ecstasy therefore brings us back to notions of the self, and specifically, the idea that the self is intrinsically fragmented and isolated, and therefore yearns for completion in another. Such ideas have various provenances: for example, one can cite again the Lacanian notion of 'lack' which I discussed briefly in Chapter 5. In fact, Lacan refers to Teresa's autobiography, and Bernini's statue of her in a rapturous pose: 'there can be no doubt that she's coming', Lacan laconically comments. Lacan also comments caustically on those theorists who have 'attempted to derive her jouissance from fucking'.[9] In this sense, Lacan is quite sympathetic to the notion that Teresa is experiencing a genuine spiritual 'overflow' or jouissance.

But the notion of the fragmented and isolated self seeking transcendence has a more ancient genealogy. For example, similar ideas were advanced within the very sophisticated psychology developed within Buddhism. Buddha argued that craving was endemic to the self, that the search of the I is the search for a home in a lonely universe. But this distinction – between I and universe, or I and not-I – is itself constituted by the assertion of I. By becoming an I, I have inevitably separated myself from the rest of reality, which becomes alien and oppressive to me:

> It is precisely this – the dichotomy of its subject/object structure – which constitutes the inherent existential ambiguity, conflict, and indeed, contradictoriness of the ego in ego-consciousness. Bifurcated and disjointed in its unity, it is delimited by, but cannot be sustained or fulfilled in, itself. Isolated and excluded in relatedness, it is restricted to yet shut off from, a world in which and to which it belongs.[10]

This compels the lonely I to search for restitution. This search takes many forms – religious, spiritual, sexual, narcotic, alcoholic and so on – and there are also many ways of masking it or dulling it – including religion and sex!

Hamlet's soliloquy – 'To be or not to be' – expresses these ideas perfectly, for the 'to be' is fraught with anguish and struggle, and one therefore yearns for the 'not to be' – ' 'Tis a consummation devoutly to be wished'. Being born is the beginning of a long separation, which lasts until death, but sex seems to provide a temporary escape from selfhood and isolation.

THE SEARCH FOR UNION

Let me recap this argument. So far from seeing sex and spirituality as opposites, it is arguable that they are intimately connected, and that the mechanical treatment of sex, its *despiritualization*, is part of the contemporary human alienation.

I would like to suggest the following rather simplistic framework, which could be described as a blend of Jungian, Lacanian and Buddhist ideas: the sexual 'drive' is not simply a physiological one, nor simply a drive for pleasure or gratification, but also involves the craving for union with another being, and for an abandonment of the ego. This craving can be seen both as a retrospective one – that is, a craving to return to a state of infantile fusion with mother's body or father's body – and also as a basic (and universal) need within human experience.

The psychoanalyst Christopher Bollas, in his book *The Shadow of the Object*, has some remarkably pregnant remarks to make about the relationship between early experience and the experience of the spiritual. He describes 'the aesthetic moment', which is

> an evocative resurrection of an early ego condition often brought about by a sudden and uncanny rapport with an object, a moment when the subject is captured in an intense illusion of being selected by the environment for some deeply reverential experience.[11]

Such experiences can be aroused by nature, by art objects, by sex, or indeed by any deeply felt interaction with the environment. Furthermore, Bollas argues that the reduction of such spiritual experience to a substratum of infantile memory, 'always strikes us as somehow an insult to the integrity of uncanny experience, as *the sacred precedes the maternal*' [added emphasis].[12]

These remarks suggest that 'spiritual' experience in fact occurs at a very early age, when the human infant becomes aware of the environment having a transformative effect on itself, changing its state radically, say from a sense of incompleteness to one of completeness. A very intense link is thereby formed between the self and the other, and the power of the other is revealed as potentially a beatific one. The split between subject and object – which haunts human beings during their adult lives – can be healed and overcome temporarily.

Bollas's analysis is of great interest, since he explains spiritual experience without reducing it or denigrating it, whereas Freud himself tended to denounce spiritual experience simply as an illusion. However, perhaps this indicates Freud's own personal blind spot towards spirituality, and at the same time, perhaps, his obsession with it: the rift with Jung revealed how much intense passion was tied up in these matters for both men.

In this light, the rather nebulous term 'spiritual' can be defined as some kind of supra-ego experience, a dissolution of normal ego-identity, and its replacement by a deeper or wider sense of self, which includes others, or includes the natural environment. The term 'spiritual' should not be confused with the notion of the 'religious', which refers much more to an institutionalized kind of experience, placed within a certain denominational register.

Further evidence concerning strong human desires for transcendence can be found in the various mind-altering procedures that exist in many human cultures, for example, the use of drugs such as alcohol, mescaline, heroin, cannabis, and so on, the use of music and dance, and also the various kinds of ritual practice, which bring about states of *participation mystique*. All of these techniques lead to an expansion of the self, or a fusion of the self with other beings or things in the environment, or even a total abandonment of the self.

Further evidence for the link between sexuality and the transpersonal can be found in mythology, where we find gods and goddesses of love who are not simply lustful or spiritual, but both. This is true of the Greek Aphrodite, who has many manifestations – as a goddess of pure love, of married love and of lustfulness, in which form she was the patron of prostitutes. The same blend can be found in the temple prostitution found in India, and in the Babylonian goddess Ishtar, who is not only the goddess of love but also of war. Here there is some evidence that functions that were to become highly differentiated in the modern Western world could be accepted as parts of a whole in the ancient world, including ideal love, sexuality and aggression.[13]

Perhaps those desert monks who fled society, only to find themselves persecuted by a barrage of sexual fantasy, had unwittingly stumbled across the deep connection between sex and spirituality. This was something that their world-view could not encompass, although other religious and spiritual traditions, such as the tantric movement in Hinduism, could.

THERE IS THIS, JUST THIS

But is there concrete evidence as to the connection between sexual and spiritual experience? Many people seem to find sexual pleasure to be so intense that they 'forget themselves', or they find that sexual union with their partner is so powerful, that the subject–object split dissolves to some extent. It is difficult to find or record first-hand accounts of such experiences, but contemporary fiction is full of them. Let me give as an example the following very graphic description of sex in Susan Fromberg Schaeffer's novel *The Madness of a Seduced Woman*:

I reached down and took his organ in my hand and began caressing it. My fingers traced its little ridges and folds; they burrowed in the fig-shaped testicles until I felt them flatten and harden under my hand. I ran my hand along the little line of fur that rose from his groin to his navel, and, just as I had forgotten what was pressing against my body, I felt the hot flesh entering mine. I felt Frank begin to move slowly inside me, and I felt the doors to my body open. I was home in my own skin. He had been separated from me for so long, and now he was back. I felt my body arching to meet his in a way that was familiar but new in its violence. A warm flush was spreading through my groin, up into my stomach, down into my thighs. And then Frank began pushing in deeper and I wanted to cry out against the pain, but my body rose to meet his, and I heard a wolfish voice, crying, and I realized that it was my voice crying out in pure pleasure and triumph.[14]

This passage eloquently describes the great sexual passion that can grip human beings, a passion that is not simply a result of physical stimulation, but arises from the utter intimacy with another, the sense of being inside each other, and lost in each other. 'My body rose to meet his' is bald enough, but encompasses a profound meeting, not just of bodies, but of selves, and also a return to oneself: 'I was home in my own skin.' The separation from another, followed by the blissful reunion, is equated with the woman's return to her own sense of self.

A novel which contains many eloquent descriptions of love-making is Brian Moore's *The Doctor's Wife*, in which a woman's life is transformed by her experience of sex with a younger man:

He put his hand out and ran the tips of his fingers over her nipples, which stood up hard. She began to undo his trousers, then pulled them down over his hips, kneeling to pull down his shorts, taking his stiff penis in her hands, watching it as he reared up over her. He lifted her up, entering her, moving in her, she beginning to move with him, so excited she felt she could come at once, she could hardly stand it, it was so great, oh, God, she cried to herself, let this go on, let it go on.[15]

It is striking how often in fiction characters cry out 'Oh God' at the moment of sexual climax: the intensity of the experience seems to make people seek religious words to express the ineffable. Elsewhere in this novel, the female character refers to the 'one-pointedness' of sexual orgasm: 'there is no past, there is this, just this'.[16] Such language is very similar to that used by mystics in describing spiritual experience, as for example, the German mystic Meister Eckhart: 'time and space are fragments, whereas God is one!' He also states: 'our whole perfection and blessing depends on our stepping across or beyond the estate of creaturehood, time and Being, and on getting at last the Cause that has no cause'.[17] That to me sounds quite close to the 'ecstatic' experiences that some people seem to have during sex.

One of the most famous passages of English prose tries to convey the flow of sexual experience through the dissolution of normal punctuation and sentence structure, as a woman lies in bed, presumably masturbating and allowing her consciousness to stream out:

> He kissed me under the Moorish wall and I thought well as well him as another and then I asked him with my eyes to ask again yes and then he asked me would I yes to say yes my mountain flower and first I put my arm around him yes and drew him down to me so he could feel my breasts all perfume yes and his heart was going like mad and yes I said yes I will Yes.[18]

In this stunning passage from Joyce's *Ulysses*, the word 'yes' is used as a rhythmical mark, suggesting the rhythmic pulse of sexual excitement, building up to the climactic final 'Yes', which is also an affirmation of life.

This is the potentially overwhelming power of sexual intimacy, a meeting place that seems absolute, not dependent on time or space or any form of ratiocination or will-power. It is not surprising that it arouses great craving in people, nor that so-called 'sex addicts' present themselves to therapists and analysts. Sex takes us to a place which seems like the source of being itself, where all contradictions are temporarily overcome. This can be seen as both a return to an infantile state, but also, if one accepts the findings of mystics in different religions, as touching upon a basic level of supra-consciousness. Or in Jungian terms, this is the experience of the Self, the centre of the psyche, which Jung saw as the source of the God-image found in many cultures.

To put it crudely, sex can make us feel god-like. Perhaps it is not surprising then that Christianity has been so suspicious about sex: this may stem from a fear of these transcendental qualities found in sexual experience, which were exploited in pagan religions, which might use sexual rituals to bring about a sense of being one with the deity.

The god-like qualities of sex can also be highly dangerous for human beings, for we can feel possessed by them, and possessed by great desire, so much so that ordinary life and its details seem to fade into irrelevance. I have worked with quite a number of people in therapy who have experienced a *coup de foudre*, and while it is clearly a momentous and overwhelming event, it can also wreck people's lives.

It is interesting to compare the passage by Teresa of Avila with the fictional passages I have just cited: the first describes an intense spiritual experience in erotic terms, the second describes sexual experiences in quasi-religious terms. But this interchange between the erotic and the spiritual is a common one, and can be found running through European literature like a thread.

SEX AND THE BLENDING OF CATEGORIES

The notion of 'transcendence' indicates that intense sexual pleasure has the ability to 'blend' categories which normally seem permanent and watertight. For example, so far from reinforcing gender stereotypes, sexual experience is able to dissolve them. 'Masculinity' and 'femininity', 'active' and 'passive', 'penetrative' and 'receptive' – these oppositions can easily melt in the heat of sex. Subject and object themselves become fragile and porous, and merge with each other. Isn't this one of the reasons that sex with a partner is so frightening to so many people, and masturbation seems a safer bet?

Sex promises a temporary nirvana where all distinctions are lost, where time itself is transcended. Thus sexual pleasure takes us into all kinds of omnipotent fantasies, as well as fantasies of utter passivity or helplessness.

It strikes me that this is one of the reasons why many men find sex difficult in so many ways – in the form of impotence, premature ejaculation, and so on: sex is a terrifying territory, where normal forms of control will not work.

It is quite striking how in psychotherapeutic work with people one often meets with a confusion between spiritual, emotional and sexual yearning. A common example of this is the situation when people meet someone whom they describe as a 'soul-mate'. This can be a very intense experience, sweeping all doubts and all thoughts about practicality away with it. But such relationships can take different forms. One route leads towards sexual passion, another towards a kind of 'soul-friendship'. But I have noticed that the first route frequently proves disastrous, and the two people often grow to hate each other. The second route seems to work much better.

What is going on here? My sense is that the experience of the 'soulmate' is an emotional and spiritual experience of kinship, close identity, and even fusion. This is the kind of love that genuinely seems to involve all the clichés about romantic love: a sense of oneness, timelessness and a breath-taking transformation of one's life-experience. But the translation of this into sexual love does not always prove a wise step; and people in such a state often find that it is impossible to live together.

In general, it is striking how many people seem to use sex to achieve experiences of openness and oneness with life. No doubt sex does bring about such feelings, but perhaps it is also true that in Western culture sex is being made to carry a heavy weight in this respect. Thus some people who have had an intense or very active sex-life can experience a kind of burn-out later in life, for sex is being asked to achieve too much.

So often in therapy one finds that sexual 'problems' are not problems to do with physical sexual technique but problems to do with being intimate with someone. Barriers come up between people – especially partners who have lived together for some time – that prevent them coming together sexually. For example, I have found the following factors to be important in this respect: fear of commitment, fear of aggression in oneself, fear of pleasure with another person, fear of being seen, and so on. But perhaps the root of all these fears is the basic fear of being close to another human being, something that brings up for many people ancient (infantile) issues to do with being suffocated or abandoned.

The other side of these problems is that they are often not experienced with strangers or in relatively new relationships. It is tempting therefore to argue that long-term relationships are simply 'boring' and kill off sexual pleasure. This is untrue; what happens is that in long-term relationships our deepest fears and barriers begin to surface, and what seems to be an idyllic relationship can become stormy or difficult. Some people therefore feel compelled to find new sexual partners, in order to keep the experience fresh and untainted by emotional difficulties.

Let me cite a brief example of how sexuality is closely linked with non-sexual issues. Jim was a middle-aged artist, who had lived with the same woman for fifteen years. They had enjoyed a good sex life until about two years previously, at which time their sexual contact began to diminish and eventually ceased altogether.

Jim and I spent some time working over the many factors affecting his identity, his sense of himself, and his sexual self-image. He didn't seem to be showing any fear of commitment or fear of intimacy – he seemed to have worked through these successfully in the early years of the relationship. However, Jim began to talk about something else. He had been a relatively unsuccessful artist for most of his life, but three years previously he had arranged an exhibition of his work in a gallery, which had been successful, and had brought him into contact with several dealers and gallery-owners who were keen on his work. In short, after spending twenty years struggling as an artist, and living in relative poverty, Jim suddenly found he was becoming quite widely known, and his income began to rise.

Eventually, after a long period of examination of all these issues, it became clear that Jim's sexual problems were tied up with his new success. He was both frightened and deeply guilty about this, and his fear and guilt counter-attacked him, tried to deflate him, and amongst other things, took away his sexual potency. He was terrified of his creative potency, and this fear 'leaked' into the sexual field.

SUBLIMATION AND ALIENATION

Within psychoanalysis, the concept of sublimation has been adduced to explain such connections between sexuality and non-sexual processes. In fact, Freud made sublimation a key to his understanding of the relationship between sexuality, repression and civilization. Basically, he argued that civilization could not permit the spontaneous satisfaction of sexual drives, but required their repression. However, sublimation – a rechannelling of sexual drives – provides an alternative solution, since the sexual drive is expressed through it, as for example, in creativity of some kind or other.[19]

One of the problems with the Freudian notion of sublimation is that it amounts to a formidable reductionism. Logically, all manner of creative processes can be described as sublimated sexual energy. For example, Melanie Klein cites children's interest in history or geography as symbolic references to parental sex.[20]

Unease with such reductive interpretations led Jung to posit a libido, a psychic energy, that was not sexual, but could be expressed sexually. The Freudian notion of sublimation is no longer needed, since the life force – the Jungian libido – can be expressed in innumerable ways, none of which is claimed to be basic to the others.[21]

Contemporary psychotherapy has also discovered the existence of 'sex addiction', which seems to argue, not for the expression of sexual drives in non-sexual ways (sublimation), but the reverse: that is, the eroticization of various feelings and needs. Thus, I have encountered a number of people, who could be described as 'sex addicts', whose root problem was by no means sexual, but flowed from a deep sense of deprivation and abandonment. Sex was one way in which such painful feelings could be anaesthetized and dispelled, for during sex one might feel cherished, adored, desired, and so on. Unfortunately, as with all narcotics, such experiences are short-lived, and have to be continually repeated.

Thus to my mind there is a *neurotic eroticization* which is fairly common in our culture – indeed, one could argue that the whole culture is possessed by it. Freud's particular relationship between sexuality and human motivation can therefore be reversed, since the massive presence of sexual acting out or sexual symbolism in our culture suggests, not the ubiquity of the sexual drives, but the mass eroticization produced by an alienated civilization.

To some extent this is turning Freud upside down, and represents a kind of challenge to his whole sexual theory. Specifically, it throws doubt on his claim that neurosis has a sexual aetiology. Rather, one can argue that neurosis often has a sexual expression! Sex is the great aspirin or tranquillizer for many people.

CELIBACY

Celibacy is something else with which I have been concerned professionally for a number of years, having worked with certain couples and individuals who spontaneously became celibate, that is, no longer felt interested in sex. This phenomenon is very difficult to deal with in a psychotherapeutic context, since one has to determine if in fact one is dealing with an antipathy to or anxiety about sex, in other words, a neurotic celibacy. I am talking about something quite different, which emerges spontaneously, and is not accompanied by any distaste for sex at all. In fact, I have seen it develop in people who had had active and enjoyable sex lives previously.

One must also distinguish this form of celibacy from an imposed one, whether for religious, moral or other reasons. The Zen teacher Philip Kapleau has an interesting description of 'voluntary celibacy':

> There's a simple test. If the renunciation comes easily, almost inevitably – which is to say without compulsion and with little

doubt or trepidation – it's fairly safe to assume that one's karma has matured in regard to sex and that one is ready for celibacy.[22]

Actually I disagree with certain elements of this formulation. In my experience, celibate people do experience trepidation, as they fear being condemned or misinterpreted by other people. None the less, I am sure Kapleau is broadly right, in that there is a celibacy which is very easy and natural, and just feels right for the individuals concerned.

For the purposes of this chapter, I am interested in celibacy as evidence for the correlation between sexuality and spirituality. The celibate person is still a sexual one, but does not have intercourse or other sexual acts. The celibate couple still have a sexual relationship, but do not physically enact it.

This kind of non-neurotic celibacy raises many questions about sexuality. How can someone get to a point where sex is no longer very interesting, or if you like, where the sex drive no longer 'drives'? One might cynically argue that this is a rationalization of the waning of sexuality in middle and old age – and certainly, celibacy tends to develop in this way in people over forty. This would be a rather reductive view – celibacy as physiological exhaustion! – and of course many people over forty continue to have an active interest in sex.

Kapleau has some further interesting comments in relation to celibate couples:

> There are many couples who eventually reach a point in their relationship in which they transcend sexuality in the narrow sense of intercourse and continue to have a rich life together. The highest love is grounded not in sexuality but in right knowledge of the interrelationship of all existence.[23]

I feel unhappy with the use of words such as 'highest' here: I don't see that a celibate relationship is 'better', 'higher' or 'more spiritual' than a sexually active one, but apart from that, I think Kapleau is right. I have met couples who had developed in this way, and their relationship felt very strong and loving to outsiders – although also puzzling.

Celibacy has become rather fashionable in the 1990s, but I don't see it as an option that one can choose. Rather, it chooses you! In other words, in the form I am describing it, it is an entirely spontaneous, indeed unconscious, development, often connected with the spiritual development of the individual or couple.

It is interesting to match this concept of celibacy against various models of sexuality. For example, can Freudian psychology accept a celibacy that is not a denial of sex? I have certainly met Freudian therapists who could and did, but I am not sure whether Freud would have. On the other hand, there is little doubt that celibacy would make perfect sense to Jung, who tended to stress the spiritual roots of sexuality.

Where Freud might say that, for the celibate individual, the sexual need has been 'sublimated' into spirituality, I would tend to reverse this: the spiritual need has been realized, and no longer needs to be expressed through sex. I see the spontaneously celibate as having discovered their spiritual roots, their spiritual purpose: sex is therefore no longer required as a 'sublimation'.

This is a rather provocative reversal of Freudian doctrine, but I have worked with a sufficient number of people in whom this development has happened to find it convincing. As one man said to me: 'Sex used to be my alpha and omega, but then I discovered something else in my life which dwarfed it, and transcended it'.

That for me is a fair summary of one kind of celibacy, and indicates the deep connections between sexuality and the inner life of the individual.

Of course, as I indicated earlier, this kind of celibacy must be distinguished from the situation in which people have renounced the body out of an unconscious distaste or fear, and cling to spirituality as a defence against sexuality.

FREUD/JUNG

I have already referred to the split between Freud and Jung, part of which was in relation to sexuality. Whereas Freud tended to see sex as a question of instinctual drives which demanded relief in the physiological sense, Jung saw sex in a much more symbolic way as the search for wholeness and union with another. Jung also desexualized the libido and argued that there was a 'life energy' which was manifest in many expressive areas, such as creativity and spirituality. This was anathema to Freud, who had beseeched Jung to preserve the 'bulwark of sexuality' against the 'occult'.[24] Looking back, it seems clear that the split was inevitable, since their views were incompatible, and in a sense each one could only develop fully by separating from the other.

But to some extent the split is being healed in contemporary psychotherapy. Psychoanalysis and analytical psychology are much more in dialogue these days: Jungians frequently cite Freud in their publications, and vice versa. This leads me to suggest that the Freud/Jung split over sexuality is indicative of two quite distinct approaches to sex, both of which are valuable and indeed essential in any overall understanding of it. Thus whilst perhaps it was once tempting to 'take sides' in the Freud/Jung debate, and to insist that one was correct and the other wrong, depending on one's own viewpoint, today it can be seen that both sides are correct, and need not form an absolute antithesis. Rather, we can speak of a 'tension of opposites', to use a Jungian phrase: such tensions can be highly creative as well as internecine.

If we bring the Freudian and Jungian views of sex into contact with each other, we are presented with human sexuality as a spectrum: at one extreme, it is a very physical appetite that human beings fulfil with great satisfaction; at the other extreme, it marks a spiritual transcendence, a recovery of wholeness, a reunion of lost fragments. And there are a whole number of positions in between those two extremes. Thus sex has a magical potency, for it seems to heal both body and soul simultaneously. Indeed, it seems to heal the split between body and soul, so that in the height of sexual pleasure or sexual intimacy with another, I am one. I am not split into intellect, body, emotions, spirit and so on, but I exist on a plane of self-existence, where I speak with one voice through my body and my emotions and my thoughts, and where I exist in a state of harmony with the other person.

Thus instead of either/or, we can move towards a position of both/and. Sex as physical gratification, and sex as spiritual transcendence: these two formulations seem so far apart, yet they need not be. The image of the lotus flower in Buddhism springs to mind: for its roots are in the mud, while its flower blooms in the air. Thus the lotus is a perfect symbol of the unification of existence that Buddhism aims at. It may seem fanciful to describe human sexuality in similar terms, yet it also seems perfectly apt. Sexual ecstasy seems at times to embrace the whole of human aspiration, yet also can be experienced in a very sensuous way that is distinctly unspiritual.

8 Feminism and the Politics of Sexuality

It is striking how the first three accounts of sexuality that I dealt with treat women and female sexuality as obscure or dangerous subjects. In Christianity, in psychoanalysis, in Foucault's work, women are either absent, or are treated as the mysterious and sinister Other. In Freudian language, women are the repressed; or to use Lacan's formulation of this, 'a woman is a symptom'.[1]

This phallocentrism is not surprising to feminists, who can argue convincingly that all non-feminist theories of sexuality have accepted patriarchal society and patriarchal forms of thought without challenge. Thus Freud assumes the 'primacy of the penis', and from this premise flows the claim that female sexuality is derivative from phallic sexuality. Women are cursed with a diminutive penis, and must spend their lives dealing with the shame and resentment (penis envy) that inevitably stem from their biological inferiority.

But these ideas bear an uncanny resemblance to Aristotle's argument that 'women are castrated men', or: 'the female is female on account of an inability of a sort, viz., it lacks the power to concoct semen'.[2] I am not suggesting that Freud was directly influenced by Aristotle: the point is that patriarchal beliefs about women have a long genealogy.

The Christian model is rather different, for here men are defined as spiritual beings who long to be with God, but who are prevented by the obstacles of materiality, passion and desire, all of which are often seen as emanating from women. Sexual desire is therefore the 'fault' of women, and men had better remain celibate or get married, so that their own desires are safely contained by a woman.

Thus all models of sex and sexuality have started from a male standpoint, and have taken male sexuality as a baseline, against which female sexuality is considered – and often not considered!

The effect of feminism on contemporary thinking about sexuality has therefore been highly disruptive, not to say explosive, since it has started from the position of women, and has relentlessly challenged every unconscious assumption, every 'masculinist' premise.

For example, ideas that sexuality is inevitably or 'naturally' linked with reproduction; that the sexual drive is innate; that men suffer most

128

of all from its fierce demands, and therefore must be indulged by women; that heterosexuality is the natural and normal expression of human sexuality; that women are best aroused sexually by the penetrating penis; that the clitoris is an 'inferior' organ to the vagina; that sexual 'liberation' benefits women as much as men; that sex is 'biological' or 'psychological'; that sex is 'private' – these and many other taken for granted ideas have been seized on by feminists and shown to be beliefs laden with ideological and political assumptions. It is true that Freud did challenge some of these ideas, but the radicalism of his insights has been blunted as psychoanalysis adapted to the norms of bourgeois society, particularly in America.

Above all, feminists have argued that sexuality is a political phenomenon: the male domination of women in patriarchal society is articulated through sexual practices and beliefs about sexuality. For example, the idea that the penis 'penetrates', while the vagina 'receives' – the active/passive polarity – can be shown to be a loaded ideological message, not a statement of 'biological' or 'natural' facts. Feminists have argued that patriarchal sexuality has treated women as sexual objects, has fetishized their bodies, and has denied women their own sexual energy and autonomy. Heterosexuality itself has been deconstructed and analysed, not as a 'natural' or biologically ordained principle, but as a politically imposed hegemony, which has been fundamentally oppressive to women. Women's sexuality has been rescued from the shadows in which it has languished within psychoanalysis and sexology.

This approach has therefore permitted a massive reappraisal of every aspect of human sexuality, including beliefs, myths, fantasies about it, as well as actual sexual practices in particular cultures. In certain cases, as with the clitoridectomy carried out in some cultures, the evidence for female sexual subordination is blatant. In other cases, there are more subtle levels of ideology to be disinterred: for example, the struggle to establish Freud's relationship to patriarchal thought has been a difficult and uneven one, as many psychoanalysts (particularly male ones) are unable to grant that Freud had such huge blind spots.[3]

In fact, feminism has also been able to use many psychoanalytic insights as part of its radical deconstruction of sexuality. It has left no stone – or assumption – unturned in its restless urge to demystify and relativize sexuality.

Feminism has perhaps been better at deconstruction than reconstruction, for it has found it more difficult to propose new models of human sexuality. However, it is not alone in this, since it is notoriously difficult to invent new sexualities, when we are all so saturated in the old beliefs and practices.

In fact, there has been considerable conflict within feminism concerning heterosexuality, lesbianism, pornography, and so on. A spectrum of political thought exists within feminism *vis-à-vis* sexuality, ranging from the liberal feminist, who wants to improve women's sexual happiness, but still sees it operating largely within a heterosexual framework, to the most radical wing of feminism, which has declared that heterosexuality is inherently oppressive, and that lesbianism is the only form of sexual expression that is liberating for women. Between these poles, feminists contest the terrain, and argue as much with each other as with non-feminists. The spectrum within feminism has been less a traditional right/left split than a divide between optimism and pessimism concerning relations with men.

One very important aspect of feminism's approach to sexuality is that it has not a detached academic but a fiercely partisan and political stance. Feminists have not been afraid to cite their own experience, or express their sense of outrage at the way women have been treated by men as sexual objects.

Perhaps the most remarkable aspect of the feminist analysis of female sexuality is that individual women have begun to speak about their own sexuality. Thus, the 'scientific' relationship of observer and observed has been shattered by a new subjectivity. Freud's famous question – 'What do women want?' – is being answered by women themselves. The object of enquiry has become the speaking subject; the mysterious Other has become the self-assertive feminist subject.

SEXUAL LIBERATION?

The so-called 'sexual revolution' that began in the 1960s is now regarded by many feminists as yet another attempt by patriarchal culture to impose its order on women. Many feminists now believe that the wave of rebellion, exploration, and political radicalism that is associated with the sixties merely helped men gain more access to women's bodies.

On the other hand, other feminists argue that sixties radicalism was of benefit to women, and that feminism itself began its new-wave resurrection at that time: 'The New Left may have been gender blind, but it did contribute, crucially, to the widening of the definition of politics to include personal life, culture and the critique of everyday life.'[4]

But certainly feminists began to separate themselves from the Left in the late sixties and seventies, as they began to perceive that many left-wing organizations were structured in just as patriarchal manner as those of the mainstream. Women were often recruited to make the tea and be available for sex. This was not what a growing number of women had entered revolutionary politics for!

Furthermore, feminists began to realize that the liberation manifestos that were being touted tended to ignore gender issues, and that the revolutionary perspectives on offer seemed to envisage a society where women's roles were not significantly different:

> The women's liberation movement arose out of the discovery that the oppressive character of relations between men and women are starkly revealed, rather than transcended, in the sexual revolution ... Free love, as it turned out, was free only for women.[5]

For some women, the Soviet Union also acted as a warning that revolutions seemed to end up strait-jacketing women in the same roles as did capitalist society. Granted, the early Soviet state did give many benefits to women, such as legalized abortion, but the Stalinist retrenchment led to a new emphasis on the mother–heroine figure.[6]

In relation to sexuality, this led to the realization that within Marxism female sexuality had either been ignored or had been defined within a masculinist paradigm. New models of female sexuality were needed, and new sexual practices were needed for women.

SEX/GENDER

Feminism began to see that more serious theorization about sexuality was called for, in particular that human sexuality could not be separated from gender structures. Everyday concepts of male and female sexuality are closely linked with stereotyped notions of masculinity and femininity: one is active, the other passive; the male is penetrating, the female is receptive; the male is also keen on sex, the female puts up with it. Male sexuality has often been seen as a ferocious unstoppable force that women have to accept and contain; female sexuality has been ignored or its existence actually denied.

In other words, sexuality is structured by patriarchal norms and expectations. Freud provides the supreme example of this: his exposition of sexuality is shot through with such comments about men and women. A typical comment is found in the *Three Essays*:

> The development of the inhibitions of sexuality (shame, disgust, pity, etc.) takes place in little girls earlier and in the face of less resistance than in boys; the tendency to sexual repression seems in general to be greater; and, where the component instincts of sexuality appear, they prefer the passive form.[7]

Of course, from a socio-political point of view, one might agree with these comments, with the proviso that such attitudes in little girls and boys are inculcated by patriarchy, intent on valorizing male sexuality, and diminishing and depreciating female sexuality. This is quite at odds with Freud's standpoint, arguing as he does that such attitudes flow from the 'instinct for mastery' possessed by boys, which leads them inexorably to a 'masculine' position, as girls are led to a 'passive' position.[8]

Freudianism shows very clearly then how conceptions of sexuality are saturated with notions about gender. Male sexuality is conceived of according to the norms of masculinity, construed as 'mastery', 'domination', 'activity' and so on; and female sexuality is seen as akin to femininity, understood as 'passivity', 'masochism', 'docility' and so on. These analogies are not peculiar to Freudian thought, but are widespread in patriarchal culture. If we say that gender is an ideological embodiment of the relations of domination and subordination between men and women, then sexuality has been thoroughly permeated with the same ideology:

> It is in the interests of the patriarchy that as many women as possible should focus their emotions on men and feel competitive with women, should depend on men's assessment of their appearance, opinions and behaviour, should easily be maneuverable into pregnancy, marriage, unpaid housework, and detachment from the public sphere.[9]

Linking sex with gender exposes the degree of sexual oppression that men have inflicted on women, in the form of rape, domestic violence, sexual harassment, and so on. But some feminists have argued that heterosexuality itself inevitably terrorizes and subjugates women; that the act of penetration itself in sexual intercourse is an act of conquest and despoliation.[10] Other feminists draw back from such a blanket statement, and argue that it is marriage that has been the means of oppressing women, and that sexual intercourse in itself is not oppressive.[11]

Also important here is the social organization of sexuality, in the form of contraception, abortion, child care, and so on, for women can argue cogently that they had been trapped for thousands of years in the procreative role, and that part of the abhorrence shown towards abortion and contraception by right-wing and 'pro-life' groups stems in fact from a barely concealed wish to keep women chained to the values of *Kinder, Kirche, Küche*. In other words, the separation of sexual pleasure from reproduction, which became a tangible reality with the development of reliable contraception, not only enabled women to claim sexual pleasure for themselves, but partially freed them from the entrapment of pregnancy and child-rearing. Reactionary groups (and governments) have never forgiven women this advance, and want to turn the clock back.

Feminists are therefore able to deconstruct patriarchal norms and expectations, and define new female sexualities, not constrained by patriarchal thought. At the same time, problems arise here, for how does one set about creating a new sexuality? Fierce debate has gone on within feminism about the constraints, if any, that should be set on female sexualities.

HETEROSEXUALITY

Whereas early feminists had tended to argue for greater female sexual pleasure within heterosexual relationships, new-wave feminists began to view the heterosexual paradigm itself as a tyrannical one, that inexorably defined female sexuality in terms of male needs. To some feminists it seemed increasingly doubtful if women really could be equal partners in a heterosexual relationship, and doubtful if intercourse itself, involving as it does the male 'penetration' of the woman, could ever be anything but a vehicle for male pleasure. The penis itself is seen as an oppressive instrument; the act of 'being penetrated' is demeaning and subjugating to women. Heterosexuality therefore has to be rejected and women have to separate from men: 'only when rape, prostitution, incest and all the other behaviors and images of heterosexual instrumentalism are eliminated will male dominance disappear'.[12]

Other feminists have argued with this, seeing it as a conservative biologist position, rather reminiscent of Victorian attitudes to men and women: men are rapacious, women have to submit, or keep away. These feminists have argued that it is possible for women to have sexual relations with men in a non-oppressive way: 'feminists have every reason to question and seek to dismantle, rather than remain in thrall to, the meanings which dominant discourse confers upon penile penetration'.[13]

This strikes me as a crucial and pivotal argument within this debate. Those feminists who condemn and reject heterosexual sex out of hand are in a sense accepting that the patriarchal definition of it is fixed, unchanging and *unchangeable*. This position flies in the face of social constructionism, which proposes that all sexual practices and meanings are historically and culturally relative.

In her book *Straight Sex*, Lynne Segal argues that sex is precisely the area of human experience where fixed identities and boundaries dissolve, and that therefore it is incorrect to state that in heterosexuality 'X happens', where X is a fixed event or feeling or relationship.[14] Thus just as we accept that patriarchal sexual relations embody stereotyped gender structures, it is also true that sexual experience is able to subvert conventional gender: men can allow themselves to feel passive and feminine, women can feel dominant and powerful.

This ties in with the debate about empiricism which I touched on briefly in Chapter 3: Juliet Mitchell criticizes some feminists for perpetrating a superficial description of social reality, without attempting to investigate deeper meanings and motives. This critique can be applied to certain feminist discussions of heterosexuality, where bewilderment is expressed that some women appear to enjoy sex with men: 'it is...a serious problem that, despite the conditions of women's oppression, women can have orgasms in heterosexual sex'.[15] Such arguments ignore the highly subjective nature of sexual experience, which can easily elude and contradict such large-scale socio-political descriptions.

Furthermore, there is a very mechanistic isomorphism within this argument: sexual relations between men and women are seen as exactly equivalent to the social relations between men and women. This ignores the implications, which I briefly discussed in Chapters 3 and 4, that flow from the notion of the unconscious: that human beings are able to have feelings and carry out acts that flatly contradict the dominant socio-political discourses or structures. In fact, we can go further: it is likely that sex is perhaps the key area of 'counter-cultural' experience, where normal gender roles can be inverted, subverted, dissolved and so on.

For example, it strikes me that defining intercourse between a man and a woman as 'an act of penetration' is itself ideologically loaded, and begs many questions. Curiously enough, those feminists who do define intercourse in this way are accepting patriarchy's own definitions. They are saying: 'yes, we agree with those brutalized men who treat women as objects for their own lust; sex between men and women is inevitably like that'. This is identification with the aggressor with a vengeance!

In other words, the equation of heterosexuality with tyranny accepts the terms of the tyrant, and does not try to formulate a feminist woman-oriented approach to male/female sex. That this can be done can be seen in the entry for 'Sexual intercourse' in the feminist encyclopedia *The Sexual Imagination*:

> A form of heterosexual activity in which the woman's vagina encloses the man's entering penis, then grips it while it is rhythmically thrust back and forth.[16]

This definition of intercourse has quite a different ideological loading, one that presents the female partner as active: 'encloses', 'grips' – these words suggest a female power in sex quite different from the abject position suggested by the anti-heterosexual feminists. I also feel that such a definition is not wish-fulfilment: many women do feel powerful during intercourse with a man; they don't feel like a victim. They can have just as much 'healthy sadism' during sex as men can. Of course, patriarchal culture has trained women to adopt passive attitudes during sex, but such training is not insuperable: it can be overturned.

One can also imagine that heterosexual feminists have experienced strong feelings of embarrassment, guilt and anger at being labelled as 'traitors' to the feminist cause by sleeping with men. Lynne Segal gives us a vivid picture of these reactions:

> Most heterosexual feminists had no intention of suppressing their desires for sexual encounters and relationships with men, but I think many of us did feel undermined and confused, if not guilty, by the accusation that we were too 'male-identified' and soft on men.[17]

Another result could be a silencing of some feminists, and therefore a closing down, rather than an opening up, of the feminist examination of sexuality. Lesbianism can easily be seen in this context as unproblematical in comparison with heterosexuality, as if being a lesbian automatically guarantees one's freedom from oppression or oppressiveness. This is a massively essentialist position: men are oppressive, women are not; heterosexual women are masochistic, lesbian women are not. One seems to be led back irresistibly to a concept of original sin!

LESBIANISM

The rejection of heterosexuality leads inexorably to a form of lesbianism: women can only find sexual pleasure with other women. But lesbianism has become more than a sexual position: it is also a political choice and a political statement. It has been conceived of not so much as a sexual relationship, as a social/emotional relationship between women. So-called 'political lesbianism' or the 'lesbian continuum' conceives of itself not as an 'option' for feminists or women, but indeed as the core of feminist belief and practice.[18]

Lesbians have contributed to many areas of feminist theorizing and practice: for example, a new sense of the erotic for women has arisen amongst some lesbians, who reject both male-dominated concepts of the female body and female sexuality, and also the more puritan wing of feminism. Lesbian theorists have developed very radical ideas about what the category of 'woman' means, and whether it needs to be abandoned as an inextricably patriarchal concept in itself. Fierce controversies have been waged over the issues of lesbian pornography and sadomasochism; the apparent hegemony of White lesbians; notions of 'correctness' in relation to feminist lesbianism, and so on.[19]

Many interesting philosophical and political problems arise in connection with lesbianism and feminist 'separatism'. In the first place, the issue of voluntarism comes up. I assume that gender and sexual relations are not simply imposed on people in a particular society, they are also internalized. In other words, they are taken into people at a deeply unconscious level. The question then arises: is it possible to exhume and change these structures and attitudes? As we have seen, some lesbian feminists express surprise that heterosexual feminists are not able – and have no wish – to change their sexual orientation, but surely this brings into question the roots of sexuality in the human being. If those roots are, as psychoanalysis argues, unconscious, then by definition one cannot simply transplant them at will. Here we see the clash between a *socio-political* approach to sexuality – which predicts that one can change one's sexuality, since it has been imposed externally – and a *psychological* approach – which predicts that one cannot, since it has been absorbed internally.

A second issue concerns the relation between separatism and freedom. If one is determined to be totally separate from something – whether it be men, the White race, or money – arguably one has to have an obsession with that very object. One has to be eternally vigilant, in order not to allow contamination from the alien Other. This strikes me as a deep paradox: how can one be free when one has already posited such a monstrous opponent? Of course, many lesbians disagree strongly with this argument – for example, in her article 'Some reflections on separatism and power', Marilyn Frye claims that the great refusal of women to be part of a male world does establish freedom: 'the woman-only meeting is a fundamental challenge to the structure of power'.[20] I agree that such acts of feminist separatism act as a *protest* to male power, but do they really challenge it? My sense is that patriarchal capitalism is perfectly able to accept and indeed accommodate such movements by feminists, gay activists, Black people and others. In other words, I would argue that such actions are reformist, not revolutionary.

At a more practical level, it is difficult to see how communities of women will become truly separate from patriarchy and capitalism. This argument can be paralleled by Black separatism, which in the end seems to amount to a Black capitalism, with Black banks, Black supermarkets and so on. However, such phenomena are not at all a challenge to the existing power structures, but a plea for a slice of the cake!

FEMALE SEXUAL PLEASURE

From the late nineteenth century and early twentieth centuries, feminism has inaugurated a reclamation of female sexual pleasure. This can be seen in such early feminist works as Marie Stopes' book *Married Love*, published in 1918.[21] Such works began the shift away from compulsory vaginal orgasm, and the requirement for the thrusting penis, and also advocated an equal sharing of sexual pleasure in marriage.

Feminists began to break down the barriers of ignorance about the female body and female sexuality, about which women had been kept in ignorance. These developments were aided by surveys such as Masters' and Johnson's *Human Sexual Response* (1962), which

exploded certain myths about female sexuality, particularly the so-
called 'immaturity' of clitoral orgasm, and announced that women
could experience multiple orgasms. None the less, it is likely that
inhibition and secrecy still shrouded female sexuality until the postwar
period.

   One of the most interesting developments in contemporary feminism is that notions of pleasure and fun in relation to sex are being
brought back into discussion, not as abstract topics but concretely. I
have been struck by books such as Grosz and Probyn's *Sexy Bodies*,
Pat Califa's *Public Sex*, and the anti-anti-pornography collections,
Sex Exposed and *Dirty Looks*, which demonstrate how enjoyable
writing (and reading) about sex can be.[22] The anti-porn movement
amongst feminists has had a grim quality about it, that made humour
and fun seem quite impermissible. This puritan strain in feminism is an
old one, dating back to the nineteenth century at least, and the moral
purity campaigns in which some feminists were involved. But while it
seemed to dominate the feminist debate during the eighties, there are
clear signs that in the nineties a more positive approach to sex is
replacing it, a celebration of female sexuality and female sexual pleasure.

   Of course, for many feminists, pornography and heterosexuality are
not humorous or fun topics; but the more 'pleasure-oriented' books
that are being published in the nineties seem to switch attention to the
positive aspects of sexuality for women. There is an energy and an
enthusiasm about these collections that itself shows an erotic kind of
commitment. Sex is not something simply to be mourned or lamented
as a lost cause, or a cause forever ruined by men – sex can be
reclaimed by women as a pleasurable, indeed ecstatic activity. It is
striking, for example, that in the collection *Sexy Bodies* there are some
pieces of creative writing about sex; there are some fun titles ('Jewels
in the crotch') and the cover of the book has a photograph by Della
Grace, entitled 'Lesbian Ladies', which is positively sexy.

   Pat Califa is well known as a sex radical who enjoys sex in all shapes
and sizes, and her writing is no different:

   The sex is better when I'm in love – whether it's giggly in the
   shower till the hot water runs out, loud and bawdy in a back-
   room bar, slow as a symphony to reach a crescendo on satin sheets,
   sneaky under a fancy restaurant table, groping in the front seat at
   ninety miles an hour until some truck driver blows his horn and
   tries to pull us over, or a grumpy quickie to cure insomnia. When

I've just barely fallen in love, nothing else matters. The world becomes an assortment of surfaces upon which to make love.[23]

In fact, quoting Califa writing in this vein makes me realize how easy it is to become earnest and ponderous about sex. Presumably this is in part a defence against the frightening and vulnerable aspects of sex, but all students of gender and sexuality owe a debt to radicals such as Califa, and to other gay and lesbian writers and activists, who have torn back the funeral shroud around sexuality, and returned some of the vitality and fun that belong to it.

CONTROVERSIES IN FEMINIST APPROACHES TO SEXUALITY

I have already mentioned some of the debates and controversies which have gone into feminist discussions of sexuality. It would be surprising if this were not so, for feminism has lifted the lid on a massive can of worms. Patriarchal thinking about sexuality had been so stereotyped, so *unthinking*, so uncritical of many weak and empty concepts, that once feminists began to throw light on the whole area, a huge number of questions began to be raised. It would seem impossible for feminists, or any group of scholars and activists for that matter, to come up with a homogeneous theory of human sexuality – indeed, there are grounds for arguing that such a model is impossible, since sexuality is so varied, heterogeneous and contradictory.

In the remainder of this chapter, I would like to briefly describe some other interesting areas which have been uncovered in the feminist explorations.

Class, Race and Cultural Differences

There are dangers that feminist theorizing and campaigns about sexuality will ignore the situation of women from very different cultures and classes. For example, feminist arguments against clitoridectomy have come in for criticism from some Muslim women, who feel that White Western women are in danger of racist campaigns against Muslim culture in general. It has been tempting for Western feminists to make a wholesale condemnation of Muslim culture as oppressive to women, but this can provoke strong indignation amongst Muslim women, who do not want to see their cultures condemned out of hand.[24]

Black women have also been critical of White women's critique of men and male sexuality. A specific example can be given: some White feminists have argued that Asian male immigrants should not be let into Britain, as 'we don't want any more men'. This has upset Black feminists, who see it not just as an attack on men, but on their own culture.[25]

Even on the subject of abortion, around which most feminists can agree, it is impossible to construct a monolithic statement, for in some cultures, women are pressurized to have their babies killed, for example if female babies are not wanted. In such a case, there may well be a struggle against abortion.[26]

These examples show a struggle between a kind of would-be homogeneous feminism, as against the fight for diversity: in an article on 'Lesbian identity', Biddy Martin argues that some lesbian theorization has constructed a monolithic lesbianism, which occludes differences of race, class and culture, and thereby suppresses the voices of, for example, Black lesbians.[27]

This anti-élitist argument can also be raised in relation to the intense theorization which has taken place in feminism. On the positive side, one can point to the radical theoretical reappraisal of gender and sexuality, so that some of the traditional underpinnings of patriarchy and capitalism have been deconstructed and shattered. On the negative side, one could argue that such theorization has been the preserve and indulgence of a White middle-class academy. There is a danger that some of the abstract reasoning can become out of touch with the harsh and oppressed life of many women from other classes and cultures, who cannot afford the luxury of such speculations.

But this has been a problem for feminism generally: in its construction of a woman-oriented philosophy and politics, it has sometimes had to ignore differences between women, which of course can be huge. In relation to sexuality, this sense of contradiction has probably been found most deeply in relation to heterosexual and lesbian women. At times, the latter have seemed to assume a natural superiority, as if heterosexual women were either betraying women, or were lagging behind in political consciousness. Naturally enough, this has infuriated other feminists, who insist that feminism does not inexorably lead to lesbianism, and that one can be a heterosexual feminist without any sense of contradiction.

These opposite tendencies – the pull towards monolithic uniformity, and the push towards diversity and heterogeneity – are in themselves fascinating poles, which seem to characterize human attitudes towards sexuality. Thus it is arguable that patriarchal ideology subsumed female sexuality within male sexuality. This monism can be found long before Freud – for example, Greek and Roman doctors argued that women's bodies were the same as men's.

What is striking therefore is that feminism has to an extent disrupted this monocular vision, and has separated out female sexuality as different from men's, but has then to an extent perpetrated another form of monism – in the argument that only lesbian sexuality is truly feminist.

The solution may lie in the direction of a model of 'diverse sexualities', that is, a spectrum of sexual orientations, feelings and acts, without the privileging of any particular one over the others. This argument is also consonant with political voices in the gay movement, who argue for the proliferation of diverse sexualities, and an escape from the relentless heterosexual hegemony (see Chapter 9).

Porn and S/M

Pornography and sado-masochism have provoked great divisions amongst feminists, for while some feminists have condemned both as objectifications of women, and expressive of the unequal power relations in patriarchy, other feminists have argued that women are not bound by such parameters, and can create their own erotic material, and can experiment with porn and S/M without necessarily falling victim to patriarchal categories. It is possible to *play* with such categories and subvert them, and not inevitably fall into a position of supine passivity towards them.[28]

This has raised the question as to whether issues of power – particularly in relation to domination and subordination – are inherently patriarchal. Does that mean that lesbians who enjoy power issues in their sexual relations, or who enjoy sado-masochistic fantasies or sexual play have 'sold out'?

These issues raise very profound questions as to the relation between 'reality' and 'fantasy', and between sexuality and the rest of life. To my mind, the argument that any enjoyment of unequal power relations in a sexual relation is 'patriarchal' manifests an extraordinarily literal-minded and determinist interpretation of culture.

There is also the question here of control and judgementalism. The spectacle of some feminists condemning others for their sexual tastes has been an uncomfortable one, since such critics themselves can be accused of being patriarchal.

In relation to the issue of pornography, the polarization amongst feminists has been striking: some have expressed vehement opposition to porn, while others have taken a more dialectical view, arguing that women should have the right to construct their own erotic material. Again, issues of censorship have loomed large – who is to control the issue of erotic material? Who is to judge what is 'erotic' and what is 'pornographic'? More left-wing feminists have been shocked at the spectacle of anti-porn activists apparently cooperating with right-wing and Christian forces in the stamping out of porn.[29]

But feminism has a long tradition of 'moral purity' and censorship:

> Feminism had very strong links with the hygiene and eugenics movements of the late nineteenth and early twentieth centuries; major political campaigns linked up with older temperance and social purity movements, so that feminist women came to embody the ideals of sexual purity that men fell so far short of.[30]

Such movements show the danger of an idealist view of gender and sexuality: if men are seen as inevitably rapacious, then women begin to be reified as the opposite polarity, that is, as creatures unsullied by male depravity. This is a highly dangerous split, and a projection onto men of all human faults.

Essentialism

There are clear signs of essentialism in some feminist positions, especially in the argument that there is a 'female sexuality' which is warmer, more caring, more reciprocal, than 'male sexuality'. The main problem with this argument is that it is empiricist: that is, ironically, it accepts the definitions that have been imposed by patriarchal society, or it accepts the surface appearance of phenomena. In a sense, it takes us back to Victorian strictures on male bestiality and female primness. Men are sexual animals, but women are loving and warm.

One can see why some feminists have been attracted to this position, for it helps women to separate from what is perceived to be the mad bad world of men. It seems very positive to construct a world of women, who care for each other, and reject masculinist ways of thought and masculinist ways of sex. But the net result is a rather undialectical view of history and human interaction.

I can cite as an example Robin Morgan's book, *The Demon Lover*, which for me is vitiated by her inability to propose a satisfactory model of male sexuality, which, she claims, is at the root of political terrorism, as indicated in the subtitle of the book, *The Sexuality of Terrorism*.[30a] She proposes that men love death, and women love life. But is this innate or are men and women trained in this by patriarchy? Morgan seems ambivalent about this.

Feminism has tended therefore to oscillate between essentialism and a socio-historical view – the idea that male and female sexualities have been constructed as part of the consolidation of patriarchal society. The first view embodies a very pessimistic view of men, who cannot be expected to change; the second is more optimistic about an overall radical change to gender and sexuality. The first position also tends to accept that patriarchal capitalism is here to stay, and women had better find a better position within it; the second position argues that there are clear signs that patriarchy is crumbling before our eyes. In some ways, therefore, the first position is more 'right-wing' than the second, and seemed to grow in influence during the eighties, when in America and Europe right-wing governments took control. However, the distinctions of 'left' and 'right' often seem inappropriate in a discussion of feminism, since the contradictions that exist within feminism cut across the conventional political spectrum.

The Female Body

The female body is a contradictory phenomenon in Western culture, and there is a wide range of views about it within feminism. On the one hand, it has been used as one of the chief icons of Western culture, and in that sense, has been appropriated by patriarchal culture as an allegorical image. On the other hand, it is possible that it has also been an image of female sexuality and power.[31]

These contradictions seem to apply to female 'icons' such as Marilyn Monroe and Madonna. Are they framed and organized as a patriarchal degradation of women, or do they also communicate something powerful about women?

Perhaps both sides have some truth in them. For example, Marilyn Monroe is often portrayed as a dumb blonde, and part of the tragedy of her life may be that her own authentic voice was not taken seriously by Hollywood, and she knew it. Madonna is quite different, for here there seems to be a greater degree of control by the artist, and a greater self-consciousness and irony about her self-presentation.

Madonna has used her sexuality in unconventional ways, and has played with images of homosexuality, masturbation, dominance and so on. Whether these images are merely shallow pop entertainment or present something more profound is arguable. But this debate is not a new one: for example, it has raged over the whole issue of women in Hollywood, or the use of the female body in fine art. Do these represent exploitation or female power, or both?[32]

SUMMARY

Overall, these arguments show that a coherent feminist theory of sexuality is difficult to arrive at, for so many perplexing questions seem to arise: should it include psychoanalytic insights, or be mainly political? Is it reformist or revolutionary? Does it reject or accept heterosexuality? Divisions are inevitable amongst feminists on all these issues, since theory is not neutral, but follows one's political and emotional predilections.

Also the attitude of feminists towards traditional feminine sexuality is complicated. While some feminists state that such displays as cosmetics, fashion, and so on, are controlled by a patriarchal urge to regulate female sexuality and render it an acceptable gift to men, other women find that they want to use cosmetics and clothes as part of their developing confidence and self-expression.

This is very clear in a psychotherapeutic context, where a wide range of attitudes is met with amongst women. For example, I have had married women clients with children who eventually came out openly as lesbian with great relief; I have also had clients who had been single and career-minded, but who eventually realized they wanted to live with a male partner and have children. Some women reject cosmetics as an artificial imposition; but others start using them as an expression of their burgeoning sexuality.

Thus the attitude of women towards already existing sexual norms and appearances is very complex, and cannot be summarized easily. Those feminists who are puzzled at how some women enjoy heterosexuality are surely trapped in their own thinking, and unable to see other people in their own world. The issue of diversity seems critically important here, for it is always tempting, when trying to construct new models of sexuality, to become quasi-imperialist: that is, to construct an ideal model, against which many people seem to fail.

To say that feminism has not arrived at a satisfactory overall theory of human sexuality can hardly count as a criticism, for it seems extraordinarily difficult to construct a theory which synthesizes biological, socio-political and psychological parameters. Furthermore, all theories are politically loaded, so the construction of a model of sexuality also poses the question: a model for whom? One might assume that it would be possible to construct a model of female sexuality that satisfied feminist credentials, but this may still be difficult, if feminists are unable to agree about certain issues.

However, focusing on the problems and controversies existing within feminist accounts of sexuality might make us overlook the huge and profound contribution that feminism has made. Certainly in the twentieth century no other field of study and exploration within sexuality has been so rich, varied and energetic, with the possible exception of psychoanalysis.

To say that feminism has politicized the study of sexuality is a bald enough statement, but one that hides a truly revolutionary breakthrough, or in fact a series of breakthroughs. One does not have to agree with all statements made within feminism to appreciate the audacity with which feminists have been able to challenge patriarchy to its foundations. Arguably, gender and sexuality are two of the key building blocks of a patriarchal society, and feminism has been able to deconstruct them and theoretically demolish them. I am reminded of the emperor's new clothes: so many apparently eternal and unquestionable aspects of human sexuality have been deconstructed and unpacked by feminism, and shown to be political constructions which are neither natural nor inevitable.

9 Homosexualities

Since the 1960s the study of homosexuality has undergone massive changes. In the first place, whereas Western sexology, medicine and psychiatry have tended to view it as a trans-historical and unchanging category which could be investigated in different cultures at different times, a new wave of sociological and political research has led to the arresting thesis that the concept of 'the homosexual' has been invented in modern times, and does not exist in other cultures and other periods in history.

Thus whereas homosexual *behaviour* can be found in cultures as different as ancient Greece, modern American prisons and the Melanesian cultures of Papua New Guinea, this does not equate with the notion of 'the homosexual' as a fixed social role or condition. This kind of searching for fixed categories throughout history – waspishly referred to by Jeffrey Weeks as the 'great queens in history' approach[1] – can be seen as an idealist and reifying one, whereas the new approach is a socio-political deconstructive one that accepts the historical relativity of categories in gender and sexuality.

The implications of this development are immense, not only for the study of homosexuality, but for other conceptualizations of sexuality. In particular, the concept of heterosexuality itself can also be historically relativized. That is, it seems likely that the two concepts exist in a structural system of co-dependence – the notion of 'the homosexual', along with other categories, such as 'perversity', 'cohabitation', and so on, has been used to draw a boundary around marital heterosexuality as the 'proper' arena for the expression of human sexuality: 'marital heterosexuality...is a core around which everything else must be seen as revolving, either in contrast to it, or as a subsidiary form'.[2]

These ideas are part of the wholesale shift away from essentialism or nativism – the idea that gender and sexual categories are constant and unchanging – towards a more historical or socio-political view, as outlined in Chapter 6. But the implications of 'historical relativity' go beyond social science into other areas such as psychology, literary criticism and so on. Furthermore, this research has helped to de-medicalize and de-pathologize homosexuality. The traditional sexological taxonomies, listing innumerable 'perversities' or 'deviations', of which the male 'invert' was one, have been largely abandoned.

But a second great shift has occurred in the study of homosexuality in the West. Whereas traditional scientific and academic disciplines boast of the 'objective' and 'impartial' nature of their methods of studying – the observer viewing the observed object in a state of so-called 'neutrality' – the study of homosexuality has seen a new subjectivity at work. The phenomenon of the 'gay sociologist' or 'gay historian' has appeared: that is, the academic who is personally involved in the subject of his study, someone who is politically committed. This phenomenon has also been found in feminism, and surely marks a critical turning point in social science, and perhaps in a wider sense, in academic studies as a whole. No longer does the student have to maintain a fictitious remoteness from his or her subject.

One great merit of this breakthrough is that it makes explicit what always happened implicitly. That is, people have always gravitated towards disciplines and topics in which they had a personal involvement, but somehow this was never mentioned, or was hinted at elliptically. The 'personal' and the 'private' were categorized as inadmissible in scientific and academic discourse, which amounts to a formidable split in consciousness that is being healed by gay and feminist scholars: the object of enquiry has become the speaking subject.

Third, these developments in the study of homosexuality have taken place within the ambit of the 'gay movement' and 'gay liberation', that is, a massive political self-assertion by lesbian and gay people. Furthermore, as part of the liberalization in Western cultures which occurred in the 1960s, homosexuality has to a limited extent been decriminalized. This is important both practically, in terms of how gay people are able to live their lives in freedom, and also philosophically, for it has taken the concept of homosexuality out of the ambit of criminology and pathology. Indeed, the categorization of homosexuality has been taken out of the hands of the medical and psychiatric professions, and has become an act of self-categorization and self-celebration: ' "Homosexuals" were once regulated and defined by "experts"; now these experts need no longer do it, for the homosexual has assumed that role for himself or herself.'[3]

Overall then, homosexuality has been *secularized*: removed from the specialist fields of medicine, law and psychiatry, and to some extent destigmatized. This process is limited – it is doubtful if the manual worker on the Ford assembly line, many school-children, and indeed many other people are free to be openly gay. Homophobia is still rampant, and is whipped up, not only by the tabloid press, but by many governments, either overtly or covertly.

This brings up the meaning of the stigmatization of homosexuality. One plausible psychological view has been that homophobia denotes a repressed homosexual desire, which is then projected and castigated. Whilst this is plausible at the individual level, it is clearly inadequate to deal with the use of homophobia as a means of social control. 'Queer-bashing' exists at all strata of society, from the actual physical violence committed on the streets against gays, to the more indirect attempts of governments to foster anti-gay sentiment, seen for example in Clause 28 of the 1988 Local Government Bill in Britain.

But systematic homophobia is not just used as a means of controlling gay people – it is used to control everyone. This can be seen in many male subcultures, where constant vigilance is needed to prevent the betrayal of a 'feminine' feeling or thought. Homophobia is used to police heterosexuals.

This backs up the idea that the whole historical development of the concept of homosexuality as a defined condition is not an isolated phenomenon, but is structurally linked to developments in heterosexuality, in the family and in class society. Hence the more prominent social role that gay men and lesbians have been able to establish in the last thirty years is clearly very threatening to many people, especially men.

RELATIVIZATION

I want to return to the notion of the social and historical relativity of the notion of 'the homosexual'. One way of approaching this is by examining terms found in other cultures, which seem to resemble the Western notion of homosexuality.

The phenomenon of the *berdache* in native American cultures has attracted considerable attention from anthropologists, and has sometimes been claimed to be an analogue of the Western 'homosexual'.[4] The berdache is a man in woman's clothing, carrying out women's occupations, and having sex with men. Such men are found in many native American societies, but the berdache seems to be defined primarily in terms of female occupation and clothing, and only secondarily by sexual object choice, whereas in the West 'homosexuality' is defined by the latter. Thus the term 'berdache' seems more akin to the English term 'transvestite'. The anthropologist Harriet Whitehead, in her study of the berdache, argues that two different gender systems are at work:

For the American Indians, occupation pursuits clearly occupy the spotlight, with dress/demeanor coming in a close second. Sexual object choice is part of the gender configuration, but its salience is low, so low that by itself it does not provoke the reclassification of the individual to a special status. In the Western system, the order of salience is virtually the reverse.[5]

This is a powerful argument against the idea that there is a pre-existing 'homosexuality', which somehow different cultures have to make provision for, by creating an institutionalized niche. It is particularly striking that although many American tribes had a social category like the berdache, some did not, suggesting that it is particular social structures that create such categories, not individual personalities or pre-existent sexual needs.[6]

A similar kind of sexual category is found in the Indian *hijras*, who are castrated men, dressed as women, who carry out certain religious rituals and frequently also work as homosexual prostitutes.[7] Thus the hijra role appears to be a very complex one, combining many attributes that are normally considered separately in Western studies of gender and sexuality: they could be described as transvestite homosexual transsexuals. Interestingly, their religious affiliation is to one of the Great Mother goddesses in Hinduism, suggesting that the castration undergone by hijras enacts an identification with the maternal body.

The anthropologist Serena Nanda makes the comment that 'the hijra role is a magnet that attracts people with many different kinds of cross-gender identities, attributes and behaviors'.[8] However, this comment implies that there are pre-existing, and presumably eternal, gender and sex identities, which seek out some kind of institutionalized position. This would suggest for example that there are always a certain number of homosexual men and women in society, who may or may not find some kind of social role. A more radical approach might suggest that the social role 'creates' or 'fosters' those identities and behaviours.

Again, a comparison between the hijra and the Western male homosexual reveals significant differences: the notion of sexual object choice does not seem to be the sole or main criterion for becoming a hijra. In fact, early Western travellers to India found it difficult to translate the word 'hijra': they have been called eunuchs, hermaphrodites, intersexed, and so on.[9]

Analysis of the berdache and hijra categories throws some interesting light on Western homosexuality, for nineteenth century and early twentieth century notions of male homosexuality often assumed that the homosexual was a 'feminized' man. Thus the homosexual was said to love men or want sex with men because he was like a woman ('a woman's soul in a man's body'). This is formalized within psycho-analysis in terms of a reverse Oedipalization: instead of identifying with his father and desiring his mother, it is claimed that the male homosexual has done the reverse. No doubt this is a very elegant theory, but how much of it stems from ideological prejudice rather than empirical evidence? Kenneth Lewes' book *The Psychoanalytic Theory of Male Homosexuality* (1988) demonstrates how the growing hostility to homosexuality amongst psychoanalysts after Freud's death was based less on empirical research than homophobic prejudice.

It is plausible that the concept of 'the homosexual' has changed its meaning in the last hundred years: from 'feminized male' to 'male with same sex object choice'. It is also striking how popular thinking still tends to see gay men as effeminate. But folk gender systems notoriously blur many boundaries in gender and sexuality: many people are surprised to learn that many male transvestites are heterosexuals; popular thinking also seems to believe that gay men desire boys. Thus folk gender/sex systems differ markedly from those systems used by social science or psychology.

A different kind of social/semantic system can be found in those cultures and subcultures which emphasize the sexual organs, and the degree of activity/passivity, used in sexual acts. Thus some prison homosexual subcultures seem to distinguish between the active pene-trators, who are considered to be 'male', and the passively penetrated, who are often considered to be 'female'. In his novel *Our Lady of the Flowers*, Jean Genet spends a considerable amount of energy analys-ing these complex differences, as for example with the character Divine:

> Though she felt as a 'woman', she thought as a 'man'. One might think that, in thus reverting spontaneously to her true nature, Divine was a male wearing make-up, dishevelled with make-believe gestures, but this is not a case of the phenomenon of recourse to the mother tongue in times of stress ... It would be curious to know what women corresponded to in Divine's mind, and particularly in her life. No doubt, she herself was not a woman (that is, a female in a skirt); *she was womanly only through her submission to the imper-ious male* [added emphasis].[10]

But this opposition according to sexual role is found in many cultures. Thus in Mexican culture the man who penetrates other men may be considered 'heterosexual', whereas the penetrated male is 'stigmatized for playing the subservient feminine role'.[11] In the Islamic society of Oman, the *xanith* denotes a man who takes a passive sexual role towards other men, and is therefore associated with women. In fact, it is possible for the xanith to 'become a man', by marrying and demonstrating his sexual potency with his wife.[12]

These examples show clearly how the dominant patriarchal gender system – which denigrates the female/feminine – is hugely influential on many social systems of sexuality. The male who takes the 'feminine' position – that is, the male who is penetrated – often seems to be separated off into an intermediate gender category, with varying degrees of social approval and disapproval. The male who penetrates other men is still considered to be 'a man'.

But these interrelationships have a further, more theoretical, corollary that is of great interest for the student of gender and sexuality. Gender and sex are seen to interpenetrate: certain kinds of sexual practices bring about a reclassification in terms of gender. Thus in the examples above, men who are anally penetrated by other men are 'not-men'. In other words, one of the important criteria for assigning a male to the gender category 'man' is whether he is sexually penetrative – either in relation to women or men.

This seems supportive of the argument – which we have also encountered in some feminist discussions – that so far from gender and sexuality being separate systems, *it is impossible to separate them*. If this idea can be backed up by further research within anthropology, psychology and sociology, it seems likely to be one of the key discoveries within contemporary gender studies, for the traditional distinction amounts to a split between biology and society. Yet the anthropological evidence demonstrates that the apparently 'biological' category of 'man' is in part determined by certain sexual practices. And gender also influences sexuality: thus the doctrines of masculinity determine what a man may or may not do sexually.

It is clear, as we survey various cultures, that sex/gender systems are made up of very different semantic categories. Some of these can be outlined as follows:

occupation
clothing
sexual object choice (man/woman/child)

sexual organ used (penis/anus/mouth/vagina)
sexual role (active/passive)
anatomical state (castrated/non-castrated)
generation (older/younger partner)
status (slaves/boys)

The berdache is defined mainly by occupation and clothing; the term 'hijra' combines anatomical state, clothing, occupation and object choice, with the addition of a specialized religious function; the term 'xanith' seems to stress sexual object choice. The Greek 'love of boys' highlights the generational dimension, which also connects with a difference in status in the two partners.[13]

It seems clear from this perfunctory analysis that there are no universal terms that might denote 'homosexuality' or 'heterosexuality', but rather a very complex set of semantic categories which are combined in different ways, depending on the particular social structure. Furthermore, when we consider the different associations which homosexuality has for different groups of people, or for different individuals, say within British society, it seems plausible that they are also using different sets of categories. In other words, gender/sex systems may not be stable even within national or linguistic boundaries.

The notion of 'the homosexual' in contemporary Western usage seems to mainly encapsulate the idea of 'same sex' object choice. A century ago it is possible that it encoded also the notion of 'feminized male'; for some people, perhaps it still does. It is perhaps preferable to speak of a cluster of meanings and associations: thus for some people 'homosexual' may mean 'same-sex sex', 'effeminate', 'anal sex', 'disgusting', 'dangerous', 'lover of boys', and so on. The crucial point is that such a selection of meanings is neither universal nor fixed.

Of course, many of these associations make up anti-homosexual prejudice, but prejudice itself can be defined as a particular kind of sex/gender system, which is not neutral but biased towards certain categories – in the West, usually heterosexuality. But then the fascinating question arises: is a neutral sex/gender system possible? Is the sociologist or the anthropologist actually able to use an 'objective' or 'scientific' set of terms and meanings that are 'value-free'? The dangers of ethnocentricity are well known in anthropological research, but it may be impossible and undesirable to avoid all ethnocentricity, just as one cannot avoid a certain amount of personal subjectivity and bias.

I have certainly found the study of prejudice to be of great value in my work as a psychotherapist. When I meet people who are anti-gay, anti-male, or anti-Semitic, I don't see it as my task to approve or disapprove of their stance, but to investigate the deeper meanings behind it. The hated Other conceals vast amounts of information about the relationship of that individual to him/herself, their early family and their 'internal objects'.

SEXUAL/SOCIAL ISOMORPHISM

Having considered societies where homosexual desire and behaviour have very different meanings, values and roles from those of British or American society, the interesting question arises as to what the relationship is between such structures of sexuality and more general socio-political values. Foucault talks of an 'isomorphism between sexual relations and social relations'. He expands upon this, in relation to Greek culture: 'pleasure practices were conceptualized using the same categories as those in the field of social rivalries and hierarchies'.[14]

Foucault is making the point that the Greeks were concerned with the notions of domination and submission, or activity and passivity, in sexual relations, just as they were concerned about these issues in society at large. Thus, Foucault claims that Greek culture did not draw the kind of demarcation between gay and straight sex that is drawn in contemporary Western culture:

> The Greeks did not see love for one's own sex and love for the other sex as opposites, as two exclusive choices, two radically different types of behaviour. What distinguished a moderate self-possessed man from one given to pleasures was, from the viewpoint of ethics, much more important.[15]

Foucault's notion of isomorphism is a useful one, and can be expanded upon. I have already argued in Chapter 6 that it is not simply the 'conceptualization' or interpretation of sexual relations that embodies socio-political meanings, but sexual practices themselves. It is not just the way that sexuality is talked about, thought about, and written about, that reveals 'social meanings' but also the way sex is practised. Edward Tejirian makes this point in his book *Sexuality and the Devil* – after arguing that *depictions* of sexuality reveal the concerns of a culture, he goes on to claim that 'sexual behaviour itself is symbolic'.[16] Tejirian is referring to the individual's symbol system, but we can enlarge this idea to include collective symbolism and meaning. Thus, referring back to the Hindu hijra, it is significant that Hinduism and Indian mythology have a very rich set of images of cross-gender identification. Serena Nanda claims that Hindu culture is more able to tolerate gender/sexual ambiguity than Western culture, which is obsessed with dichotomous or binary categories.[17]

Another clear example concerns the obloquy which has often been attached to oral sex in Western cultures, presumably because it is non-procreative, and blurs the heterosexual boundaries – two men or two women can practise the same kinds of oral sex as a male/female couple. Hence mouth/penis or mouth/clitoris sex tends to escape from the dominant paradigm of sex as a penis/vagina activity.

What then is the significance of the Western division between homosexuality and heterosexuality? Or to put this question more provocatively, what lies behind the *construction* of the concepts of homosexuality and heterosexuality? Why has Western culture formed such a clear-cut distinction between them, when other cultures have not? Why has the homosexual become a 'species'? Why has so much opprobium been attached to homosexual behaviour, when in other cultures it is not?

It is probably dangerous to pursue single-track theories that try to explain everything in terms of a single foundation such as Freud's Oedipal theory. However, it is useful to begin with the close connection in many societies between sexuality and social structure. If we consider those societies with complex kinship systems, those systems are created by the principles of endogamous and exogamous marriage. In modern Western societies, the nexus between marriage, kinship and property is a very powerful one: for example, the stress on female virginity and fidelity seems to be related to the reliability of male inheritance and the emphasis on primogeniture in capitalist society.[18]

Let me state this baldly: sex helps create society. Or rather, structured forms of sexual relations help create social structure. For example, I argued in Chapter 6 that the incest taboo guarantees endogamy. If you like, a ring is drawn around certain sexual forms, which are validated by church and state, and others are severely prohibited. In the West the ring has been drawn around marital genital heterosexuality; the proscriptions have involved non-procreative sex (anal, oral, with contraception); same-sex sex; sex with oneself; public sex; anonymous sex; and so on. Note that this does not mean that sexuality *causes* social structure – that would be yet another form of idealism – rather, it is one of the instruments that brings it about.

This argument can be summarized rather crudely in relation to the construction of 'the homosexual': in the development of capitalism in the nineteenth century, the links between sexuality and property were intensified, since capitalism is a culture centred on property. Those forms of sexual desire and activity which do not reinforce the links between sex, kin and property were stigmatized as fundamentally hostile to society. In other words, 'homosexuality' is a concept invented by bourgeois society in an attempt to purge itself of all sexual practices that might subvert the 'sanctity of marriage' and the sanctity of property and its inheritance. But many other sexual activities were also stigmatized, for example, premarital sex, abortion, female adultery, and so on. Male adultery was not condemned as fiercely because it does not threaten the inheritance of property in the family.

In this light, it is interesting to consider the contemporary relaxation of certain taboos in Western society. For example, non-procreative sex is widely accepted; same-sex sex less so, but it is surely less prohibited than formerly. What does this tell us about contemporary social structures? Are they in the process of transformation? Are capitalism and patriarchy about to disappear? Or are we witness to a brilliant Foucaultian manoeuvre by patriarchal capitalism, controlling by liberalizing?

HOMOSEXUALITY FOR WHOM?

The invention of homosexuality may also be witness to more primitive needs to construct images of the 'Other', to replace those lost through the decay of religion. Demonization must take different forms in a more secular age, and race, gender and sexuality provide a rich harvest of witches, demons and scapegoats.

Without doubt homosexuality functions as the repository for all kinds of negative myths and fantasies, leading to a kind of scapegoating. This has been exacerbated by the rise of AIDS, which has seen much public rhetoric concerned with the themes of crime and punishment, along with the suggestion that since sex is basically sinful, someone has to pay. Gay people are paying, since their sexuality is particularly heinous.

But there is a further complication in the creation of 'homosexuality': gay identity contains much that is unconsciously desired by straight people. The Other contains elements towards which very ambivalent feelings exist: hatred and longing, for example. Thus while the concept of 'the homosexual' has been frequently used to constrain or police heterosexual people, it is possible that it also acts as a safe repository of *forbidden desires*. In other words, the gay man and lesbian are acting out those desires which are deeply repressed in heterosexuals. There beyond the pale, at a safe distance, exist these hedonistic people who pursue each other for sex in public lavatories, shove their penises through holes in the toilet wall, suck each other's penises at the drop of a hat, and so on. The respectable heterosexual can turn away in disgust, yet may remain unconsciously fascinated by the whole business.

This paradoxical quality to homosexuality is reminiscent of the values attached to menstruation in many cultures. Of course it is well known that this has attracted a vast array of taboos. But some anthropologists have also pointed out that the menstruating woman is not simply seen as a loathsome figure, but as an extremely powerful one. Menstrual blood has the same dual quality: the anthropologists Terence and Patricia Hays report that the Ndumba people of Melanesia see this as potentially lethal to men.[19] But menstrual blood is clearly symbolic of the dangers posed by women and femininity to the masculinity of men, who must be protected against the temptation of regressing to an earlier feminine identity. If you like, male castration anxiety conceals a castration wish, which must be strenuously denied.

Here then is a basic principle in psycho-social structures: the taboo is both hated and desired. Quite simply, male homosexuality is not a matter of indifference to patriarchal culture. On the contrary, it excites intense feelings of anxiety, repulsion, and so on, sure signs that quite primitive feelings are being unconsciously evoked.

Thus one has to ask the question: 'Homosexuality for whom?' For homosexuals or heterosexuals? One can draw a parallel with ethnicity: for Black people have been projected very much as fantasy figures for Whites, and as the containers for fantasies to do with sexuality, 'primitiveness', and so on.

There is therefore an interesting ironic ambiguity about the contemporary politicization of homosexuality. If it was created as a 'species', as part of the consolidation of heterosexuality, as a kind of limit or parameter, it has now become a place of celebration for gay men and lesbians; there has been a positive acceptance of the stigmatized, as in the use of the terms 'queer', 'dyke', and so on.

PATHOLOGY

The construction of 'the homosexual' seemed to go hand in hand with a process of pathologizing and demonization. Homosexuality became an obsessive theme of medicine and psychiatry, and was also regulated by means of legal and criminological statutes and procedures.

We have already noted that this suggests the exile of homosexual desire from the heterosexual norm: the homosexual was figured as 'the Other', who must be shunned, feared and persecuted, if the family and other institutions of bourgeois life were to be kept intact. This can be seen very clearly in the furore which went on in the British public schools at the end of the nineteenth century. Whereas earlier in the century public school ideology had praised the virtues of male friendship extensively, and had inculcated a kind of homoerotic culture of sport, physical prowess and military discipline, the Victorian Establishment seemed to take fright at the possible implications of this in terms of homosexual relations between boys, or between boys and masters. A series of stern denunciations rang out, castigating the evils of male/male love.[20]

In other areas, homosexuality was ineluctably associated with the concept of 'perversion'. The new science of sexology classified the male homosexual as an 'invert'; in psychoanalysis, it was claimed that homosexuality represented an immature diversion from the broad mature stream of heterosexuality. Furthermore, as an added insult, the homosexual was said to be indulging in a regressive fantasy, for he was still trying to make love to his father and identify with his mother.

The demonization of homosexuality reached extraordinary levels within psychoanalysis. Kenneth Lewes records some of the intemperate language used by analysts, particularly about gay men, and describes some of the bizarre attempts to 'cure' them. Is this so far removed from the Nazi persecution of homosexuals?

The imputation of pathology and demonology to gay men and lesbians continues to the present day. Its greatest impetus has been AIDS, which has led to extraordinary depths of obloquy and hatred, particularly in the tabloid press, and in the mouths of certain politicians and other public figures. Thus at the height of the heated and hysterical panic in the eighties, various newspapers and commentators suggested that people with AIDS should be locked up in camps, sterilized, or exiled into ghettos. Those on the religious right were not slow to suggest that AIDS was a punishment from God for the sin of homosexuality, or that AIDS was a precursor to the Final Judgement.

POLITICIZATION

Up to now, I have been pursuing a largely theoretical approach to different kinds of homosexual behaviour, in order to demonstrate the non-universality of the concept of 'the homosexual' found in Western society. But in the last thirty years, academic approaches to homosexuality have been overshadowed by the intense political struggles waged by gay men and lesbians against criminalization and discrimination, and the struggle to create a gay lifestyle. These struggles began initially in opposition to the attempts of the state to pathologize and criminalize homosexuality, but they have become much more positive than this: 'gay culture' is a tangible influence, certainly within British and American society, in areas such as popular music and dance, fashion, literature, art and cinema. Gay men and lesbians have been able to come out of hiding, to abandon an apologetic stance towards their own sexuality, and to proclaim instead its virtues. In the words of Foucault, a 'reverse discourse' began to be counterpoised to the hegemonic discourse which had pronounced homosexuality to be sick and bad.[21]

In America this struggle is often dated from the Stonewall riots of 1969, when gay men and lesbians fought back against the repressive measures used by the police. In Britain, there is less of a specific turning point, but various campaigns in the last thirty years have demonstrated the political potency and attractiveness of the gay movement.

Perhaps more than anything else, AIDS has transformed the gay movement, for it brought about a new solidarity, a sense of fellow-feeling, and it also led to a sustained campaign against the homophobic publicity found in the press and other media.

As with feminism, one can say that 'the Other' began to find its own voice; the 'object' of medical, psychiatric and legal procedures and taxonomies became the 'subject', able to argue for itself and defiantly assert its own identity.

The gay community also began to present a formidable theoretical analysis of sexuality and gender, arguing that the heterosexual family – so often used to denigrate homosexuality as perverse – was neither natural, inevitable nor particularly wholesome. Social constructionism was a godsend in these arguments, for gay scholars and activists could argue cogently that sexual relations were not a universal constant throughout human history and society, but could be shown to vary enormously. The family was not unchanging, and attitudes towards homosexual behaviour differed widely from culture to culture. Sexuality was a socio-political construction, not a moral or biological given.

Gay men and lesbians were also able to point to the negative aspects of heterosexuality and conventional marriage: in a sense, traditional morality and sexology were turned upside down – the gay lifestyles seemed creative and energetic in comparison with the moribund status of heterosexuality and marriage. In particular, lesbians have been able to present a ferocious dissection of the claustrophobic and repressive effect of marriage on many women: 'a long grey stream of heterosexual misery'.[22]

DIVERSITY AND CHOICE

The gay liberation movement has indicated that a repressive heterosexuality can be replaced by an acceptance of diverse sexualities, none of which seeks to dominate the others, or claims to be the 'norm' or the non-perverse. Jeffrey Weeks has presented a sustained defence of 'diversity' in his books, arguing for 'the celebration of desire as many-sided and many-shaped'.[23] The same idea can be found in feminism, where attempts to construct a monolithic 'female sexuality' have inevitably foundered in the face of the great variety of sexual tastes and activities of women.

The notion of 'diversity', allied with that of 'choice', in sexual orientation and gender, marks a complete reshaping of the traditional concepts of 'perversion' and 'deviance'. These latter terms are utterly normative: each perversion is implicitly or explicitly measured against the gold standard of marital heterosexuality, and seen to fail. In a sense, gay radicals advocate a new morality which has come off the gold standard completely: no sexual or gender orientation need be judged in terms of any other.

These ideas are very attractive – however, as a project they remain intensely utopian unless one considers the socio-political and psychological contexts of sexual relations. In particular, I question how much 'choice' we have over these matters. Can heterosexual people enjoy homosexual sex if they 'choose' to? Can gay men and lesbians enjoy heterosexual sex if they choose to?

My own feeling is that we have very little choice in these areas. Even within a particular sexual orientation, there seems to be little leeway about whom one is turned on by. If you are turned on by remote beautiful people, it is going to be enormously difficult for you to switch to people who are different from that. Or if you like thin people, how would you 'decide' to be turned on by less thin people?

I am really saying that diversity and choice are quite distinct terms within this debate: the first term is about tolerance, the second is about will-power. This is the voluntarist argument: that I can reinvent myself as I choose. Crucially, this ignores the unconscious, which tends to act like God in the old joke: 'make God laugh by telling him your plans'.

PLEASURE

Gay sex is non-procreative. This is part of its affront to Christianity and other conservative moral codes, but it has opened the door to a new consideration of sexuality as a set of diverse choices about bodily pleasures, which may not be necessarily genital. Lesbians in particular have pushed back the frontiers of 'correctness', as they have explored the possibilities of lesbian pornography, sado-masochism, and other pleasures, often causing consternation to the more conservative wing of feminism.

It is interesting to note in this light how much of the theoretical work that has been done on gender and sexuality is extremely earnest, as if somehow the mention of the word 'pleasure' would scandalize the academic audience. In this sense, the contribution of gay activists has been highly disruptive, and brings into question the conventional divisions between 'theory' and 'life', or 'intellect' and 'pleasure'. Gay culture brings the body right to the forefront of discussions about sexuality, and offers a much needed sense of relief from the rather disembodied speculations of Lacanian and Foucaultian research.

CLASS

As a minor footnote in the history of male homosexuality, the concept of 'rough trade' – the older middle or upper-class man associating with working-class youth – is fascinating, since it brings together gender, sexuality and class. The working-class youth seems to be seen as an image of masculinity by the older man, and there is an element of 'patronage' in the relationship: the education of the youth in cultural matters.[24]

This cross-class and generational relationship also seems to have excited considerable disapproval – it is possible that Oscar Wilde was hounded so viciously partly because of his socializing with working-class youth. Certainly the Irish patriot Roger Casement was probably refused commutation of his death sentence because of the 'Black Diaries', detailing his homosexual encounters with youth all over the world, which the British Government circulated while pleas were being made on his behalf.[25]

In his article 'Across the great divide', the gay journalist Peter Burton argues that the great period for such relationships was before 1940, and that today social structure has levelled out more, so that 'patronage' does not take place.[26]

Certainly, this kind of relationship maximizes otherness across the class and age divides, and raises interesting theoretical questions about desire and otherness. Since homosexuality is by definition about 'sameness', it is interesting to consider those relations where other forms of otherness are exploited. We could speculate that sexual desire must find some source of tension or difference between partners: if not sex identity (male/female), then gender (masculine/feminine); if not gender, then social class, ethnicity, generation, and so on. Sexual excitement may hinge on some type of 'difference': I desire something that is foreign to me.

SUMMARY

The impact of gay men and lesbians in the study of sexuality has been threefold. At the theoretical level, gay scholarship has revolutionized the field, since the traditional concepts of 'perversion' and 'normality' have been overturned. The idealist views that heterosexuality and homosexuality are simply 'human nature', eternal and unchanging, have been shattered in the face of the new historical research, which demonstrates conclusively that different cultures and different epochs have quite distinct gender/sex systems.

Gay scholars have also been able to deconstruct the heterosexual family, another concept that has been reified in many disciplines, such as psychology, sociology and anthropology.

Second, sexuality has been politicized. Or rather, it has been *consciously* politicized, since gay historians have been able to demonstrate that the heterosexual/homosexual split is intrinsically a socio-political demarcation, and that sex is subject to covert political construction in all cultures.

Third, gay culture has brought an effervescence and style that has had considerable impact on areas such as music, art, fashion and literature.

Without doubt, the gay movement is second only to feminism as a revolutionary influence in contemporary thinking about gender and sexuality. In both cases, the revolutionary quality stems in part from the concreteness of the movement. What I mean is that gay men and lesbians have not only posed very profound theoretical and political questions about sexuality, they have also demonstrated by their lives that many traditional concepts are hidebound, reactionary and repressive. 'Im Anfang war der Tat' – deeds speak louder than theories perhaps, but in the case of the gay movement, the deconstruction of traditional accounts of sexuality has proceeded at both levels – theory and practice – and has been explosive, disruptive and highly creative.

10 Male Sexuality

Amidst the contemporary ferment in the study of gender and sexuality, male sexuality remains something of an enigma, and is surprisingly under-researched. Yet in political terms, it is also easy to understand why this should be so, since traditional conceptions of sex and sexuality have been dominated by the male heterosexual viewpoint. Hence most radical critics and researchers have tended to steer clear of this area, or have taken up quite negative standpoints towards 'masculinist heterosexism'.

For example, some feminists have tended to treat male sexuality monolithically, as a unidirectional terroristic onslaught on women. This strikes me as a form of philosophical idealism, encompassing a vision that is unchanging and unchangeable, as in the writings of Mary Daly:

> Phallic lust, violent and self-indulgent, levels all life, dismembering spirit/matter, attempting annihilation....This lust is *pure* in the sense that it is characterised by unmitigated malevolence. It is *pure* in the sense that it is ontologically evil, having as its end the braking/breaking of female be-ing. Its goal is the obliteration of natural knowing and willing, of the deep purposefulness which philosophers have called *final causality* – our innately ordained Self-direction towards happiness [original emphasis].[1]

Daly is one of the most idealist of all feminists, and she posits such categories as 'natural knowing' and 'innately ordained Self-direction' which are ahistorical and asocial. Hence male sexuality itself is 'pure', 'unmitigated', 'ontologically evil'. Such categories are rather reminiscent of theological concepts such as 'original sin', and in an odd way Daly's is a comforting vision for women – for there is nothing one can do about it, except avoid it!

It is also a strangely traditional, quasi-Victorian view, and moreover one that ignores contradictory evidence, of which there is an abundance. Thus in my work with men in therapy, I have found that many feel sexually confused and inadequate, and definitely do not seem to feel in a position of mastery *vis-à-vis* women. Of course, one has to distinguish between the general patriarchal framing of sexuality, within which undoubtedly male sexuality has been dominant over women's – not to say obliterative of women's – and those individual males who may have suffered damage or deprivation, resulting in sexual misery and autism. However, I would argue that patriarchy does damage men considerably, and that male sexuality and its traditional parameters have been a prison for men.

Men certainly seem to have many problems with sex. For example, the performance ethos seems to imprison many men in a strait-jacket, which narrowly defines what they can and cannot do and feel sexually. Part of the pay-off of this is the large number of men who suffer from impotence, infertility, premature ejaculation, and other forms of sexual dysfunction. Again we see the close connection between gender and sexuality: the constraints of masculinity have operated quite fiercely in the sexual domain, so that men have felt afraid to feel 'feminine', or 'passive', or gentle – anything that contradicted the particular requirement of their culture's code of manhood.

What is striking here is that the rise in political articulateness that is evident in the women's movement and the gay movement has not been found in the 'men's movement'. Of course, arguably part of the reason for this is that patriarchy has permitted men to speak for thousands of years, and therefore it is time for others to speak. But in the new wave of political liberation that has swept Western cultures since the war, men have remained silent on the subject of their own problems. But then part of the cult of machismo is that men do not admit to weakness and vulnerability. Masculinity has 'spoken' about many things, but it is afraid to speak of its own fragility and its own needs.

My own work with men convinces me that male sexuality is not monolithically macho, impersonal or domineering. It is very difficult to make generalizations about it, since the category 'men' includes a very wide variety of human beings – heterosexual, homosexual, bisexual, masculine, feminine, bold, timid, and so on. Of course, I tend not to see in my work the brash young males who see women as trophies, and sex as a kind of competitive game with each other, women the almost incidental targets for their lust. Such men undoubtedly exist, but so do very different kinds of men, for example, those who are terrified of sexuality, terrified of women, and of their own sexual needs.

It is also likely today that male sexuality, as with many other aspects of male identity, is in a considerable crisis, as the familiar traditional forms of patriarchal society falter and partially disintegrate. Part of this disintegration can be ascribed to the developments made by women, who have increasingly rejected the traditional role of breeding machine, and have claimed their own right to sexual pleasure and agency. The traditional passivity of women in sexual matters has been partially overturned, and without doubt this has placed question marks over male 'activity' and performance. Some men are afraid of the idea of sexually active women, demanding their own pleasure and their own preferred form of sexual activity, let alone women who are not sexually interested in men.

I would also like to refer briefly to the two chapters on Freudian thought in this book, and in particular the idea that the notion of the unconscious militates against a simple one-to-one transmission between patriarchal ideology and human identities. Let me cite again the comment by Jacqueline Rose: 'Because there is no continuity of psychic life, so there is no stability of sexual identity, no position for women (or men) which is ever simply achieved.'[2]

This aspect of psychoanalytic thought has great importance, for it implies that the view, propounded by some feminists, that men are agents of patriarchal oppression can only be partly true. Male psychology and male sexuality are more complex and contradictory than that, once we accept the postulate of the unconscious, which contains desires that are taboo in the normal social world. To paraphrase Freud's famous comment about women: '*What do men want?*' Do they simply want to dominate women sexually? To be rampantly phallic? To rape and destroy?

Such an analysis of male sexuality would be one-sided, blinkered and thoroughly empiricist. One can reply that men also want the reverse: to be dominated; to be non-phallic; to be raped. Of course, such desires present many problems for men, for they are outside the aegis of patriarchal masculinity. None the less, there is plenty of evidence for the existence of such desires in the concrete work with men that goes on in psychotherapy.

But before we look at contemporary changes to gender and sexuality, it is important to gain some impression of the traditional patterns.

PATRIARCHAL MALE SEXUALITY

Traditionally men have treated women as their sexual property, both to act as the vehicle for their own sexual pleasure, and as breeding machines. Christianity has provided the supreme ideological justification for this: sex is for procreation, and also to keep male lust within proper bounds. The woman has often been seen therefore as the necessary container for male desire, civilizing it and making it suitable for polite society. The woman is seen as a *vessel*, quite literally, for male desire, and as a vessel, her own desires are of no consequence.

In fact, there is a huge split in the perception of female sexuality, for alongside this view of woman as the virtuous (asexual) vessel, goes the image of the carnal slut, Mary Magdalen to the Virgin Mary. The various images of the Virgin Mary are of great symbolic importance here, for she is the container of the male God, and also bereft of any sexuality of her own.[3] At the other extreme, the persecution of witches in Europe marked the climax of the punishment of women for their sexuality.[4]

Within patriarchal ideology, one of the common views of male sexuality has been that it is a raw force of nature, which somehow has to be satisfied, and women had therefore better put up with it. The idea has been that men are somehow possessed of an overwhelming sexual drive, for which they are not really responsible. Thus until recently in Western cultures, rape has often been treated as an unfortunate by-product of this male drive, and the concept of marital rape did not exist in most societies. In the married state, women just had to submit to male sexual demands, and could not be said to be 'coerced' into sex, since the marriage vows involved their agreement to sex at any time, whether they felt like it or not. The same was true of domestic violence: it is only since the 1980s that the police in Britain have started to take this seriously; before that, it was almost considered a man's right to beat up his wife.

These ideas about male sexuality have been so widespread, so deeply engrained in patriarchal society, that probably all commentators, scholars and scientists have been influenced by them. For example, the nineteenth century psychiatrist Krafft-Ebbing:

> It is beyond doubt that man has livelier sexual demands than woman. Following the impulse of nature from a certain age he wants a woman. His love is sensual, his choice is limited by physical advantages. Following nature's urge, he is aggressive and tempestuous in his wooing.[5]

This paragraph contains some of the key words that have been used to define male sexuality: 'nature', 'impulse', 'urge', 'aggressive'. It is almost as if men have no choice in the matter! Nature simply dictates that they are swept by overwhelming urges, and women can only submit in turn.

A more eloquent sermon on the 'male impulse' can be found in D.H. Lawrence, who never tired of expounding on the transcendental nature of the male sexual drive, and the sickness of modern women who have forgotten how to submit to it:

> He was aware of the old flame shooting and leaping up in his loins, that he had hoped was quiescent for ever. He fought against it, turning his back to her. But it leapt, and leapt downwards, circling in his knees....Her tormented modern-woman's brain still had no rest. Was it real? And she knew, if she gave herself to the man, it was real. But if she kept herself for herself, it was nothing. She was old; millions of years old, she felt. And at last, she felt she could bear the burden of herself no more. She was to be had for the taking. To be had for the taking.[6]

Notable here is Lawrence's portrayal of his hero 'fighting against' his sexual urges, which he had hoped had faded away. This repeats the idea that the male is not in control of his sexuality, in fact, *he is not responsible for it*. This astonishing idea is clearly an ancient one, for we have already observed it in certain Christian documents, where it is seen as the promptings of the devil. The Lawrentian cosmology is rather different: both sexes have to submit to the male sexual drive, otherwise they will know no peace of mind. But this idea can also be used to justify all manner of sexual terrorism, just as the idea of an innate male aggression can be used to justify war and violence.

Granted, Lawrence's sexological map is a complex one, and includes intense emotional and spiritual feelings, but at the heart of it is a kind of phallic renaissance:

> Out of his utter, incomprehensible stillness, she felt again the slow momentous surging rise of the phallus again, the other power. And her heart melted out with a kind of awe.[7]

Lawrence seems bitter that women have lost their awe before the 'surging phallus', and men are too wimpish to exert their phallic authority.

Right across Western patriarchal culture, then, we find a kind of worship of the phallus, not expressed with Lawrence's eloquence or passion, but expressing the same ideas: male sexuality exists *sui generis*, as a ferocious force of nature, and women's role is to submit to it, to provide a container for it. In this sense, there is a real connection between traditional marital heterosexuality and acts of sexual violence, including rape. One is legalized, the other illegal, yet it is plausible that both enforce male sexual oligarchy and terrorism.

Feminism has carried out a brilliant feat of socio-historical scholarship by showing the connection between 'normal' male sexuality with the terrible acts of sexual violence that have been carried out by men against women. In other words, there is an unbroken continuum between the 'respectable' theories that male sexuality is 'natural', 'urgent', 'irrepressible' and so on, and the sexual violence committed against women: one tacitly justifies the other. That is why rape was treated mildly in the lawcourts and why marital rape did not exist as a legal concept. In this sense, sexual terrorism has existed at the heart of patriarchal society and at the heart of marriage. I still meet women in my work who submit on a daily basis to sex with their husbands, because that is 'what is expected'.

But what is the origin of this type of male sexuality? Some feminists, such as Mary Daly and Robin Morgan, have argued that sexual rapacity is intrinsic to men. If this is correct, the consequences for both sexes are terrifying. For women, the separatist agenda becomes utterly compelling, but even so perhaps no woman can ever be totally free of the image of the destructive male. But for men also the prospect is terrible. What am I to do, as an adult male, if it is true that I am a latent sexual terrorist? Indeed, one meets men in therapy with precisely that fantasy, and it tends to totally incapacitate them emotionally and sexually.

However, if male rapacity is socially constructed, as one of the building bricks of patriarchy, a different perspective opens up. Male sexual terrorism is a relative not an absolute condition: it has socio-historical roots and a development, and conceivably an end. Both collectively and individually one can then conceive of a male sexuality that is not coercive or oppressive.

THE SOCIAL CONSTRUCTION OF MASCULINITIES

As with feminism and the gay movement, the study of masculinity has been revolutionized by social construction theory. The quasi-biological, quasi-religious arguments that men are 'naturally' aggressive, violent, sexually demanding, and so on have been overthrown in favour of socio-historical research demonstrating that a variety of 'masculinities' has been constructed as part of patriarchal rule. For example, R.W. Connell argues in an article entitled 'The state, gender and sexual politics', that as the modern state has evolved, it has required differing forms of masculinity to consolidate and enact its rule:

> The states of the *ancien régime* were integrated with, indeed operated through, a hegemonic form of masculinity which prized personal and family honour, worked through patronage and kinship obligations, and connected the exercise of authority with a capacity for violence...
>
> The hegemonic masculinity of the old regime was displaced during the nineteenth century by a hegemonic masculinity organized around themes of rationality, calculation, orderliness.
>
> This change in gender was not a *consequence* of the bourgeois revolution, it was *a central part* of it, part of the dynamic that created modern industrial capitalism as an already-gendered social order [original emphasis].[8]

Crucially, Connell argues that gender structures are not a by-product, but are one of the key means by which such social changes occur. Furthermore, as Connell shows, the 'liberal state' is perfectly able to recreate forms of masculine violence when this is required for the suppression of political opposition. This is shown most clearly in the rise of European fascism in the thirties, a crucial part of which was the recruitment of violent gangs of men, who terrorized Jews, left-wingers, union activists and so on.[9] In addition, most liberal states train considerable numbers of men in the practice of violence – in the armed forces, the police, riot squads, and so on. Liberal democracy has never been shy of using the 'iron fist' to exert its influence, as seen for example in the Gulf War, when many thousands of Iraqi troops were massacred by Western forces.

Thus the use of the term 'masculinities' in the plural is of great importance in this socio-historical approach: 'masculinity' is not conceived of as a monolithic and unchanging principle, but one that changes according to the requirements of the patriarchal state. Furthermore, many different kinds of masculinity can co-exist in the same society, each with its own social function and symbolism. Thus in British society, class and gender intersect in complex and interesting ways: one finds the aloof masculinity of the public school élite, the aggressive masculinity of certain working-class men, and the 'respectable' demeanour of others. It strikes me also that different masculinities can coexist in the same individual male, and are expressed on different occasions according to the social context. For example, some

British 'football hooligans' are found to have 'respectable' jobs in the City of London during the week.

A huge amount of research is being undertaken into the various forms and practices of the various masculinities that exist in patriarchy. For example, considerable interest has been aroused in the 'public face' of men at work, since this kind of masculinity is of great importance in the large-scale organization of work, and the exclusion or subordination of women.[10] Research is being pursued into a wide variety of topics, including the use of sport in the construction of masculinity, the relationship between violence, criminality and male control, and the relationship between the rise of feminism and a possible 'crisis in masculinity'.[11]

The use of the term '*construction* of masculinities' must be balanced by the term 'deconstruction'. This has two senses: at the theoretical level, it has been possible for radical historians and social scientists to expose the mystified and covert nature of these masculinities and their vital role in the patriarchal state. But there is a more concrete sense of the word 'deconstruction': that men and women are able to organize in opposition to such hegemonic masculinities. In the words of Jeff Hearn, 'we need to fully recognize and change men's powers, and to support women's liberation, and yet at the same time to undermine "our" identities as men'.[12]

Constraints of space do not allow me to expound a fully worked out approach to male sexuality using social constructionism, but one can sketch out a number of interesting topics. First, as I pointed out in Chapter 6, male and female bodies have not always been considered to be very dissimilar. A historical approach might therefore consider those critical periods when a 'two sex' approach began to supersede a 'one sex' approach: what implications does this have for the construction of male sexuality? Second, fruitful lines of research open up in relation to the Renaissance, and the new empirical approaches to reproduction that emerged at that period – was male sexuality conceived of differently from the medieval paradigm, and how does this relate to the changes in social structure in the sixteenth and seventeenth centuries? Here one might tie in Connell's thesis regarding the masculinities of the *ancien régime* and the bourgeois state. Third, the relation between the family, marriage and male sexuality is of great importance – for example, as we have seen, in the nineteenth century, great emphasis was laid on female virtue, while male sexuality was still permitted its excesses. Fourth, the particular function and meaning of male homosexuality is clearly of great importance in the evolution of modern male sexualities in the West. Fifth, fascinating avenues of research are opened up in relation to the Lacanian notion of the phallus: for example, how does this abstract concept relate to the penis, and the emphasis placed on the penis in male sexuality?[13]

This is not a comprehensive list by any means, but demonstrates the extremely fertile ground that has been opened up by the new historical approach to masculinities.

MISOGYNY

Hostility to women seems to be built into male sexuality in many cultures. Thus anthropologists report that in many pre-industrial cultures, male culture is heavily distinguished from female culture, and women are treated with aggression, fear and disdain. At times, there is also the view that sex is dangerous and should be infrequent – for example, T. and P. Hays found amongst the Ndumba people that newly wed couples might wait months, or even a year, before having sexual intercourse.[14]

What is the function and meaning of this distancing and hostility between the sexes? A feminist view might be that such attitudes are built into all patriarchal societies, and help men to keep control of women. Women are treated as lesser beings, their sexuality is demeaned or dismissed, and women's bodies are seen as vehicles for male sexual satisfaction and for reproduction.

Other theories have been put forward: for example, in his study of rituals amongst the Sambia people of Papua New Guinea, G.H. Herdt describes how 'in all facets of one's existence...the differences between maleness and femaleness are fetishized, exaggerated and blown up'. His explanation of this is quite different from the feminist one:

> This symbol structure suggests that in male erotic life, constant hostility is often needed to create enough of a distance, separateness and dehumanization of women to allow there to occur the ritually structured sexual excitement necessary for culturally tempered heterosexuality and the 'reproduction' of society.[15]

This theoretical understanding of heterosexuality has interesting connections with other issues to do with 'otherness'. For example, many researchers have argued that masculinity itself is constructed as a defence against femininity. Part of being a man is to demonstrate visibly that one is not a woman, thereby maintaining the requisite distance between the sexes. The construction of masculinity is maintained by a set of severe taboos and punishments awaiting any transgression, so that the man who falls short is condemned as 'less than a man'. This also suggests that men are terrified of falling back into a regressive feminine identification, and therefore have to keep up a constant hostility towards their own feminine side, for fear of betraying the masculine ethic.[16]

The idea of 'distance' between the sexes also seems to connect with incest, for the incest taboo can be seen as maintaining a distance from a desired sexual object – one's parent, child or sibling. Thus, incestuous relations between parents and children, or between siblings, often seem to be 'too close', and those people who have experienced them seem to have great difficulty in separating from the relationship, and tend to seek out similar patterns in later life. The failure of the push outwards towards exogamous relationships results in a profoundly regressive sexuality.[17]

In this light, it is interesting that it is men who predominantly carry out incestuous sexual acts with their children, as if they have not become sexually autonomous beings themselves, and crave sexual union with a child, not an adult. Of course, again feminism might argue that paternal incest shows another facet of patriarchal hostility towards women: even a man's daughters are not immune from his rapacity. On the other hand, one might argue that men who commit incest are in fact severely damaged individuals, whose sense of individual existence has been badly compromised, so that an adult sexual relationship has become impossible. Some therapists working with incest offenders also argue that the male offender is seeking in his daughter a distorted trace of his own lost contact with the feminine.[18]

But incestuous desire has wider implications, for the incest taboo causes great problems for many individuals in the West, since the taboo splits love and sexuality: one learns that one must not desire the person whom one loves most intensely. Thus, it is quite common to meet people who do not desire the people they like, and do not like the people they desire. In Freud's words, 'they seek objects which they do not need to love, in order to keep their sensuality away from the objects they love'.[19]

Herdt's theory of erotic distance can be also be used to explain part of the hostility felt towards homosexuality in some cultures: the homosexual is refusing to desire the stipulated 'other', that is, the opposite sex, and desires 'the same' sex.

There is also the fascinating phenomenon of sexual boredom: for example, married people often seem to get jaded with each other sexually. Why should this be so? The 'distance' theory predicts it, since married people often become companionable, and certainly live in proximity to each other.

One can also tie in certain feminist ideas – for example, that heterosexuality is an intrinsic injury to women. This is predicted in Herdt's theory, since he is claiming that in order to desire women, men have to objectify them and feel hostile towards them.

But what about women's hostility to men? It is striking in this context to see how feminism has permitted women to feel openly hostile to men – in this sense, hatred between the sexes has been too one-sided, since men have had a monopoly of it. Women have traditionally not been allowed such feelings, at least in public.

It strikes me that desire for 'the Other' always involves a degree of hatred – since one feels incomplete without the other person, one needs them, and so on. Certainly, in therapeutic work, one often uncovers a degree of hate between men and women – however, such hatred is not problematical if it is integrated into the full personality and accepted. But the patriarchal organization of sexuality and emotions has stipulated that men are permitted – even encouraged – to act out such hostility – whereas women are taught to express theirs in a much more veiled manner.

THE OPPRESSION OF MALE SEXUALITY

The arguments as to the oppressive nature of male sexuality are highly persuasive. But they are one-sided. The political structuring of sexuality by patriarchy has not been of 100 per cent benefit to men. One can argue that whilst it places women in the strait-jacketed role of sexual servant to the male, he too is narrowly defined. His role is to 'perform', to fertilize the woman and produce many children, and then to work hard to provide for wife and children. Without doubt men have had the advantage over women, since sexual double standards (with regards to extramarital affairs and prostitution) always provided an escape from married tedium for men, while the woman was shackled to kitchen and nursery, often denied sexual pleasure within marriage and fiercely condemned for having affairs. None the less the split between passion and duty has also had serious consequences for men.

These ideas are presented brilliantly in fictional form in Edith Wharton's *The Age of Innocence* (1920), in relation to the 'wild oats' that young men sow in upper-class New York society, specifically in this novel the affair with a married woman from which the main male character, Newland Archer, is recovering:

> The affair, in short, had been of the kind that most of the young men of his age had been through, and emerged from with calm conscience and an undisturbed belief in the abysmal distinction between the woman one loved and respected and those one enjoyed – and pitied. In this view they were sedulously abetted by their mothers, aunts and other elderly female relatives, who all shared Mrs Archer's belief that when 'such things happened' it was undoubtedly foolish of the man, but somehow always criminal of the woman. All the elderly ladies whom Archer knew regarded any woman who loved imprudently as necessarily unscrupulous and designing, and mere simple-minded man as powerless in her clutches. The only thing to do was to persuade him, as early as possible, to marry a nice girl, and then trust her to look after him.[20]

Wharton writes ironically about the double standards which are involved in such situations, for these affairs are seen as part and parcel of young men's growing pains, but as reprehensible on the part of the woman involved. Therefore he has affairs with disreputable women as a kind of necessary rite of passage, before he marries a 'nice girl'. The nice girl has to 'look after him', that is, in part regulate the man's sexuality, involve him in the production of children, and the establishment of a home, so that he is fit for civilization. In fact, the hero of *The Age of Innocence*, Newland Archer, realizes too late that he has married without passion, as demanded by the social norms that suffocate him, while the woman he loves intensely is forever lost to him.

Wharton portrays this sexual ethic in tragic terms for both men and women. The two main female characters in the novel are wronged, one by losing the man she loves, the other by being married to a man who does not love her; but the male character himself is shown as making a profound sacrifice, one that is demanded by the mores that he castigates half-hysterically, half-bitterly:

> 'The individual, in such cases, is nearly always sacrificed to what is supposed to be the collective interest: people cling to any convention that keeps the family together – protects the children, if there are any'.[21]

His words are prophetic, for his own hopes of pursuing the woman he really loves are dashed when his wife announces her pregnancy: his fate is sealed by her words, for while he can just about contemplate leaving his wife for another woman, he cannot leave his pregnant wife. He also realizes that he has been brilliantly managed by his own family and his wife's family, who all along were aware of his infatuation for another woman:

> He guessed himself to have been, for months, the centre of countless silently observing eyes and patiently listening ears, he understood that, by means as yet unknown to him, the separation between himself and the partner of his guilt had been achieved, and that now the whole tribe had rallied about his wife on the tacit assumption that nobody knew anything, or had ever imagined anything...
>
> It was the old New York way, of taking life without 'effusion of blood'; the way of people who dreaded scandal more than disease, who placed decency above courage, and who considered that nothing was more ill-bred than 'scenes', except the behaviour of those who gave rise to them.
>
> As these thoughts succeeded each other in his mind Archer felt like a prisoner in the middle of an armed camp. He looked about the table and guessed at the inexorableness of his captors.[22]

Wharton is even-handed in showing the tragic effects of sexual hypocrisy and repression, for while women are either stigmatized as 'criminal' whores or revered as 'innocent' madonnas – described by the hero as 'that terrifying product of the social system he belonged to, the young girl who knew nothing and expected everything'[23] – the men are trapped in the confines of marriage and procreation. Love and sexual passion come off second-best to 'form'.

It would be tempting to analyse such a brilliant work as an exposé of sexual hypocrisy and the cruelty of a social élite, but it is important to grasp that this élite is concerned with its own preservation. It does not pursue 'form' simply for its own sake, but as a means to an end. The constriction of sexuality for both men and women is necessary if the tightly knit social group is to regulate itself, and perpetuate itself, by means of inheritance, kinship and property relations. Thus men are permitted a degree of illicit sexual pleasure, whereas women are condemned for the same; but both sexes are required to fall into place within the great strictures of marriage, family and property.

Edith Wharton's book, like many other novels in English, demonstrates with great clarity the connections between sexuality, procreation and property. There is a kind of endogamous law in force: one must marry in the right class, and in the right income bracket. In *The Age of Innocence*, the woman whom Archer loves – Countess Ellen Olenska – is marked as a woman contaminated by her excessive contact with European decadence, particularly her Polish husband, and her possible affair with her secretary. This is a theme familiar in the novels of Henry James, and it marks a fascinating twist on the notion of 'the Other', for in such literature European and American families regard each other as precisely that, and therefore as both exotic and attractive, but dangerous. To marry across the Atlantic risks disaster.

Another splendid illustration of the relations between sexuality, property and endogamy can be found in the novels of Jane Austen, who ironically counterpoises the opposed demands of love and property, and constantly seeks some acceptable compromise between them. How often in Austen's works are characters mentioned with a sub-clause about their financial standing: 'Mr Smith, with twenty thousand a year'. In her novel *Persuasion* (1817), as in all her major novels, love and property are eventually united harmoniously: the main male character, Captain Wentworth, returns to his old sweetheart, Anne Eliot, who had previously turned him down, not only a sadder and wiser man, but a richer one. Austen comments rather acidly:

> Captain Wentworth, with five-and-twenty thousand pounds, and as high in his profession as merit and activity could place him, was no longer nobody. He was now esteemed quite worthy to address the daughter of a foolish spendthrift baronet, who had not had principle or sense enough to maintain himself in the situation which Providence had placed him, and who could give his daughter at present but a small part of the share of ten thousand pounds which must be hers hereafter.[24]

This remarkable paragraph, redolent with financial imagery, contrasts two kinds of men: Wentworth, who is now 'somebody', because of his financial and professional advancement, and Anne Eliot's father, who by contrast has frittered away his money, and therefore leaves her poor by comparison. Wentworth, although *nouveau riche*, is therefore an entirely respectable sexual/marital partner for Anne: sexuality and money are woven together in a tight interlocking pattern. It is not money that makes Wentworth desirable to Anne – that is the vulgar view of a character such as Mrs Elton in *Emma* – but it makes him socially irreproachable. Austen abhorred marriage without love, but was hard-headed enough to see the folly of marriage without money. Or as David Cecil commented: 'It was wrong to marry for money, but it was silly to marry without it.'[25]

Of course the social mores portrayed by Edith Wharton and Jane Austen are specific to the times they are writing about, but we can see an interesting point in common between them in relation to both male and female sexuality. Women must be seen to be utterly virtuous, but men are required to be outwardly respectable in sexual matters *and affluent*. Thus sexuality is tightly constricted and regulated according to a fine web of rules, and men are required to bring with them an adequate fortune as well as a prepossessing manner.

In fact, this conjunction of sex and property appears to run like a deep vein through patriarchal society, cutting across many apparently distinct cultures. In his book *Manhood in the Making*, David Gilmore itemizes the fierce requirements placed upon men in many cultures, and in relation to Mediterranean machismo he comments that men are required to produce many children and also provide for them:

> Honor is about being good at being a man, which means building up and buttressing the family or kindred – the basic building blocks of society – no matter what the personal cost...Manhood, then, as call to action, can be interpreted as a kind of moral compunction to provision kith and kin.[26]

It is interesting to make the connection between this analysis – which Gilmore extends to African, Asian, Pacific, South American, as well as European cultures – and the central tragic structure of Wharton's *The Age of Innocence*. For Newland Archer is trapped by his own family and his wife's family precisely on the issue of 'kin': it is his wife's pregnancy which closes the door to freedom for him. And his wife ensures her victory by first informing Ellen Olenska of her pregnancy, sure that the 'other woman' will now concede defeat in the face of her pregnancy. The unborn child carries a tremendous social and moral weight, and for the man in question acts as an insuperable obstacle to his bid for emotional and sexual liberation. He has sown his seed, and now he must 'provision' both mother and child.

CRISIS

As we turn from the world of upper-class New York society in the nineteenth century to the late twentieth century, it is striking how the iron bands which constrict both sexes in Wharton's novels seem to have partially disintegrated. This has a double effect: in part, there is a sense of liberation, but also an atmosphere of fear and crisis.

Certainly anyone who works in depth with men on the question of their sexual and gender identity will be struck by the sense of uncertainty that pervades these issues. So far from having a sense of solidity, certainty or absoluteness, many men appear confused and vulnerable in relation to their sexuality. It could be argued that this is partly a reaction to the rise of feminism, and the developing confidence of contemporary women.

No doubt this is true; but I also want to suggest that male sexuality contains an inherent fragility. It can never be certain of its aim or its identity, and therefore constantly seeks to assert itself brashly and even violently. But is sexual violence an expression of strength? Not necessarily – it can also involve an attempt to refute feelings of inadequacy and impotence.

If we speak of a 'crisis' in male sexuality in Western culture, what does this mean? A whole range of issues can be adduced here: the rise of feminism and other 'counter-cultural' movements, such as the gay movement, changes to the traditional family structure, the loss of traditional occupations such as heavy engineering and coal-mining, which diminishes the male sense of social potency, and so on.

Overall, there seems little doubt that traditional machismo has been strongly challenged externally. But I am more interested in this context in aspects of male sexuality that can be challenged from the inside, aspects that must be unpacked and explored if men are to feel a sense of sexual freedom.

Performance

Male sexuality is heavily tied up with performing, and with the secret fears of not being able to carry out one's duties. The male sexual agenda is a heavy one: first, the man has to have an erection and maintain it, and as men get older, their fears about erections increase considerably, as for different reasons erections become less reliable. Tiredness, stress, emotional disturbance, lack of desire – many factors can reduce that ability to have 'instant erections' which young men often boast about.

But the erection is only the beginning of a man's arduous duties, according to the standard paradigm of male sexual responsibility. The erect penis must penetrate the woman; intercourse must be sustained for a reasonably long time; the man must postpone his own ejaculation, so that the woman (considered to be slower to orgasm) has time; ideally, the man must time his orgasm to coincide with the woman's; the man must have 'prepared' the woman, by stimulation of the clitoris, and so on. I could go on – my point is that this is not a caricature, but an assessment of how many men see their sexual duties. The word 'duty' strikes an ironic note here, since sex is supposed to be about carefree abandonment, yet for many men it is anything but. There is a kind of utilitarian or puritan strain in this list of duties that seems absurd – yet tragic. The joys of sex are turned into a kind of Calvinist work ethic.

But what keeps this fearful set of burdens going? Simply the stipulation that being 'masculine' involves such duties – therefore a man who shirks them is 'less than a man'. The solution is obvious: for men to be able to act as they feel, not as they feel they ought. Yet this would represent a revolution in male sexuality and within masculinity itself.

Emotion

Male sex traditionally lacks emotion. That is, men have often adopted a rather stoical grim-faced demeanour during intercourse. How many women complain that their male partner buries his head in the pillow, does not have any eye-contact with them, seems unable to be light-hearted about it, is too active and aggressive, and so on? The problem here is surely the wider issue within the ambit of masculinity itself: men feel emotionally constrained, not to say constipated. Feelings are for women; men *act*.

Yet so much of this is a lie. How often do I hear men say that during intercourse they surprised themselves and their partners by bursting into tears? What is difficult for many men is to stay emotionally responsive and finely tuned during sex – thus, to be able to feel humorous, silly, vulnerable, frightened, and so on. These are some of the feelings that go against the masculine code, and the lack of them eventually spells death to sexual intimacy and pleasure.

Intimacy

Intimacy is what makes sex work over a long period for two people. Without intimacy, sex becomes boring, and then the temptation is strong to find new partners, so that sex becomes interesting again. But it is intimacy that is problematic for many men. I am not denying that many women also find this a problem, but somehow Western culture has made a terrible division of labour, so that women are used to relating to other people, while men are used to going out into the world and doing things.[27]

Thus many men find it unnatural to be intimate. It strikes them as effeminate, or just plain dangerous and terrifying. Sex therefore turns into a contest, an armed camp, a struggle. At times, sex like this can be great fun, but sex can also be something simpler, more gentle, more meandering. The word that comes to mind here is 'goal'. For many men, sex is goal-driven, and the goal is orgasm. They drive relentlessly towards it, and feel refreshed when the goal is reached.

But there is another kind of sex – without goals, which is a kind of sexual being-with-each-other. I think this is more difficult for men, who find this kind of intimacy distinctly embarrassing and unnerving.

Aggression

Strangely enough, I have found that many men have great problems with aggression in sex. I say 'strangely enough' since one of the key accusations made by feminists about male sexuality is that it is predicated upon aggression and violence towards women. This may be true at the macro level, but large numbers of men seem to find it very disturbing.

This can make a man impotent, for he is afraid to believe that anyone can love his erect penis, which to him seems like a deadly weapon. It also seems so vulgar, so obvious, so crude. I am not saying that the penis is inherently aggressive, but rather that sex between two people often has an element of aggression in it. This is as true for women as men, and again many women find it difficult to enjoy their own aggressive feelings during sex.

The solution to these problems is to educate people to accept their own aggressive feelings, to be able to enjoy them, and to come to realize that 'aggression' does not equal 'destruction'. If I put my penis inside you, it does not follow that you will be wrecked or damaged by the experience. Yet many men have this belief, no doubt stemming in part from the Oedipal taboo: 'I love Mummy very much, but I must never have sexual feelings about her.' The penis can then come to seem a 'debased' and vulgarized organ compared with a fleshless love.

The word 'flesh' seems a key one in this context. Flesh is something that Christianity has often abhorred; and for many men, the flesh is a dangerous realm, compared with the realm of ideas, thought, logic. Sex is one way that human beings have of becoming incarnate, of being embodied, of finding a concrete home in the universe. Yet many men feel distinctly disembodied, yearn to be in their bodies, yet also feel terrified of the consequences.

SUMMARY

Male sexuality is a very difficult subject to understand, since it is made up of so many contradictory factors. There is the pressure to be macho, the sense of performance and 'masquerade' which drives many men to 'do sex' well. This is sex as an external act, muscular, ardent, with a beginning and an end. What a relief when it is over! A relief no doubt for many partners of such men, but also for the men themselves, who are off the hook for another period. I am talking very much of penile sex, since the penis seems to be for some men the be-all and end-all of sex.

Yet the penis is also a very fragile organ: it is definitely not a ten-inch steel bar! It is quite floppy, unpredictable, and often not subject to the individual's will-power. One can even say it is comical in its alternations between flaccidity and rigidity.

But this is the aspect of sexuality that frightens many men. The ability not to have an erection, the ability to enjoy body to body contact without rushing to intercourse, the ability to have intercourse without rushing to orgasm. Of course, these abilities can be set, not just against the Western code of masculinity, but against the whole Western notion of goal-oriented behaviour. Sex has become teleological.

It is fascinating therefore, as a man, to read lesbian accounts of sex that is not like this, that is sensual as well as sexual, that doesn't drive to orgasm, that pertains to the whole of the body. Yet I see no reason why such experiences are forbidden to men – except within the codes of masculinity that terrorize us.

Male sexuality cannot therefore be understood without an understanding of the masculinities that exist in our culture, and that for many men act as fierce codes of honour. Masculinity is driven by shame and fear, and the terrible possibility of being found to be 'not a man'. Yet such masculinities are not set in stone: both at the collective level and individually, it is possible to change them.

11 Conclusions

I have not written this book in order to arrive at any definitive conclusion as to what human sexuality is, but rather to outline some parameters within which it can be studied. In fact, it seems impossible to attempt a conclusive description and explanation, for the reason that sex has been given different meanings by different groups of people, and has also been studied in different ways. Over the past two thousand years, one can see a succession of paradigms within which sex has been described: the moral/religious framework of Christianity; the biological analysis beginning in the Renaissance, which provides a more empirical and anatomical approach, but also contains covert ideological messages; the psychological approaches, headed by the dominant figure of Freud; and more recently, socio-historical analysis which has argued that 'sexuality' itself is not a fixed unchanging entity, but has been constructed as a concept.

Within these very complex paradigms, one can isolate a number of parameters that have been prominent.

SIN AND GRACE

The idea that sex is sinful and should be avoided if one wants to attain spiritual purity is not found in all religions, but achieved a fierce intensity within Christianity. A stark dualism between body and soul has therefore dominated Western culture up to the present day, and even in the 'post-permissive' age, when pre-marital sex is widespread in countries such as Britain and America, it is common to find that people are haunted by feelings of guilt about sex.

One can certainly point to the control aspect of Christian moralizing over sex – it enabled the churches to wield a formidable influence over their congregations – yet surely there are other reasons for the equation of sex with sin. The development of rationality in Western culture has led to a deep suspicion of the irrational and primitive experiences provided in sex. At the same time this also makes sex intensely desirable as an escape from rationality.

One can also adduce the need of all societies to proscribe those forms of sexual behaviour which are seen as inimical to that society's survival. Such proscriptions will then be elevated and transformed into the level of taboo or 'morality'.

A simple example concerns procreation: many societies have encouraged the production of many children, since they are a vital economic resource; on the other hand, modern China sees this as potentially catastrophic and attempts to restrict families to one child.

In the former case, the requirement for large families means that it is seen as 'manly' to procreate – for example, in Mediterranean societies the socio-economic requirement for children is 'ideologized' and becomes a moral imperative, and a gender stipulation for both men and women. A fertile man is a 'manly' man; a 'barren' woman is viewed with pity and scorn. In some societies, childlessness is grounds for divorce.[1]

These strike me as strong arguments for claiming that sexual morality does not float above society in a realm of its own, but follows societal requirements.

ESSENCE VERSUS CONSTRUCT

The notion of essentialism or innateness runs like a thread through the ancient and modern study of sex. We can see Freud struggling for forty years to reconcile his notion of the sexual instincts, born out of the biological matrix of the human body, with his entirely psychological psychology. There is a kind of split vision here: sex is both instinctive and mental, both primitive and sophisticated. But as a mental or psychic phenomenon it appears highly plastic and subject to the early impressions of childhood, and definitely not inborn or 'constitutional'.

But Freud's model is a very sophisticated one; more often there has been a crude kind of nativism preached on the subject of sexuality. For example: there is a male sexual drive which must be satisfied, or there will be trouble. In many ways, this is akin to the notion of original sin which, Augustine argues, is transmitted through conception.

But essentialist notions are also found in contemporary feminist thinking: the notion that as there is a rapacious male sexuality, there is a 'warm', 'loving' female sexuality.

In a sense, essentialism is both highly attractive and also something of a dead end. It is attractive since it silences all doubts and queries: men are just like that, or women are just like that, or gay people are born like that. However, according to this view, sexuality is not creative – we all submit to our biological or genetic fate. One can see at once why Freud struggled to transcend a reductive biological framework, for about that psychology could have little to say.

At the time of writing, in the mid-nineties, within radical social science a massive tide is running against essentialism in favour of 'social constructionism': the idea that gender and sexuality are created in society, and arise historically. This thesis has overthrown many previously held shibboleths. For example, the idea that the homosexual role was 'invented' in modern times sheds much light on the social meanings that homosexuality has in the West, and the quite different meanings that homosexual behaviour may have in other cultures, which have quite distinct social niches.

CONSCIOUS/UNCONSCIOUS

The notion of the unconscious is one of the most radical themes in all theories of sexuality, for it proposes that our sexual desires are inaccessible and unknowable, and contradict our outer personality. In a sense, this shatters all empiricist approaches, which take the surface of events as a truthful description of them. And many arguments in relation to sexuality do seem to have an empiricist bent: for example, the feminist argument that heterosexuality inevitably demeans women. Such an argument posits a one-to-one relation between certain desires and acts and their meanings that is simply untenable in a non-empiricist theory such as psychoanalysis.

A model of sexuality that embraces the unconscious will therefore tend to be both more complex and more contradictory than one that does not. This is both an attraction – for human sexuality certainly does not seem to be a simple affair – and perhaps also at times an evasion, for it is quite easy to describe some awkward fact that will not fit into a particular theory as an 'aspect of the unconscious'. In other words, the unconscious can become a kind of dustbin.

None the less, my own profession convinces me that concrete work with people on sexual problems is going to be very difficult without the notion of the unconscious, for one does find repeatedly that people begin to discover desires within themselves that do not fit with the rest of their personality, or desires that they have never been aware of, but that may have affected their lives considerably.

Furthermore, if one accepts the Freudian notion of the unconscious, sexual desire is shown to be irrevocably primitive, concerned with re-enacting infantile bodily needs: the need to be held, to be stroked, to suck, to bite, to penetrate, and so on. Thus in the 'adult world', sexuality floats like an iceberg, concealing a massive underworld of primitive and irrational desires, which may be repressed but which still exert a massive influence on personality and the conduct of our daily life.

SEX/GENDER

The connection between sexuality and gender is one of the most important ideas to emerge from research in feminism and the gay movement. For example, heterosexuality seems intimately associated with certain notions of 'masculinity' and 'femininity', and notions of 'man' and 'woman'. The idea that men are 'penetrative', while women are 'receptive', for example, has dominated traditional thinking about sexuality.

One can also cite the common view that gay men are feminine: this correlation may often be false – especially in view of the macho movement amongst gay men – but it demonstrates the close association between sex and gender in popular thinking.

But this link has also been held in more scientific models such as Freud's. Freud smuggled many gender traits into his ideas about sexuality: for example, that women are passive, or are more ashamed than men, and so on.

Certainly in Western culture sexual feelings and sexual acts are classified according to particular gender categories. It is 'manly' to feel and do certain things sexually, and 'womanly' to do certain other things.

Part of the deconstruction of conventional sexuality and gender therefore consists of breaking these links, which seem to be neither 'natural' nor innate.

SUBJECTIVITY

One of the most striking developments in the contemporary study of sexuality is the rise of subjectivity. Whereas neurologists, psychologists and sexologists have studied human sexuality and its variants much as they might study insects or plants – by means of an 'objective' taxonomic approach – the post-1970s rise of feminism and the gay movement have allowed the 'objects' of study to become the subjects, who speak, who describe their own desires, and who have therefore shattered the traditional subject–object split.

This is surely a revolutionary change in methods of study. One can compare it to Marx's distinction between philosophy and revolutionary politics: the traditional detached academic attitude was redundant, since the world had to be changed. In Marx's eyes, the working class must become the subject of history.

I am not claiming that feminism and the gay movement have aped Marx's words, but rather that a parallel process has been going on. Those who have been marginalized, oppressed and pathologized begin to speak, begin to make their own demands, begin to describe their own lives, not in a spirit of scientific objectivity, but with passion, indignation and exhilaration.

Thus polemic has forced its way into academic enquiry. In relation to sexuality, this seems to be a healing process, since it has always seemed quite odd that sex – that most passionate and primitive of human activities – might be described as a kind of laboratory experiment, or in terms of stimulus–response theory. It seems quite evident that human beings are not sexually aroused by a particular set of physiological stimuli alone, but also by emotional and spiritual factors which are very personal and idiosyncratic.

SAMENESS/OTHERNESS

The notion of the other has dominated Western thinking about sex. Homosexuality has been defined as deviant or perverse, precisely because it does not seek out the opposite sex, but the same sex. Thus otherness has been favoured, sameness abhorred.

Similarly one might argue that masturbation has excited disapproval partly because sex with oneself denied the possibility of another as the object of one's desire. Or to take oneself as the other offends the predilection for alterity in patriarchal sexual relations.

But what is the meaning of this bias for otherness? There are those who simply invoke the statutes of biology or other forms of nativism: people simply are heterosexual, simply seek the other in order to feel complete, to become one, and so on. This explanation has the great virtue that no further comment is needed. It is rather like the suggestion that God created heterosexuality – our enquiry is ended!

Others, such as Plato and Jung, have argued for a craving for unity in the human being, stemming from some ancient sense of incompleteness, from having been split from one's 'other half'.

Interesting psychological arguments describe the human being craving another through a sense of loss. In Lacanian language, desire seeks to fulfil the loss of the other, but can never replace it. One might say, desire guarantees the presence of loss. Or even that a sense of I is bound up with loss and incompleteness.

These ideas have interesting relationships with Buddhist and other Eastern ideas that suggest that the I intrinsically leads to craving for otherness. The paradox here is that a primary split in reality, which leads to the creation of the I, also leaves the I with a terrible sense of fracture, which sexuality promises to heal. Such theories are attractive in terms of an understanding of the individual, but they lack a socio-political dimension. Here we might be interested in the historical development of sexual relations, the creation of monogamous heterosexuality, the history of the family, and so on. Here we are more concerned with the proscription of sexualities that do not conform to the patriarchal norm, which is very much concerned with the links between sex, reproduction and property.

The notions of sameness and difference form massive motifs in the human approach to sexuality. On the one hand, there has been the constant attempt to subsume one kind of sexual practice within another; on the other hand, there has been the striving to differentiate. Thus, for example, patriarchal ideology has tended to subsume female sexuality within male sexuality. As we have seen, both Aristotle and Freud argue that women are really castrated men.

But feminism breaks away from this monolithic tendency and asserts that a female sexuality exists *sui generis*, and does not depend on men for its pleasures. But at the same time, some feminists have carried out a further monistic take-over by arguing that only lesbianism is truly feminist, and that heterosexuality is irretrievably patriarchal and a hostage to male domination. Heterosexual feminists have therefore had to struggle to reclaim their own territory.

There seems to be a strong tendency to create monolithic groupings in relation to sexuality. Of course, this tendency exists in other areas such as class and ethnicity: it seems to be very difficult for human beings to consider another viewpoint apart from their own.

All human cultures have been highly ethnocentric, even, one might say, narcissistic.

DIVERSE SEXUALITIES AND UTOPIA

Many areas of modern sexual study point towards the reclamation of sexualities formerly dismissed as 'perverse', 'abnormal' or marginal. These include female sexualities, homosexualities, sado-masochistic sexualities, the use of fantasy in sex, erotic or 'pornographic' art, and so on.

But the project of accepting such a broad spectrum, whilst attractive, remains entirely utopian unless one attends to the socio-political context. This is one of the key problems for feminist activists and theoreticians: how is it possible to change the world so that women and women's sexuality are celebrated? Can this be done within the confines of patriarchal capitalism? Some feminists, it strikes me, operate under the fantasy that they can change their own particular world while the larger world goes on its way. Is this really possible?

The same arguments apply to the gay movement, and to all groups that campaign for their own sexualities to be recognized and validated. To whom are we appealing? Of course, political groups are able to form their own cultures and live within them, to a degree, as the gay movement has shown convincingly. None the less, feminists and gay activists still live under the roof of patriarchy and capitalism. There is a strong danger of falling into a kind of reformism. This is all very well and good, but as the twentieth century has shown all too graphically, reforms can easily be taken away again. Furthermore, this century has shown how sexuality can easily become an arena for punitive reaction, as right-wing governments seek to banish and obliterate radical groups. 'Back to the family!' is the inevitable cry of tyranny.

SEXUAL SIGNS

Sex can mean so many things – materiality, pleasure, an infantile paradise, the endless search for a 'lost object', the recreation of desire, control over other people's bodies, a commodity, a meeting place – the list is endless. In fact, one problem with many theories of sexuality is precisely that they strive to anchor it to one principle, whether it be the 'sexual drive', the 'sexual instinct', the 'search for pleasure', the 'need to relate', and so on. It strikes me that any monistic model can only in the end restrict and reduce human sexuality. But it refuses to be pinned down in this way – no sooner has one apparently neatly defined it than we see it emerging in some corner of human experience that is unexpected and extra-limital.

How can we ever define what turns people on? Some are turned on by physical beauty; some by close intimacy; some by aggression and power struggles; some by anonymity; some by intellectual achievement; some by their own suffering; some by hatred. Surely human beings are capable of being turned on by anything, not excluding degradation and death. Hence human sexuality must be seen as a kind of theatre of the imagination and the body, a theatre in which many forces come together.

I find it useful therefore to consider the notion of *sexual signs* – meaning that all varieties of sexual feeling and expression function as a dense semiotic by means of which meanings are transmitted between people and within people. Being 'turned on' is in a sense to be excited by a set of signs that have particular meaning for you.

All descriptions of sexuality – be they biological, psychological, historical or sociological – are therefore necessarily one-sided, and one cannot criticize them for that. But perhaps it is useful to take a bird's eye view, and thereby grasp the sheer ubiquity of sexuality in modern human existence. In one of his more provocative moments, Jacques Lacan announces to his listeners: 'perhaps we are fucking right now'. Surely Lacan is right in the sense that an erotic relationship can go on in any medium: it is not restricted to the body. The concept of 'sublimation' in psychoanalysis grasps this point – sexuality can be expressed through any human endeavour or expression.

Naturally enough, many empirical enquiries into sexuality have focused on the physical parameters of sex – the nature of 'foreplay', the sensitivity of certain organs, the structure of orgasm and so on. But such enquiry tends to fall into a kind of behaviourist trap: as if sex were about physical technique. Of course, partly it is, but it is also about the imagination and fantasy. Hence a caress from one person is exciting; from another, repugnant; from another, uninteresting. The body must be at the centre of the study of sexuality, but so must the imagination and the emotions. Indeed, when we consider the links between sexuality and spirituality that I sketched out in Chapter 7, we can conclude that through the sexual, human beings have the capacity to express any feeling, any thought, any wish.

At the same time, there seems little doubt that the last two hundred years have seen an expansion (Foucault's 'intensification') in the use made of sexuality as a sign system, so much so that contemporary culture is replete with sexual signs. Just as religion or politics or mythology or magic have been the key symbolic systems in other cultures, sexuality has become one of the central 'signifying systems' in Western culture in the modern epoch.

I construct my own sexual identity not simply to obtain pleasure or love, but also to communicate who I am, what I feel, what I think. But I do not exist simply as an individual: the reason I am able to use sexuality in this complex manner is because I take part in a socialized sexual system. Social groups construct complex systems of sexual signification which permit a vast communication network to operate. Students of sexuality have only begun to scratch the surface of this awesome system, or set of systems: much remains to be explored.

Notes

2 CHRISTIANITY AND SEX

1. Jon Sobrino, *Christology at the Crossroads: A Latin American Approach* (London: SCM, 1978), p. 296.
2. Robert Markus, *The End of Ancient Christianity* (Cambridge: CUP, 1990), pp. 27 ff.
3. J. Sobrino, *Christology at the Crossroads*, p. 294.
4. See Christopher Hill, *The Century of Revolution: 1603–1714* (London: Sphere, 1969).
5. E.J. Tejirian, *Sexuality and the Devil: Symbols of Love, Power and Fear in Male Psychology* (New York and London: Routledge, 1990), p. 175.
6. See Estelle Roith, *The Riddle of Freud: Jewish Influences on his Theory of Female Sexuality* (London and New York: Tavistock, 1987), pp. 89 ff; Uta Ranke-Heinemann, *Eunuchs for the Kingdom of Heaven: Women, Sexuality and the Catholic Church* (Harmondsworth: Penguin, 1991), pp. 16–20; Harriett Gilbert (ed.), *The Sexual Imagination: From Acker to Zola* (London: Jonathan Cape, 1993), under 'Judaism', pp. 134–5.
7. Christopher Rowland, *Christian Origins: An Account of the Setting and Character of the Most Important Messianic Sect of Judaism* (London: SPCK, 1985).
8. Alan Richardson (ed.), *A Dictionary of Christian Theology* (London: SCM, 1969), p. 56; J. Sobrino, *Christology at the Crossroads*, pp. 195–8.
9. Alan Richardson (ed.), *A Dictionary of Christian Theology*, under 'Gnosticism', pp. 133–7; Uta Ranke-Heinemann, *Eunuchs for the Kingdom of Heaven*, *passim*; Elaine Pagels, *The Gnostic Gospels* (Harmondsworth: Penguin, 1982), pp. 129–39.
10. E.C. Whitmont, *Return of the Goddess* (London: Arkana, 1987).
11. Hilda Graef, *Mary: A History of Doctrine and Devotion* (London: Sheed & Ward, 1985), p. 32.
12. St Augustine, *Concerning the City of God against the Pagans* (Harmondsworth: Penguin, 1984), p. 286.
13. Elaine Pagels, *Adam, Eve and the Serpent* (Harmondsworth: Penguin, 1988), p. 80.
14. Luke 12: 49–53.
15. E. Pagels, *Adam, Eve and the Serpent*, p. 15.
16. Ibid., p. 59.
17. Aline Roussel, *Porneia: On Desire and the Body in Antiquity* (Cambridge, Mass.: Blackwell, 1993), p. 193.
18. Luke 16: 13.
19. See R. Markus, *The End of Ancient Christianity*, chapters 3 and 5; Aline Roussel, *Porneia*, chapters 9 and 10.
20. C. Rowland, *Christian Origins*, pp. 285–94.
21. Mark 13: 30.
22. E. Pagels, *Adam, Eve and the Serpent*, p. 113.

23. Augustine, *The City of God*, p. 551.
24. Ibid., p. 589.
25. Ibid., p. 588.
26. Ibid., p. 581.
27. Ibid., p. 581.
28. Ibid., p. 577.
29. Ibid., p. 854.
30. Ibid., p. 857.
31. Ibid., p. 220.
32. R. Markus, *The End of Ancient Christianity*, chapter 4.
33. E. Pagels, *Adam, Eve and the Serpent*, p. 129.
34. For a negative view of Augustine, see Uta Ranke-Heinemann, *Eunuchs for the Kingdom of Heaven*, chapter 6; for a more positive view, see R. Markus, *The End of Ancient Christianity*.
35. Augustine, *The City of God*, p. 584.
36. Ean Begg, *The Cult of the Black Virgin* (London: Arkana, 1985).
37. See Hilda Graef, *Mary: A History of Doctrine and Devotion*; Marina Warner, *Alone of All her Sex: The Myth and the Cult of the Virgin Mary* (London: Picador, 1976), pp. 34–49.
38. M. Warner, *Alone of All her Sex*, chapter 13.
39. See Marion Woodman, *The Pregnant Virgin* (Toronto: Inner City Books, 1985).
40. E. Pagels, *The Gnostic Gospels*, chapter 3.
41. Ean Begg, *The Cult of the Black Virgin*, p. 139.
42. P.F. Palmer (ed.), *Mary in the Documents of the Church* (London: Burns Oates, 1953), p. 52.
43. Genesis 3:16.
44. Herbert McCabe, *The Teaching of the Catholic Church: A New Catechism of Christian Doctrine* (London: Catholic Truth Society, 1985), p. 43.
45. Ibid., p. 44.
46. See Michel Foucault, *The History of Sexuality: An Introduction* (Harmondsworth: Penguin, 1990), part 5.
47. Ibid., pp. 58–64.
48. M. Foucault, *The History of Sexuality*, vol. 2, *The Use of Pleasure* (Harmondsworth: Penguin, 1992), chapter 3.
49. *The Cloud of Unknowing and Other Works* (Harmondsworth: Penguin, 1978), p. 140.
50. St John of the Cross, *The Dark Night of the Soul* (Cambridge: James Clarke, 1973), pp. 19–20.
51. Sigmund Freud, *The Ego and the Id*, in *On Metapsychology: The Theory of Psychoanalysis* (Harmondsworth: Penguin, 1991), p. 362; Jacques Lacan, *Ecrits: A Selection* (London: Routledge, 1989), p. 52.
52. E. Pagels, *Adam, Eve and the Serpent*, pp. 146–8.
53. C.G. Jung, *Answer to Job*, in H. Read, M. Fordham and G. Adler (eds), *The Collected Works of C.G. Jung*, vol. 11, *The Psychology of Religion: West and East* (Princeton and London: Routledge & Kegan Paul, 1969).
54. See E. Pagels, *Adam, Eve and the Serpent*, pp. xx and 10.

3 FREUD I: FROM BIOLOGY TO PSYCHOLOGY

1. M.J. Sirks and C. Zirkle, *The Evolution of Biology* (New York: The Ronald Press, 1964), pp. 121–5 and 149–53.
2. M. Foucault, *The History of Sexuality: An Introduction*, p. 18.
3. Ibid., pp. 36–73.
4. S. Freud, *Three Essays on the Theory of Sexuality,* in *On Sexuality* (Harmondsworth: Penguin, 1979), pp. 56–7 n.
5. Ibid., p. 60.
6. S. Freud, 'The dissolution of the Oedipus complex', in *On Sexuality*, p. 318.
7. M. Foucault, *The History of Sexuality: An Introduction*, p. 69.
8. See the discussion in Louis Breger, *Freud's Unfinished Journey* (London: Routledge & Kegan Paul, 1981), chapter 2, 'Psychoanalysis is not a science'.
9. S. Freud, *An Outline of Psycho-analysis*, in *Historical and Expository Works on Psychoanalysis* (Harmondsworth: Penguin, 1993), p. 385.
10. S. Freud, *The Ego and the Id*, pp. 371 ff.
11. S. Freud, *Three Essays on the Theory of Sexuality*, p. 101.
12. Ibid., pp. 101 ff and 128.
13. Jeffrey Masson (ed.), *The Complete Letters of Sigmund Freud and Wilhelm Fliess 1887–1904* (Cambridge, Mass.: Belknap, 1985), p. 2.
14. For a commentary on the Freud/Fliess relationship see Masud R. Khan, 'Montaigne, Rousseau and Freud', in *Privacy of the Self* (London: Hogarth, 1986), pp. 99–111.
15. J. Masson, *The Complete Letters of Sigmund Freud and Wilhelm Fliess*, p. 42.
16. Ibid., p. 266.
17. Ibid., p. 300.
18. Ibid., p. 326.
19. Ibid., p. 291.
20. Ibid., p. 296n.
21. For a negative view of this episode, see Jeffrey Masson, *The Assault on Truth: Freud and Child Sexual Abuse* (London: Fontana, 1992), chapter 3; a more circumspect view can be found in Lisa Appignanesi and John Forrester, *Freud's Women* (London: Weidenfeld and Nicholson, 1992), pp. 119–20 and 134–41.
22. J. Masson, *The Complete Letters of Sigmund Freud and Wilhelm Fliess*, p. 459.
23. Ibid., p. 459.
24. For a chilling example, see Jeffrey Masson, *Final Analysis: The Making and Unmaking of a Psychoanalyst* (London: Fontana, 1992), pp. 189–90.
25. Ibid., p. 191.
26. Ibid., p. 212.
27. J. Masson, *The Assault on Truth*, pp. xxiii, 11, 187.
28. Juliet Mitchell, *Psychoanalysis and Feminism* (Harmondsworth: Penguin, 1990), pp. 352–4.
29. J. Masson, *Final Analysis*, pp. 149–80.
30. See, for example, the collection of papers on sexual abuse in *Journal of Analytical Psychology* 40: 1 (1995).

31. For a critical view, see Jacqueline Rose, 'Dora: Fragment of an analysis' in *Sexuality in the Field of Vision* (London: Verso, 1986), pp. 27–47; also L. Appignanesi and J. Forrester, *Freud's Women*, pp. 146–67; the original case-study is S. Freud, 'Fragment of an analysis of a case of hysteria (Dora)', in *Case Histories I* (Harmondsworth: Penguin, 1991).

32. Lou Andreas-Salomé, *The Freud Journal* (London: Quartet, 1987), pp. 91–2.

33. See J.R. Greenberg and S.A. Mitchell, *Object Relations in Psychoanalytic Theory* (Cambridge, Mass.: Harvard University Press, 1983), pp. 119–50.

34. See the essays in *British Journal of Psychotherapy* 12: 3 (1996).

35. See Eric H. Lenneberg, *Biological Foundations of Language* (New York: John Wiley, 1967).

36. See H. Solomon, 'The transcendent function and Hegel's dialectical vision', *Journal of Analytical Psychology* 39: 1 (1994), pp. 77–100.

37. On timelessness, see S. Freud, *The Unconscious*, in *On Metapsychology*, pp. 190–1.

38. S. Freud, *Three Essays*, p. 155.

39. Jeffrey Weeks, *Sexuality and its Discontents: Meanings, Myths and Modern Sexualities* (London and New York: Routledge, 1985), p. 148.

40. Maria Torok, 'The significance of penis envy in women', in J. Chasseguet-Smirgel (ed.), *Female Sexuality: New Psychoanalytic Views* (London: Maresfield, 1988), p. 159.

41. See Kenneth Lewes, *The Psychoanalytic Theory of Male Homosexuality* (London: Quartet, 1988).

42. J. Lacan, *Ecrits*, p. 171.

43. R.D. Laing, *Self and Others* (Harmondsworth: Penguin, 1971), p. 32.

44. S. Freud, 'Two principles of mental functioning', in *On Metapsychology*, p. 36.

45. James Strachey, 'Sigmund Freud: A sketch of his life and ideas', in *On Metapsychology*, p. 22.

46. S. Freud, *Introductory Lectures on Psychoanalysis* (Harmondsworth: Penguin, 1991), p. 453.

47. Estelle Roith, *The Riddle of Freud*, p. 138.

48. See, for example, S. Freud, *Civilization and its Discontents*, in *Civilization, Society and Religion* (Harmondsworth: Penguin, 1991), p. 296.

49. Jacqueline Rose, 'Femininity and its discontents', in *Sexuality: A Reader*, ed. *Feminist Review* (London: Virago, 1988), p. 97.

50. J. Mitchell, *Psychoanalysis and Feminism*, p. 354. Mitchell's reference to 'Millett' denotes Kate Millett, *Sexual Politics* (New York: Doubleday, 1970).

51. J. Rose, 'Femininity and its discontents', p. 184.

4 FREUD II: MALE AND FEMALE SEXUALITY

1. See, for example, Jacques Lacan, *The Four Fundamental Concepts of Psycho-analysis* (London: Hogarth, 1977), p. 49.

2. S. Freud, *Three Essays on the Theory of Sexuality*, p. 87.
3. Ibid., p. 67 n.
4. Ibid., p. 127.
5. Ibid., pp. 141–4.
6. Ibid., pp. 144–5.
7. S. Freud, 'On female sexuality', in *On Sexuality*, p. 373.
8. See E. Roith, *The Riddle of Freud*, pp. 32, 116 and 120.
9. S. Freud, 'On female sexuality', p. 380.
10. Ibid., p. 391.
11. Ibid., p. 382.
12. J.R. Greenberg and S.A. Mitchell, *Object Relations in Psychoanalytic Theory*, p. 146.
13. W.R.D. Fairbairn, *Psychoanalytic Studies of the Personality* (London: Routledge & Kegan Paul, 1952), p. 34.
14. J.R. Greenberg and S.A. Mitchell, *Object Relations in Psychoanalytic Theory*, p. 157.
15. Michael Balint, 'Changing therapeutical aims and techniques in psychoanalysis', in *Primary Love and Psycho-Analytic Technique* (London: Maresfield, 1985), p. 230.
16. M. Balint, 'Character analysis and new beginning', in *Primary Love and Psycho-Analytic Technique*, pp. 159–73.
17. S. Freud, *Three Essays*, pp. 141–4.
18. Ibid., pp. 159–60.
19. S. Freud, 'Fetishism', in *On Sexuality*, p. 356.
20. See Elizabeth Grosz, *Jacques Lacan: A Feminist Introduction* (London and New York: Routledge, 1990), p. 68.
21. S. Freud, 'Some psychical consequences of the anatomical differences between the sexes', in *On Sexuality*, p. 336.
22. Ibid., p. 335.
23. Ibid., p. 341.
24. S. Freud, *New Introductory Lectures on Psychoanalysis* (Harmondsworth: Penguin, 1991), p. 160.
25. Ibid., p. 162.
26. For example, R.J. Stoller, *Sexual Excitement: Dynamics of Erotic Life* (London: Maresfield, 1986), chapter 2, 'Primary femininity'.
27. S. Freud, *New Introductory Lectures*, p. 151.
28. Ibid., p. 161.
29. These arguments are summarized in E. Roith, *The Riddle of Freud*, pp. 11–34.
30. Ibid., chapter 5.
31. S. Freud, *On the History of the Psychoanalytic Movement*, in *Historical and Expository Works on Psychoanalysis* (Harmondsworth: Penguin, 1991), p. 116.
32. S. Freud, 'Some psychical consequences of the anatomical differences between the sexes', p. 337.
33. E. Grosz, *Jacques Lacan*, p. 157.
34. Michel Foucault, 'Truth and power', in Paul Rabinow (ed.), *The Foucault Reader* (Harmondsworth: Penguin, 1991), p. 73.
35. S. Freud, *Civilization and its Discontents*, p. 304.

36. See Jill L. Matus, *Unstable Bodies: Victorian Representations of Sexuality and Maternity* (Manchester: Manchester University Press, 1995).
37. See Donna Haraway, '"Gender" for a Marxist dictionary: The sexual politics of a word', in *Simians, Cyborgs and Women: The Reinvention of Nature* (London: Free Association Books, 1991), pp. 127–48.
38. K. Lewes, *The Psychoanalytic Theory of Male Homosexuality*, p. 148.
39. J. Lacan, *Ecrits*, p. 50.
40. S. Freud, *On the History of the Psychoanalytic Movement*, p. 115.

5 LACAN: LACK AND DESIRE

1. J. Lacan, *Ecrits*, p. 42.
2. Ibid., p. 44.
3. See Bradley A. Te Paske, *Rape and Ritual: A Psychological Study* (Toronto: Inner City Books, 1982).
4. S. Freud, *New Introductory Lectures*, p. 47.
5. S. Freud, *The Ego and the Id*, p. 368.
6. J. Lacan, *Ecrits*, pp. 171–2.
7. J. Lacan, *The Four Fundamental Concepts of Psycho-analysis*, pp. 168 ff.
8. S. Freud, *Three Essays*, pp. 116–17.
9. J. Lacan, *The Four Fundamental Concepts of Psycho-analysis*, pp. 178 ff.
10. John Donne, 'The Canonization', in Herbert Grierson (ed.), *The Poems of John Donne* (London: OUP, 1933), p. 14.
11. J. Lacan, 'God and the Jouissance of The Woman', in Juliet Mitchell and Jacqueline Rose (eds), *Feminine Sexuality: Jacques Lacan and the Ecole Freudienne* (Basingstoke: Macmillan, 1982), p. 143.
12. J. Lacan, 'Seminar of 21 January 1975', in J. Mitchell and J. Rose (eds), *Feminine Sexuality*, p. 170.
13. J. Lacan, *Ecrits*, pp. 81, 147, 160, 166, 172, 234.
14. Ibid., p. 106.
15. J. Lacan, 'The Meaning of the Phallus', in J. Mitchell and J. Rose (eds), *Feminine Sexuality*, p. 78.
16. Lacan's most accessible papers on the phallus are 'The signification of the phallus', in *Ecrits*, pp. 281–91, and 'The meaning of the phallus', in J. Mitchell and J. Rose (eds), *Feminine Sexuality*, pp. 74–85.
17. F. de Saussure, *Course in General Linguistics* (New York: McGraw-Hill, 1966), pp. 111 ff.
18. See Lynne Segal, *Straight Sex: The Politics of Pleasure* (London: Virago, 1994), pp. 130–40.
19. R.J. Stoller, *Sexual Excitement*, p. 123.
20. J. Lacan, *The Four Fundamental Concepts of Psycho-analysis*, p. 195.
21. Further analysis of the horror film can be found in Roger Horrocks, *Male Myths and Icons: Masculinity in Popular Culture* (Basingstoke: Macmillan, 1995), chapter 7.
22. See Alice Miller, *Banished Knowledge: Facing Childhood Injuries* (London: Virago, 1990).

23. The relation of Kristeva to Lacan is considered by E. Grosz, *Jacques Lacan*, pp. 150–67.
24. See Elizabeth Wilson, 'Psychoanalysis: Psychic law and order?', in *Sexuality: A Reader*, pp. 157–76.
25. On Lacan's Hegelian influences, see Ross Skelton, 'Lacan for the faint hearted', *British Journal of Psychotherapy* 10: 3 (1994), pp. 418–29.
26. Karl Marx, 'Economic and philosophical manuscripts', in *Early Writings* (Harmondsworth: Penguin, 1975), p. 385.
27. K. Marx, 'Critique of Hegel's doctrine of the state', in *Early Writings*, p. 70.
28. Ibid., p. 80.
29. Ibid., p. 98.
30. Lucio Colletti, 'Introduction', in K. Marx, *Early Writings*, p. 33.
31. K. Marx, *Grundrisse: Foundations of the Critique of Political Economy (Rough Draft)* (Harmondsworth: Penguin, 1993), p. 84.
32. M. Foucault, *The History of Sexuality: An Introduction*, pp. 103 ff.

6 SEXUALITY AS A MODERN CONCEPT

1. M. Foucault, *The History of Sexuality: An Introduction*, p. 78.
2. Ibid., p. 105.
3. David Halperin, 'Is there a history of sexuality?', in H. Abelove, M.A. Barale and D.M. Halperin (eds), *The Lesbian and Gay Studies Reader* (New York and London: Routledge, 1993), pp. 416–31.
4. Ibid., p. 424.
5. K. Marx, 'Concerning Feuerbach', *Early Writings*, p. 423.
6. K. Marx, *Grundrisse*, p. 84.
7. K. Marx, 'Economic and philosophical manuscripts', *Early Writings*, p. 347.
8. D. Haraway, *Simians, Cyborgs and Women*, p. 132.
9. Alexandra Kollontai, 'Sexual relations and the class struggle', *Selected Writings* (London: Alison & Busby, 1977), pp. 237–49.
10. See Alix Holt, 'Morality and the new society', in A. Kollontai, *Selected Writings*, pp. 201–15.
11. Leon Trotsky, *Women and the Family* (New York: Pathfinder, 1973), p. 53.
12. Maurice Florence, 'Foucault, Michel, 1926–', in Gary Gutting (ed.), *The Cambridge Companion to Foucault* (Cambridge: CUP, 1994), p. 314.
13. P. Rabinow (ed.), *The Foucault Reader*, p. 223.
14. See L. Segal, *Straight Sex*, pp. 178–88.
15. Friedrich Nietzsche, *Beyond Good and Evil: Prelude to a Philosophy of the Future* (Harmondsworth: Penguin, 1973), pp. 29 and 154.
16. James Miller, *The Passion of Michel Foucault* (London: Flamingo, 1994), p. 67.
17. Ibid., pp. 42–5.
18. David Ingram, 'Foucault and Habermas on the subject of reason', in Gary Gutting (ed.), *The Cambridge Companion to Foucault*, p. 223.

19. M. Foucault, *The History of Sexuality: An Introduction*, p. 17.
20. Ibid., pp. 77–8.
21. R. Barthes, 'Myth today', in *Mythologies* (London: Vintage, 1993), pp. 109–59.
22. M. Foucault, *The History of Sexuality: An Introduction*, p. 24.
23. Ibid., p. 23.
24. Ibid., p. 143.
25. Lois McNay, *Foucault: A Critical Introduction* (Cambridge: Polity Press, 1994), p. 70.
26. M. Foucault, *The History of Sexuality: An Introduction*, p. 100.
27. Ibid., p. 151.
28. Discussion of 'scripts' can be found in R.J. Stoller, *Sexual Excitement*, pp. xiv–v, 13–14, 207–9.
29. M. Foucault, *The History of Sexuality: An Introduction*, p. 109.
30. Aline Roussel, *Porneia*, p. 150.
31. Carole S. Vance, 'Negotiating sex and gender in the Attorney General's Commission on Pornography', in L. Segal and M. McIntosh (eds), *Sex Exposed: Sexuality and the Pornography Debate* (London: Virago, 1992), p. 41.
32. Cate Haste, *Rules of Desire: Sex in Britain: World War I to the Present* (London: Pimlico, 1992), pp. 178–82.
33. M. Foucault, *The History of Sexuality: An Introduction*, pp. 139–40.
34. Ibid., pp. 104–5.
35. Ibid., pp. 92–3.
36. Ibid., pp. 95–6.
37. M. Foucault, *The Use of Pleasure*, p. 6.
38. Ibid., p. 32.
39. J. Miller, *The Passion of Michel Foucault*, chapters 8 and 10.
40. Ibid., p. 373.
41. See J. Weeks, 'Uses and abuses of Michel Foucault', in *Against Nature: Essays on History, Sexuality and Identity* (London: Rivers Oram, 1991), pp. 157–69.
42. Thomas Laqueur, *The Making of Sex: Body and Gender from the Greeks to Freud* (Cambridge, Mass.: Harvard University Press, 1990).
43. J.L. Matus, *Unstable Bodies*, p. 123.
44. Ibid., chapter 1.
45. Judith Butler, *Gender Trouble: Feminism and the Subversion of Identity* (New York and London: Routledge, 1990), p. 31.
46. L. Segal, *Straight Sex*, pp. 34–40, 223–6.
47. See Celia Kitzinger, 'Problematizing pleasure: Radical feminist deconstructions of sexuality and power', in H.L. Radtke and H.J. Stam (eds), *Power/Gender: Social Relations in Theory and Practice* (London: Sage, 1994), pp. 194–209.
48. I.M. Lewis, *Social Anthropology in Perspective: The Relevance of Social Anthropology* (CUP, 1985), p. 238.
49. Ibid., p. 239.
50. Ibid., pp. 239–40.
51. L. Appignanesi and J. Forrester, *Freud's Women*, pp. 331 and 473.
52. Judith Butler, *Gender Trouble*, p. 31.

53. Monique Wittig, 'One is not a woman', in H. Abelove, M.A. Barale and D.M. Halperin (eds), *The Lesbian and Gay Studies Reader*, p. 105.
54. E. Pagels, *Adam, Eve and the Serpent*, p. 11.
55. J.L. Matus, *Unstable Bodies*, chapter 4.
56. See Linda Williams' discussion of pornography: *Hard Core: Power, Pleasure and the 'Frenzy of the Visible'* (London: Pandora, 1991).
57. Caroline Ramazanoglu, *Feminism and the Contradictions of Oppression* (London and New York: Routledge, 1989), pp. 138–70.
58. These issues are discussed in Don Milligan, *Sex-Life: A Critical Commentary on the History of Sexuality* (London: Pluto, 1993).

7 SEXUALITY, SPIRITUALITY, AND ALIENATION

1. See J. Weeks, *Sexuality and its Discontents*, pp. 61–95.
2. *The Life of St Teresa of Avila by Herself* (Harmondsworth: Penguin, 1957), p. 123.
3. Ibid., p. 210.
4. See J.P. Dourley, 'The religious implications of Jung's psychology', *Journal of Analytical Psychology* 40: 2 (1995), pp. 189–91.
5. *The Verse in English of Richard Crashaw* (New York: Grove, 1949), p. 46.
6. Ibid., p. 205.
7. S. Freud, 'The future of an illusion', in *Civilization, Society and Religion*, p. 212.
8. C.G. Jung, *Memories, Dreams and Reflections* (London: Flamingo, 1983), p. 192.
9. J. Mitchell and J. Rose (eds), *Feminine Sexuality*, p. 147.
10. Richard de Martino, 'The human situation and Zen Buddhism', in E. Fromm, D.T. Suzuki and R. de Martino (eds), *Zen Buddhism and Psychoanalysis* (London: Souvenir Press, 1960), p. 145.
11. Christopher Bollas, *The Shadow of the Object: Psychoanalysis of the Unthought Known* (London: Free Association Books, 1987), p. 39.
12. Ibid., p. 39.
13. On Aphrodite, see *New Larousse Encyclopedia of Mythology* (London: Hamlyn, 1968), pp. 130–3. See also W. Colman, 'Love, desire and infatuation: Encountering the erotic spirit', *Journal of Analytical Psychology* 39: 4 (1995), pp. 497–514.
14. Susan Fromberg Schaeffer, *The Madness of a Seduced Woman* (London: Pan, 1989), p. 237.
15. Brian Moore, *The Doctor's Wife* (London: Corgi, 1978), p. 66.
16. Ibid., p. 70.
17. *Meister Eckhart* (New York: Harper & Row, 1941), pp. 131 and 135.
18. Harry Levin (ed.), *The Essential James Joyce* (Harmondsworth: Penguin, 1963), p. 50.
19. See S. Freud, *Introductory Lectures*, pp. 47–8, 389–91, 422–4.
20. See, for example, Melanie Klein, 'Early analysis', in *Love, Guilt and Reparation and Other Works: 1921–1945* (London: Virago, 1988), pp. 77–105.

21. C.G. Jung, 'On psychic energy', in H. Read, M. Fordham and G. Adler (eds), *The Collected Works of C.G. Jung*, vol. 8, *The Structure and Dynamics of the Psyche* (Princeton and London: Routledge & Kegan Paul, 1969).
22. Roshi Philip Kapleau, *Zen: Dawn in the West* (London: Rider, 1980), p. 78.
23. Ibid., p. 78.
24. See the chapter 'Sigmund Freud', in C.G. Jung, *Memories, Dreams and Reflections*; also p. 283 on libido. Freud's comments can be found in *Three Essays*, p. 140; *On Narcissism*, in *On Metapsychology*, pp. 72–4; *On the History of the Psychoanalytic Movement*, pp. 119–27.

8 FEMINISM AND THE POLITICS OF SEXUALITY

1. J. Mitchell and J. Rose (eds), *Feminine Sexuality*, p. 168.
2. Aristotle, *Generation of Animals*, quoted in A. Rousselle, *Porneia*, p. 30.
3. See Siân Morgan, 'The dream of psychoanalysis: Irma's dream, some commentaries and a contemplation of its navel', in *British Journal of Psychotherapy* 12: 2 (1995), pp. 160–9.
4. L. Segal, *Straight Sex*, p. 24.
5. L. Appignanesi and J. Forrester, *Freud's Women*, p. 455.
6. See Alix Holt, 'Women and the Revolution', in A. Kollontai, *Selected Writings*, pp. 113–22.
7. S. Freud, *Three Essays on the Theory of Sexuality*, p. 141.
8. Ibid., pp. 106 and 117.
9. H. Gilbert (ed.), *The Sexual Imagination*, p. 114.
10. See Sue Wilkinson and Celia Kitzinger (eds), *Heterosexuality: A 'Feminism and Psychology' Reader* (London: Sage, 1993).
11. See L. Segal, *Straight Sex*.
12. S.P. Schacht and Patricia H. Atchison, 'Heterosexual instrumentalism: Past and future directions', in Sue Wilkinson and Celia Kitzinger (eds), *Heterosexuality*, p. 131.
13. L. Segal, *Straight Sex*, p. 244.
14. Ibid., pp. 245–53.
15. Celia Kitzinger, 'Problematizing pleasure: Radical feminist deconstructions of sexuality and power', in H.L. Radtke and H.J. Stam (eds), *Power/Gender*, p. 201.
16. H. Gilbert (ed.), *The Sexual Imagination*, p. 239.
17. L. Segal, *Straight Sex*, p. 58.
18. See Adrienne Rich, 'Compulsory heterosexuality and lesbian existence', in H. Abelove, M.A. Barale and D.M. Halperin (eds), *The Lesbian and Gay Studies Reader*, pp. 227–54.
19. See the debates in 'Issues around lesbianism', in *Sexuality: A Reader*, pp. 201–304.
20. Marilyn Frye, 'Some reflections on separatism and power', in H. Abelove, M.A. Barale and D. M. Halperin (eds), *The Lesbian and Gay Studies Reader*, p. 95.

21. See Cate Haste, *Rules of Desire*, chapter 4.

22. E. Grosz and E. Probyn (eds), *Sexy Bodies: The Strange Carnalities of Feminism* (London and New York: Routledge, 1995); Pat Califa, *Public Sex: The Culture of Radical Sex* (Pittsburgh: Cleis, 1994); L. Segal and M. McIntosh (eds), *Sex Exposed*; P.C. Gibson and R. Gibson (eds), *Dirty Looks: Women, Pornography, Power* (London: BFI, 1993).

23. Pat Califa, '*Un*monogamy: Loving tricks and tricking lovers', in *Public Sex*, p. 202.

24. C. Ramazanoglu, *Feminism and the Contradictions of Oppression*, pp. 143–4.

25. *Sexuality: A Reader*, p. 224.

26. C. Ramazanoglu, *Feminism and the Contradictions of Oppression*, pp. 157–61.

27. Biddy Martin, 'Lesbian identity and autobiographical difference[s]', in H. Abelove, M.A. Barale and D.M. Halperin (eds), *The Lesbian and Gay Studies Reader*, pp. 274–93.

28. See Susan Ardill and Sue O'Sullivan, 'Upsetting an applecart: Difference, desire and lesbian sadomasochism', in *Sexuality: A Reader*, pp. 277–304.

29. The two wings are illustrated by the anti-porn book, Catherine Itzin (ed.), *Pornography: Women, Violence and Civil Liberties* (Oxford: OUP, 1993); and the anti-anti-porn collection, L. Segal and M. McIntosh (eds), *Sex Exposed*.

30. L. Appignanesi and J. Forrester, *Freud's Women*, p. 68.

30a. Robin Morgan, *The Demon Lover: The Sexuality of Terrorism* (London: Mandarin, 1990).

31. On the use of allegory, see Marina Warner, *Monuments and Maidens: The Allegory of the Female Form* (London: Picador, 1987).

32. See Camille Paglia, 'Madonna I: Animality and artifice', and 'Madonna II: Venus of the radio waves', in *Sex, Art and American Culture* (London: Viking, 1992); for a more complex view, see M.J. Hardie, ' "I embrace the difference": Elizabeth Taylor and the closet', in E. Grosz and E. Probyn (eds), *Sexy Bodies*, pp. 155–71.

9   HOMOSEXUALITIES

1. Jeffrey Weeks, 'Discourse, desire and sexual deviance: Some problems in a history of homosexuality', in Kenneth Plummer (ed.), *The Making of the Modern Homosexual* (Totowa: Barnes and Noble, 1981), p. 77.

2. Mary McIntosh, 'The homosexual role', in K. Plummer (ed.), *The Making of the Modern Homosexual*, p. 46.

3. Kenneth Plummer, 'Homosexual categories: Some research problems in the labelling perspective of homosexuality', in K. Plummer (ed.), *The Making of the Modern Homosexual*, p. 50.

4. The following material is taken from Harriet Whitehead, 'The bow and the burden strap: A new look at institutionalized homosexuality in native

North America', in H. Abelove, M.A. Barale and D.M. Halperin (eds), *The Lesbian and Gay Studies Reader*, pp. 498–527.

5. Ibid., p. 513
6. Ibid., pp. 502–3.
7. The detail about hijras is taken from Serena Nanda, *Neither Man nor Woman: The Hijras of India* (Belmont: Wadsworth, 1990).
8. Ibid., p. 19.
9. Ibid., p. xi.
10. Jean Genet, *Our Lady of the Flowers* (London: Panther, 1969), pp. 209–10.
11. Tomas Almaguer, 'Chicano men: A cartography of homosexual identity and behavior', in *The Lesbian and Gay Studies Reader* p. 257.
12. S. Nanda, *Neither Man nor Woman*, pp. 129–43.
13. See Michel Foucault, *The Use of Pleasure*, pp. 193–5.
14. Ibid., p. 215.
15. Ibid., p. 187.
16. E. Tejirian, *Sexuality and the Devil*, p. 156.
17. S. Nanda, *Neither Man nor Woman*, pp. 19–23.
18. A point made by Friedrich Engels, *The Origin of the Family, Private Property and the State* (Harmondsworth: Penguin, 1986), pp. 95–6.
19. T.E. Hays and P.H. Hays, 'Opposition and complementarity of the sexes in Ndumba initiations', in Gilbert Herdt (ed.), *Rituals of Manhood: Male Initiation in Papua New Guinea* (Berkeley: University of California, 1982), pp. 201–38.
20. See Jeffrey Richards, '"Passing the love of women": Manly love and Victorian society', in J.A. Mangan and J. Walvin (eds), *Manliness and Morality: Middle Class Masculinity in Britain and America, 1800–1940* (Manchester: Manchester University Press, 1987), pp. 92–122.
21. M. Foucault, *The History of Sexuality: An Introduction*, p. 101.
22. Celia Kitzinger and Sue Wilkinson, 'Theorizing heterosexuality', in S. Wilkinson and C. Kitzinger (eds), *Heterosexuality*.
23. Jeffrey Weeks, *Sexuality* (London and New York: Routledge, 1986), p. 75; see also J. Weeks, *Sexuality and its Discontents*, chapter 9; and J. Weeks, *Against Nature*, chapter 11.
24. Peter Burton, 'Across the great divide', in *Amongst the Aliens: Some Aspects of a Gay Life* (Brighton: Millivres, 1995), p. 103.
25. Brian Inglis, *Roger Casement* (London: Coronet, 1974), pp. 373–405.
26. Peter Burton, 'Across the great divide', p. 107.

10   MALE SEXUALITY

1. Mary Daly, *Pure Lust: Elemental Feminist Philosophy* (London: Women's Press, 1984), p. 2.
2. J. Rose, 'Femininity and its discontents', in *Sexuality: A Reader*, p. 184.
3. See Marina Warner, *Alone of All her Sex*, pp. 50 ff.
4. See Uta Ranke-Heinemann, *Eunuchs for the Kingdom of Heaven*, chapter 19.
5. R. v. Krafft-Ebbing, *Aberrations of Sexual Life: The Psychopathia Sexualis* (London: Panther, 1965), p. 25.

6. D.H. Lawrence, *Lady Chatterley's Lover* (Harmondsworth: Penguin, 1961), p. 120–1.
7. Ibid., p. 182.
8. R.W. Connell, 'The state, gender and sexual politics: Theory and appraisal', in H.L. Radtke and H.J. Stam (eds), *Power/Gender*, p. 150.
9. Ibid., p. 150.
10. See David H.J. Morgan, *Discovering Men* (London and New York: Routledge, 1992), chapters 4–6; Jeff Hearn, *Men in the Public Eye: The Construction and Deconstruction of Public Men and Public Patriarchies* (London and New York: Routledge, 1992).
11. On sport, see R. Horrocks, *Male Myths and Icons*, chapter 9; on criminality, see T. Newburn and E.A. Stanko (eds), *Just Boys Doing Business: Men, Masculinities and Crime* (London: Routledge, 1994); on men and feminism, see Lynne Segal, *Slow Motion: Changing Masculinities, Changing Men* (London: Virago, 1990).
12. Jeff Hearn, *Men in the Public Eye*, p. 231.
13. See Tony Jefferson, 'Theorising male subjectivity' in T. Newburn and E.A. Stanko (eds), *Just Boys Doing Business*, pp. 10–31.
14. T.E. Hays and P.H. Hays, 'Opposition and complementarity of the sexes in Ndumba initiation', pp. 206–8.
15. G.H. Herdt, 'Fetish and fantasy in Sambia initiation', in *Rituals of Manhood*, p. 91.
16. See R.J. Stoller, *Presentations of Gender* (New Haven and London: Yale University Press, 1985); David Gilmore, *Manhood in the Making: Cultural Concepts of Masculinity* (New Haven and London: Yale University Press, 1990).
17. Evangeline Kane, *Recovering from Incest: Imagination and the Healing Process* (Boston: Sigo, 1989), pp. 48 ff.
18. Ibid., chapter 1.
19. S. Freud, 'On the universal tendency to debasement in the sphere of love', in *On Sexuality*, p. 251.
20. Edith Wharton, *The Age of Innocence* (Harmondsworth: Penguin, 1984), pp. 83–4.
21. Ibid., p. 96.
22. Ibid., pp. 279–80.
23. Ibid., p. 39.
24. Jane Austen, *Persuasion* (Harmondsworth: Penguin, 1965), p. 250.
25. Jane Austen, *Emma* (Harmondsworth: Penguin, 1966), p. 12.
26. D. Gilmore, *Manhood in the Making*, pp. 43–4.
27. See Vic Seidler, 'Fear and intimacy', in Andy Metcalf and Martin Humphries (eds), *The Sexuality of Men* (London: Pluto, 1990), pp. 150–80.

11 CONCLUSIONS

1. E. Pagels, *Adam, Eve and the Serpent*, pp. 11–12.

Index